Making Race Visible:
Literary Research for Cultural Understanding
STUART GREENE and DAWN ABT-PERKINS, Editors

The Child as Critic: Developing Literacy through
Literature, K–8, FOURTH EDITION
GLENNA SLOAN

Room for Talk: Teaching and Learning in a
Multilingual Kindergarten
REBEKAH FASSLER

Give Them Poetry!
A Guide for Sharing Poetry with Children K–8
GLENNA SLOAN

The Brothers and Sisters Learn to Write: Popular
Literacies in Childhood and School Cultures
ANNE HAAS DYSON

"Just Playing the Part": Engaging Adolescents in
Drama and Literacy
CHRISTOPHER WORTHMAN

The Testing Trap: How State Writing Assessments
Control Learning
GEORGE HILLOCKS, JR.

The Administration and Supervision of Reading
Programs, THIRD EDITION
SHELLEY B. WEPNER, DOROTHY S. STRICKLAND,
and JOAN T. FEELEY, Editors

School's Out! Bridging Out-of-School Literacies
with Classroom Practice
GLYNDA HULL and KATHERINE SCHULTZ, Editors

Reading Lives: Working-Class Children and
Literacy Learning
DEBORAH HICKS

Inquiry Into Meaning: An Investigation of Learning
to Read, REVISED EDITION
EDWARD CHITTENDEN and TERRY SALINGER,
with ANNE M. BUSSIS

"Why Don't They Learn English?" Separating Fact
from Fallacy in the U.S. Language Debate
LUCY TSE

Conversational Borderlands: Language and Identity
in an Alternative Urban High School
BETSY RYMES

Inquiry-Based English Instruction
RICHARD BEACH and JAMIE MYERS

The Best for Our Children: Critical Perspectives on
Literacy for Latino Students
MARÍA DE LA LUZ REYES and
JOHN J. HALCÓN, Editors

Language Crossings:
Negotiating the Self in a Multicultural World
KAREN L. OGULNICK, Editor

What Counts as Literacy?
Challenging the School Standard
MARGARET GALLEGO and
SANDRA HOLLINGSWORTH, Editors

Critical Encounters in High School English:
Teaching Literary Theory to Adolescents
DEBORAH APPLEMAN

Beginning Reading and Writing
DOROTHY S. STRICKLAND and
LESLEY M. MORROW, Editors

Reading for Meaning:
Fostering Comprehension in the Middle Grades
BARBARA M. TAYLOR, MICHAEL F. GRAVES,
and PAUL van den BROEK, Editors

Writing in the Real World
ANNE BEAUFORT

Young Adult Literature and the New Literary
Theories
ANNA O. SOTER

Literacy Matters: Writing and Reading the Social Self
ROBERT P. YAGELSKI

Building Family Literacy in an Urban Community
RUTH D. HANDEL

Children's Inquiry:
Using Language to Make Sense of the World
JUDITH WELLS LINDFORS

Engaged Reading:
Processes, Practices, and Policy Implications
JOHN T. GUTHRIE and
DONNA E. ALVERMANN, Editors

Learning to Read:
Beyond Phonics and Whole Language
G. BRIAN THOMPSON and
TOM NICHOLSON, Editors

So Much to Say: Adolescents, Bilingualism, and
ESL in the Secondary School
CHRISTIAN J. FALTIS and PAULA WOLFE, Editors

Close to Home: Oral and Literate Practices in a
Transnational Mexicano Community
JUAN C. GUERRA

Authorizing Readers: Resistance and Respect in the
Teaching of Literature
PETER J. RABINOWITZ and
MICHAEL W. SMITH   (Continued)

LANGUAGE AND LITERACY SERIES (*continued*)

On the Brink:
Negotiating Literature and Life with Adolescents
SUSAN HYNDS

Life at the Margins: Literacy, Language, and
Technology in Everyday Life
JULIET MERRIFIELD, et al.

One Child, Many Worlds:
Early Learning in Multicultural Communities
EVE GREGORY, Editor

Literacy for Life: Adult Learners, New Practices
HANNA ARLENE FINGERET and
CASSANDRA DRENNON

The Book Club Connection
SUSAN I. MCMAHON and TAFFY E. RAPHAEL,
Editors, with VIRGINIA J. GOATLEY and
LAURA S. PARDO

Until We Are Strong Together:
Women Writers in the Tenderloin
CAROLINE E. HELLER

Restructuring Schools for Linguistic Diversity
OFELIA B. MIRAMONTES, ADEL NADEAU, and
NANCY L. COMMINS

Writing Superheroes: Contemporary Childhood,
Popular Culture, and Classroom Literacy
ANNE HAAS DYSON

Opening Dialogue: Understanding the Dynamics of
Language and Learning in the English Classroom
MARTIN NYSTRAND, et al.

Reading Across Cultures
THERESA ROGERS and ANNA O. SOTER, Editors

"You Gotta Be the Book": Teaching Engaged and
Reflective Reading with Adolescents
JEFFREY D. WILHELM

Just Girls:
Hidden Literacies and Life in Junior High
MARGARET J. FINDERS

The First R: Every Child's Right to Read
MICHAEL F. GRAVES, PAUL VAN DEN BROEK,
and BARBARA M. TAYLOR, Editors

Exploring Blue Highways:
Literacy Reform, School Change, and the Creation
of Learning Communities
JOBETH ALLEN, MARILYNN CARY, and
LISA DELGADO

Envisioning Literature:
Literary Understanding and Literature Instruction
JUDITH A. LANGER

Teaching Writing as Reflective Practice
GEORGE HILLOCKS, JR.

Talking Their Way into Science
KAREN GALLAS

Whole Language Across the Curriculum:
Grades 1, 2, 3
SHIRLEY C. RAINES, Editor

No Quick Fix: Rethinking Literacy Programs in
America's Elementary Schools
RICHARD L. ALLINGTON and
SEAN A. WALMSLEY, Editors

Nonfiction for the Classroom:
Milton Meltzer on Writing, History, and Social
Responsibility
E. WENDY SAUL, Editor

When Children Write
TIMOTHY LENSMIRE

Dramatizing Literature in Whole Language
Classrooms, SECOND EDITION
JOHN WARREN STEWIG and CAROL BUEGE

The Languages of Learning
KAREN GALLAS

Partners in Learning:
Teachers and Children in Reading Recovery
CAROL A. LYONS, GAY SU PINNELL, and
DIANE E. DEFORD

Social Worlds of Children Learning to Write in an
Urban Primary School
ANNE HAAS DYSON

The Politics of Workplace Literacy
SHERYL GREENWOOD GOWEN

Inside/Outside:
Teacher Research and Knowledge
MARILYN COCHRAN-SMITH and SUSAN L. LYTLE

Literacy Events in a Community of Young Writers
YETTA M. GOODMAN and
SANDRA WILDE, Editors

Whole Language Plus: Essays on Literacy in the
United States and New Zealand
COURTNEY B. CAZDEN

Process Reading and Writing:
A Literature-Based Approach
JOAN T. FEELEY, DOROTHY S. STRICKLAND, and
SHELLEY B. WEPNER, Editors

Literacy for a Diverse Society
ELFRIEDA H. HIEBERT, Editor

Making Race Visible

Literacy Research for Cultural Understanding

EDITED BY

Stuart Greene
Dawn Abt-Perkins

FOREWORD BY
Gloria Ladson-Billings

AFTERWORD BY
Sonia Nieto

Teachers College
Columbia University
New York and London

Published by Teachers College Press, 1234 Amsterdam Avenue, New York, NY 10027

Library of Congress Cataloging-in-Publication Data

Making race visible : literacy research for cultural understanding / edited by Stuart Greene,
    Dawn Abt-Perkins ; foreword by Gloria Ladson-Billings ; afterword by Sonia Nieto.
        p. cm. — (Language and literacy series)
    Includes bibliographical references and index.
    ISBN 0-8077-4392-5 (cloth : alk. paper) — ISBN 0-8077-4391-7 (pbk. : alk. paper)
        1. Reading—United States.   2. Multicultural education—United States.
    3. Race awareness in children—United States.   I. Greene, Stuart.   II. Abt-Perkins, Dawn.
    III. Language and literacy series (New York, N.Y.)
    LB1050.2.M37 2003
    370.117—dc21   2003056366

ISBN 0-8077-4391-7 (paper)
ISBN 0-8077-4392-5 (cloth)

Printed on acid-free paper

Manufactured in the United States of America

10   09   08   07   06   05   04   03   8   7   6   5   4   3   2   1

Contents

Foreword   **vii**
    Gloria Ladson-Billings

Introduction   How Can Literacy Research Contribute
           to Racial Understanding?   1
    Stuart Greene and Dawn Abt-Perkins

Part I. Recognizing Teacher and Student Racial Identities

1. Teacher and Student Attitudes on Racial Issues:
   The Complementarity of Practitioner Research and
   Outsider Research   35
       Courtney B. Cazden

2. Parallax: Addressing Race in Preservice Literacy Education   51
       Arlette Ingram Willis

3. "Are You Makin' Me Famous or Makin' Me a Fool?"
   Responsibility and Respect in Representation   71
       Deborah Appleman

Part II. Working Against "Color Blind" Practices and Contexts

4. Negotiating Race in Classroom Research:
   Tensions and Possibilities   89
       Joanne Larson

5. Successful Strategies of Latino Students:
   Bringing Their Worldviews to Their Studies   107
       Marilyn S. Sternglass

Part III. Making Visible Power and Discrimination

6. Tenth-Grade Literacy and the Mediation of Culture,
    Race, and Class   131
        Melanie Sperling

7. Reading Discrimination   149
        Patricia E. Enciso

8. Diversity Discourses:
    Reading Race and Ethnicity in and around Children's Writing   178
        Colette Daiute and Hollie Jones

Afterword   **201**
        Sonia Nieto

About the Contributors   **207**

Index   **211**

Foreword

Gloria Ladson-Billings

Stuart Greene and Dawn Abt-Perkins have assembled a group of first-rate literacy and language scholars to take on the challenge of race and racism. This work meets the dual criteria of educational research in that it is both theoretically substantive and practically significant.

This work made me think back to an earlier point in my own career. When my professional dossier was submitted for tenure review by my university's social sciences divisional committee, it contained the two requisite scholarly pieces my university requires for "objective" evaluation. One piece was my then recently published book (1994), *The Dreamkeepers: Successful teachers of African American Children.* The second piece was an article I coauthored with William Tate (1995) entitled, "Toward a Critical Race Theory of Education." I felt relatively confident about the book. It contained empirical research that was funded by my postdoctoral fellowship. Although I thought of what I was doing as "path breaking," I had honored enough of the canons of research to know that most scholars would recognize it as "scholarship." However, the critical race theory piece was entirely conceptual. It raised troubling ideas about the fixed place of racism in our society and it suggested that much of the work that had gone before was unlikely to serve as a corrective. It was what many in the scholarly community might consider a "dangerous" move for a junior scholar to make. The short answer was that it was not a dangerous move, since I was indeed tenured. However, as a part of my state's open records laws I was permitted to see my entire tenure file and read the external review letters.

The letters written by senior colleagues were flattering and humbling. I was gratified to learn that many of the people I looked to for scholarly wisdom and guidance held my work in high esteem. There was, however, one "interesting" letter. One scholar commented that while she or he thought my work in culturally relevant pedagogy was "important," "outstanding," and "cutting edge," she or he was "less sanguine about my work on critical race theory." This work, the letter went on to say, was divisive and destructive in the social sciences and had no place in education.

My own reaction to this individual's response might be seen by others as curious. Instead of being discouraged, I read those words as an indicator that I was on the leading edge of important work. Yes, it made established scholars uncomfortable. Yes, it was about speaking the previously unspoken and yes, it offered scholarship infused with confrontation and critique.

Similarly, this volume offers scholarship infused with confrontation and critique. This confrontation and critique is not offered for its own sake. Rather, it forces us to deal with the ongoing and seemingly never-ending choreography of race that has been present since the early founding of the United States. The contributors to this volume have taken up critical race theory as a rubric for making sense of literacy, and literacy as a rubric for making sense of race.

The opening chapter sets the stage for discussing race. It looks at the epistemological, ontological, and symbolic meanings of race in our society. It asks questions about our difficulty in speaking about race aloud. Why, whenever the subject is race, do we struggle to stay on topic and sustain attention? Race, according to Toni Morrison (1992), "has become metaphorical—a way of referring to and disguising forces, events, classes, and expressions of social decay and economic division far more threatening to the body politic than biological 'race' ever was" (p. 63).

In an earlier work I argued (Ladson-Billings, 1998), "Our notions of race (and its use) are so complex that even when it fails to 'make sense' we continue to employ and deploy it . . . that our conceptions of race, even in a postmodern and/or postcolonial world are more embedded and fixed than in a previous age" (p. 9).

I have tried to use critical race theory (CRT) in my work because it offers not only new ways to consider race and its various permutations, but also new methodologies to consider a variety of persistent social injustices and inequities. Chief among these new methodological tools is narrative: storytelling and counter storytelling. CRT uses storytelling to "analyze the myths, presuppositions, and received wisdoms that make up the common culture about race and that invariably render Blacks (and other people of color) one down" (Delgado, 1995, p. xiv).

This volume is filled with stories, from Cazden's retelling of Vivian Paley's stories, to Willis's students' journal narratives, to Sperling's stories of two very different 10th grade English classrooms, to Enciso's fourth and fifth graders and their multiple readings of a single text. These stories serve as both scaffold and edifice for the volume; the authors use them to explore the complexities and insistence of race in the classroom and our lives. But the volume is also filled with tensions. These tensions revolve around the role of the researcher and the researched, the knower and the known, the subject and the object. They also revolve around subject matter and social matters. And they revolve around theory, practice, and praxis.

It is no accident that literacy serves as a site of racial struggle and potentially of racial understanding. Historically, in the United States being literate was a marker of humanity and served as the criterion for citizenship. Cornelius (1991) points out that literacy literally meant survival to Black people. The ability to read and write allowed enslaved Africans access to information that was vital to their liberation struggle. In fact, literacy was seen as so powerful that, in order to protect the interests of White slave owners people were legally prohibited from teaching enslaved Blacks to read and write. According to Cornelius (1991), "For enslaved African-Americans, literacy was more than a path to individual freedom—it was a communal act, a political demonstration of resistance to oppression and of self-determination for the black community" (p. 3).

Literacy has been an interesting racial battleground. Prendergast (2003) argues that literacy became the site of struggle for racial justice while it simultaneously served as a site of racial injustice, since it was sometimes used to rationalize White privilege. An example of this injustice was the pervasive use of literacy tests as arbitrary tools to deny voting privileges to newly emancipated Blacks.

Literacy became one of the primary weapons in the modern civil rights movement. People like Septima Clark and Esau Jenkins worked tirelessly in Citizenship Schools throughout the South to improve the literacy of a people one to two generations out of enslavement. To be able to read and write was (and continues to be) about power. From a CRT perspective, literacy represents a form of property. It is a property that traditionally was "owned" and "used" by Whites in the society. Its possession signified the superiority of its possessor. Clark and Jenkins used their Citizenship Schools to empower illiterate sharecroppers in ways that government-sponsored programs could not (Morris, 1984).

As splendid as this collection is, it still leaves the reader with a number of questions about issues of race and literacy. One of the questions springs out of an observation. Why are so few men engaged in this work? Perhaps the limited number of men is a function of who comprises the professional ranks of literacy education scholars. However, it seems consonant with critical race theory to note that those who have experienced social marginalization and alienation—in this case, women—may be better positioned to recognize and address inequity and injustice found in other realms.

Another question that this volume raises is what my students now know as the "so what" question. We have crafted elegant theory, we have mined the literature, we have meticulously collected the data, and we are confident in our results. These steps work well in the conventional dissertation "exercise." However, when the issues we study are of such grave import, we need to know what difference, if any, our results will make in the lives of real people. While I am not suggesting that researchers should only engage in policy- and/or practice-oriented work, I fear we do not have the luxury to merely wring our collective hands about the sorry state of race relations in schools and classrooms. What do practitioners and policy makers know (or know better) as a result of this volume? Each chapter provides a number of new insights. How teachers, administrators, and teacher educators make use of these insights is crucial for increasing access to literacy and opportunities for racial reconciliation.

A third question this volume provokes is: "What's next?" The chapter authors have presented us with some beautifully crafted descriptions of close-to-the-shop-floor practices at a variety of levels. Their descriptions are complex, rich, and nuanced. Like a kaleidoscope they shift and change with every new turn and reading. We see race and literacy through the lens of classroom teachers. We see it through the lens of researcher. We see it through the lens of classroom teachers who are researchers and we see it through the lens of researchers who are classroom teachers. We get glimpses of how students see the classroom and a small peek at how parents experience their children's literacy learning. But, what are our next steps?

As researchers we must ask ourselves if we can be satisfied with reporting and interpreting inequity and injustice or do we have some greater obligation toward advocacy? From my perspective there is only one ethically defensible response to that question. If we hold ourselves to the standards of physicians who pledge, "first, do no harm," than we have many opportunities for intervention. We have an obligation to the students we teach never to avoid the knotty and uncomfortable issues of race, class, and gender that persist in our society. We have an obligation to our colleagues to challenge their resistance and ignorance to how these issues are made manifest in their work. We have an obligation to our institutions to push them to confront the "corporateization" of the university and to work against exclusionary and discriminatory policies. And we have an obligation to our profession to disrupt the canonization and reinscription of curricula and dogma that offer no space for new ideas about the nature and scope of our work.

The obligations I outlined above speak to a broader group of professionals than just the literacy education community. Indeed, if the charge were theirs alone I would feel more confident of the likelihood that it would be met. But this charge falls to a broad and diverse range of scholars, some who are actively engaged in working against racial understanding, a much larger contingent who sits on the sidelines content to ignore and diminish the issue, and a tiny fraction, like the authors in this volume, who insist on pushing the issues in rigorous and creative ways. It is to this latter group we look for leadership and hope. Their dogged determinism will help us all to do research for racial understanding.

REFERENCES

Cornelius, J. D. (1991). *When I can read my title clear: Literacy, slavery, and religion in the antebellum south.* Columbia, SC: University of South Carolina Press.

Delgado, R. (Ed.). (1995). *Critical race theory: The cutting edge.* Philadelphia: Temple University Press.

Ladson-Billings, G. (1994). *The dreamkeepers: Successful teachers of African American children.* San Francisco: Josey-Bass.

Ladson-Billings, G. (1998). Just what is critical race theory and what's it doing in a "nice" field like education. *International Journal of Qualitative Studies in Education, 11*(1), 7–24.

Ladson-Billings, G., & Tate, W. F. (1995). Toward a critical race theory of education. *Teachers College Record, 97,* 47–68.

Morris, A. D. (1984). *Origins of the civil rights movement: Black communities organizing for change.* New York: Free Press.

Morrison, T. (1992). *Playing in the dark: Whiteness and the literary imagination.* Cambridge, MA: Harvard University Press.

Prendergast, C. (2003). *Literacy and racial justice: The politics of learning after Brown v. Board of Education.* Carbondale, IL: Southern Illinois University Press.

Making
Race Visible

How Can Literacy Research Contribute to Racial Understanding?

Stuart Greene and Dawn Abt-Perkins

At a National Council of Teachers of English (NCTE) conference, we attended a session entitled, "Color-Blindness in the Classroom: Can Black and White Students Talk Meaningfully across the Barrier of Race?" Conducted by Sharon Lewis and Sarah Jonsberg (2001), the session was intended to help teachers find ways to engage their students in multiracial conversations about texts. One of the exercises the presenters asked us to complete entailed reading the graduation scene from Maya Angelou's *I Know Why the Caged Bird Sings* and to discuss our thoughts in small, mixed-raced groups. During the discussion, Dawn's group talked about many topics—discrimination, feelings of being an outsider, feelings of helplessness and anger, our own experiences with achievement. Despite the focus of the sessions, none of the participants talked about race—our own or the narrator's—or racism, the indisputable central topic of the piece. Sharon Lewis then asked us to consider why it was difficult to maintain a conversation focused on race even with a text ostensibly about race. The question hung in the air unanswered. Then stories from White teachers in the room emerged, each story illustrating teachers' frustration and anxiety about working on racial issues and racial texts in their classrooms. Again the discussion wandered into other related territory—censorship, working with African American parents, and the like. The teachers present never directly addressed Sharon's question.

Why could we not keep a conversation focused on racial discrimination, on racialized experience, or on how who we were affected our reading of this text? This experience illustrated for us that, as educators, we may very well lack strategies and experiences with having conversations about race or racism across multiracial experiences.

We had a similar experience at the NCTE Assembly for Research conference entitled, "Talking Reading, Writing, and Race: Contributions of Literacy Research to Racial Understanding," which inspired this book. As cochairs of the conference, we challenged the researchers present to consider the ways in which race influences the work they do as literacy researchers, particularly the questions they ask, their theories of race, and their investments in the outcomes of their investigations in urban settings. They, too, had difficulty, a symptom perhaps of the ill-defined nature of race (e.g., duCille, 1996). All too often equated with the color of one's skin, race is a powerful determinant of social status, where one lives, works, or goes to school; race is also a process of social stratification that may be, paradoxically, transparent in literacy research. As Weis, Fine, Weseen, and Wong (2000) observe, "'Race' is a social construction, indeed. But 'race' in a racist society bears profound consequences for daily life, identity, social movements, and the ways in which most groups *other*" (p. 40). The real question is how we can talk and write about race.

Thus, it may not be surprising that speakers at the conference focused less on race than on discussions of differences in language use (cf., Ball, 1996; Cazden, 1994; Lee, 1993; Michaels, 1991), community literacy patterns (cf., Heath, 1983; Schaafsma, 1993), and culturally informed literacy practices (cf., Dyson, 1997; Gutierrez, 1992). We do not wish to diminish the recent history of literacy research on cultural differences. However, we do not believe this body of work addressed the concerns of the teachers in that crowded room—concerns about cross-racial communication in multiracial literacy classrooms; achievement and tracking issues; and about establishing classroom cultures where race, discrimination, and privilege could be safely and productively addressed.

The researchers whose projects make up this volume foreground race in their inquiries into literacy instructional practice at a time when census figures tell us what many teachers already know: that we live in an increasingly multiracial society and that despite the advances made toward integration after the Civil Rights Act in 1964, minority students living in poverty are more segregated than at any time since the Supreme Court ruled that segregation was a violation of the Fourteenth Amendment (Orfield & Gordon, 2001). Although Latino enrollments have exploded during the past 10 years, little has been done to provide desegregated education for Latino students. As well, they have for some time been more segregated than Black students, not only by race and ethnicity but by poverty as well. Data also demonstrate that the United States has increasingly become a metropolitan society, dominated by the suburbs where Black and Latino middle-class students are equally segregated. As Orfield and Gordon observe, "The suburbs are becoming far more differentiated by race and ethnicity and the lines of social change have moved out far beyond the central cities" (p. 2). More than ever before, they also argue, "Teachers are faced with a major set of challenges to the future of the minority middle class"

(p. 2). If we expect teachers to be effective, insuring that students acquire the social and cultural capital they will need to have in the 21st century, then they need to understand more fully the complexities of learning across both race and class.

As the editors of this volume, we argue that, as teachers and researchers, we need to engage more fully in the process of making race visible, both as a mark of difference and privilege, and ways that the institutions of schooling and society have placed minority students in poverty at distinct disadvantages in achieving access to quality education, housing, health care, and employment. To do this, we believe it is necessary to interrogate our sense of privilege in the research we conduct, the power we wield as we create racialized categories to describe students and teachers, and present what we find. This means reading our projects and ourselves as "racial texts" written through the experience we bring as people of different racial backgrounds (Cochran-Smith, 2000). More than this, we argue that researchers should examine their own investments as they study the literate practices of minority students, blurring the line between researcher and activist. If our research is to make a difference, we must be willing to challenge, even transform, the structures of schooling that have insured that we have a position of privilege and that have also disenfranchised generations of poor minority students.

Questions we raised in planning our NCTE Assembly for Research Conference several years ago remain on our minds today:

- How do researchers in education negotiate the decisions they make in creating racial categories in their work?
- What political, social, and personal investments do they bring to studies of race in the classrooms they observe?
- What are the consequences of focusing on race in reporting what researchers find?
- In what ways do their studies transform their own thinking about how race plays itself out in their investigations of literacy?

Our sense is that few studies have confronted race in significant ways, despite the urgency expressed in reviews, reports of research, and the like. For example, Michelle Fine and her colleagues (1997) observed that such research is imperative. After all, they argued that "race is a critical and defining feature of lived experience that young and old and people of all colors reflect upon, embody, challenge, and negotiate" (p. 251). In the recently published *White Reign: Deploying Whiteness in America* (Kincheloe et al., 2000), the editors conclude that educators at every level not only need to teach about and discuss issues of racial identity, but foreground the ways in which power operates in their classrooms. Similarly, issues related to race and social justice have gained prominence in a multipart series of articles in the *New York Times* (Correspondents, 2001) describing "how race is lived in America." As teachers and researchers, we cannot ignore the call for making schools more equitable for all of our students. This is especially true at a time when the impact of *Brown v. The Board of Education* (1954) continues to erode through such Supreme Court decisions as *Board of Education of Oklahoma City v. Dowell* (1991), *Freeman v. Pitts* (1992), and *Missouri v. Jenkins* (1995), in each case the Court ruling in favor of rapid restoration of local control as the primary goal of desegregation cases; George Bush Sr.'s first presidential veto of civil rights legislation in American history; and George Bush Jr.'s emphasis on school accountability through high-stakes testing in lieu of the federal government's taking responsibility for the structural inequities that create disadvantages for the low-income minority students many of us teach.

WHY FOCUS ON RACE?

Like others, the contributors to this volume have been concerned with the policies of housing and schooling that have led to the unequal distribution of opportunities to those people who are both poor and minority. Where people attend school is determined by the politics of "racial geography" (Santow, 2002), a notion that describes the ways in which minority groups have been contained in urban spaces where there is a lack of such resources as health care, nutrition, jobs, and safe housing. Recent research (e.g., Orfield & Gordon, 2001) indicate that families who are minority and poor are isolated in urban areas where housing and schools have devastating effects on the psyches of those who inhabit those spaces. Based on this research, it is not surprising that Black and Latino students constitute 80% of the public school populations in such cities as New York, Boston, and Detroit.

One consequence of these inequities have led to what Jencks and Phillips (1998) have termed the Black-White achievement gap. They observed that:

> African Americans currently score lower than European Americans on vocabulary, reading, and mathematics tests, as well as on tests that claim to measure scholastic aptitude and intelligence. This gap appears before children enter kindergarten, and it persists into adulthood. It has narrowed since 1970, but the typical American Black still scores below 75 percent of American Whites on most standardized tests. On some tests the typical American Black scores more than 85 percent of Whites. (p. 1)

Of course, this gap is not an inevitable fact of nature.

A glance at histories of education reveal circumstances more than a century ago in American education that inform exclusionary practices in our schools today. David Tyack (1974), for example, explained that, "During the nineteenth century no group in the United States had a greater faith in the equalizing power of schooling or a clearer understanding of the democratic promise of education" (p. 110) than African Americans. James Anderson (1988) as well has provided accounts of the "unique system of public and private education that was developed by and for Black southerners between 1860 and 1935" (p. 2). His accounts offer a much-needed corrective to the distortions and half truths in histories that describe the role that northern White philanthropy played in fostering the education of ex-slaves. Although Anderson points to a strong tradition of education and desire to sustain Black schools for themselves, he also underscores the tactics of federal and state governments and extralegal organizations that disenfranchised, segregated, or cheated Black pupils across the nation. Similarly, Carl Kaestle (1983/1999) has observed that despite the stress the founders of the republic placed on education—that education put citizens on equal footing—even the "most ringing statements about the equality of all men were not taken to include women or Black people" (p. 92). Indeed, as Tyack concluded, "Blacks learned that the educational system was not meant for them" (Tyack, 1974, p. 110).

One unfortunate consequence of these exclusionary practices is to think of Black children living in poverty as "culturally deprived" or "culturally deficient." Thus the role of school, some would argue, is to compensate for children's presumed lack of cultural and social resources (Ladson-Billings, 1999). In turn, the prevailing question is what schools can do to raise the achievement of Black students. Ladson-Billings outlined three possible responses that teachers have made in the past. The first is to improve achievement through remediation or acceleration without regard to students' social or cultural background. The second is to resocialize urban Black students into mainstream behaviors, values, and attitudes while simultaneously teaching them basic skills (e.g., Delpit, 1995). And the third, to which we ascribe, is to facilitate learning by building on students' language and culture as a bridge to school achievement (e.g., De La Luz Reyes, 2000; Gay, 2000; Lee, 1994; Ladson-Billings, 1994; Nieto, 1999).

Although Latin American children living in poverty in such major cities as Chicago have performed somewhat better than Black students (Orfield et al., 1996), patterns of underachievement for poor Black and Latino students compared to those living in White suburban areas can be seen in the National Assessment of Educational Progress findings. As Orfield and his colleagues point out, "only 19% of disadvantaged urban seventeen-year olds had 'adept' reading skills in 1984 compared to 50 to 55 percent in advantaged suburban communities" (p. 66). They conclude that the "concentration of minority and low-income students in low-performing schools creates a vicious cycle of failure, as these students have little exposure to the culture of achievement that characterizes many suburban schools" (p. 66). Oakes's (1985) study of tracking, too, affirms that low-income minority students are not exposed to the kinds of "high-status" knowledge or cultural capital that characterizes this culture of achievement. Unfortunately, recent studies of tracking (e.g., Oakes & Guiton, 1995; Yonezawa, Wells, & Serna, 2002) and achievement (Orfield & Gordon, 2001) underscore the perpetuation of structural inequalities and minority student underachievement in urban settings where they attend segregated schools.

However, identifying structural inequities in the organization of schools does not fully explain the achievement gap in performance across racial categories (e.g., Oakes & Guiton, 1995). Part of the responsibility rests on teachers' attitudes and experiences specifically tied to race. Ferguson's (1998) survey of teacher expectations led him to draw four conclusions that underscore the ways in which teachers define difference in the assumptions they bring to the classroom:

- Teachers have lower expectations for Blacks than Whites.
- Teachers' expectations have more impact on Black students' performance than White students.
- Teachers expect less of Blacks than of Whites because Black students' past performance and behavior have been worse.
- Teachers perpetuate racial disparities through basing their expectations on past performance.

Although we know that teacher expectations influence student outcomes for children of color, we know little about how researchers' expectations have shaped the outcomes of literacy research. Those teachers who are most interested in bridging racial differences find that both traditional research on literacy development and instructional practice are too far removed from their own experiences. They have difficulty translating the dictates of "expert" accounts into things they can do to improve the growth and development of their students (cf., Freedman, Simons, Kalnin, Casareno, & The M-Class Teams, 1999). We know that teachers are concerned about issues of race and how they affect students' investments in classrooms and school cultures, engagement in reading and the study of literature, and their progress as writers. In turn, teachers seek research that will guide their reflections, inspire them in developing their own research projects, and inform their perspectives on their work in racially diverse literacy classrooms.

DEFINING RACE: ARE YOU CALLING ME A RACIST?[1]

As we have suggested, keeping a conversation in research or teaching communities focused on race is difficult to accomplish. Landsman (2001) offers a useful explanation in recognizing that White teachers stand in front of classrooms and populate administrative offices. The percentage of teachers of color, at around 10%, is diminishing, despite the increase of students of color in our classrooms. She writes: "For those of us who are white, I believe avoidance comes because we are afraid of our own racism. At the same time, we want to remain comfortable with our interpretations of race, even if they are inaccurate or just plain wrong. Such a discussion makes people uncomfortable, uncertain" (p. xii). For that matter, Landsman suggests that "those of us who are white do not want to talk about our white skin or explore what 'whiteness' has to do with all that is going on in our own lives or the lives of our students" (p. xii). But there may be an equally profound reason for avoiding the topic or issues surrounding race. Ian Lopez (1995), a legal scholar, puts the problem succinctly when he observes that, "Despite the pervasive influence of race on our lives in U.S. law, a review of opinions and articles by judges and legal academics reveals a startling fact: few seem to know what race is and is not" (p. 193; see also Tatum, 1997). What does appear true, Lopez points out, is that one's ancestry and appearance—for example, one's hair, complexion, and facial features—remain dominant in determining one's economic prospects and fate in a "race-conscious market" (p. 192).

The definitional issue surrounding race is compounded by the fact that most would agree that race is a fluid, unstable fiction, a "social construction" (Weis, Fine, Weseen, & Wong, 2000, p. 39; see also Omi & Winant, 1994). Yet, Lopez offers a useful definition of race: "a group loosely bound together by historically contingent, socially significant elements of their morphology and/or ancestry . . . Neither an essence nor an illusion, [race] is an ongoing process of social and political struggle" (Lopez, 1995, p. 193). Seen in this way, race resists simple definition, especially once we see that there is no biological basis for race and "no genetic characteristics possessed by all the members of any one group" (Ladson-Billings, 2000, p. 259). Race is at once "part skin color, part privilege, and part social construction" (Landsman, 2001, p. xv).

By defining race in individual terms, it is possible to view racism more tangibly; in turn, individual acts are judged to be racist or not. However, this definition of racism as an individual, ethical act shuts down discussions about racism—especially among White people or in mixed-race groups—because people do not want to be put in the position of being judged. White researchers/teachers then avoid this work, either thinking they have nothing of meaning to contribute or out of fear of being judged as racist. Race is not "their" project. And African Americans find themselves preferring conversations with White colleagues in which racism is silenced because individualized definitions of race puts Black researchers and teachers in the uncomfortable role of judging the personal ethics of their colleagues. As White researchers, we have both made the mistake of turning to an African American colleague and asking the question, "Does what I am writing make me sound racist?" locating racism as something that may or may not exist and only within me.

Viewing racism as an individual phenomenon is reductive and shuts down dialogue. As an alternative, we argue with others that race is a social phenomenon that is open to critique. This places responsibility on those in power to change policies in order to distribute opportunities more equitably. Specifically, critical race theory (Ladson-Billings & Tate, 1995) offers an alternative definition for the type of conversation about racism we believe is necessary and productive in literacy research. Critical race theory defines racism as a present and unavoidable force in the construction of our social reality. Racism is a system of privileged discourses and discriminatory institutionalized practices, which act upon our individual perceptions of reality. Our understanding of what is real is intrinsically racist because we have grown up in and live in a society with racist institutions and discursive practices. As Gerardo Lopez (2001), in his review of critical race theory in educational research, states:

> Critical race theory abandons the neutral concept of a "color blind society" in favor of a critical perspective that recognizes the normality—and thus invisibility—of racism in our daily lives. (p. 30)

Critical race theorists challenge definitions of racism that locate racism in individual acts. Race is undeniably an element of social status and is, therefore, negotiated as a social process rather than as a biological determinant. Although critical race theory is not in any way monolithic, we might summarize some key conclusions that come out of recent work: that racial categories are fluid, systems of racial classification vary across cultures, members in a particular category are not immutable, and racial categories vary within a culture over time (Flagg, 1998). Most importantly, critical race theorists begin with the premise that race is a permanent feature of American society (Bell, 1992; Delgado, 1995).

The permanence of racism in our social reality means that we have a personal responsibility to understand racism and work against its effects. We are challenged to use race as a construct to examine the limitations of our interpretations, to wonder continually about the ways in which our racial identities are playing out in the work we do, and the extent to which our discursive practices maintain inequity and injustice. The questions that we should ask and now do ask in this work are:

- How is racism present in my interpretations?
- How is it working in these situations I am describing?
- Where are the "multiple faces of racism" (G. Lopez, 2001, p. 30) present?

In asking these questions, we accept that racism is always present and that our role is to make it as visible and open to scrutiny as possible. Our responsibility is to "scrutinize the often very subtle messages about identity and difference that float between the lines of the curriculum and consciously work to construct opportunities . . . in which all the members of the community are able to interrogate their construction of self and other" as Cochran-Smith (2000) suggests. The challenge that we see before us and that scholars of color have raised is not "solely about racism . . . it is also about truth and reality" (Ladson-Billings, 2001, p. 259).

More than critique and analysis, we need to develop through our research on literacy useful and strategic ways to combat racism in its various forms and manifestations. After all, people who are poor and of color live in a different America than those who are in power, continually living in disproportionate numbers in inner cities and attending inferior and inadequate primary and secondary schools. To combat inequities, the Bush administration has embraced a policy of increased testing, standards, and accountability to close the achievement gap between socially and economically disadvantaged students and their more advantaged peers. In short, the rhetoric of change is, "No Child Left Behind." However, research not only demonstrates key flaws in the assumptions used to justify high-stakes testing and accountability (Orfield & Kornhaber, 2001), but indicates such an approach to achieving equity has the potential to harm the very students policy has sought to help.

In fact, Natriello and Pallas (2001) reveal that graduation rates for minority students will likely fall with increased high-stakes testing. Their review of outcomes in three different states shows the ethnic and racial disparities in performance in Texas, New York, and Minnesota, concluding that "we should be concerned about their [high-stakes testing's] potential to exacerbate already substantial inequities in schooling" (p. 37). For example, Natriello and Pallas show that one could predict the number of students who would receive a Regents diploma by examining those schools with the lowest proportion of minority students and students living in poverty. The greater the proportion of students of color in a class or those receiving a free lunch in 1995–1996, the chances of students who receive a Regents diploma is diminished. Thus, given the potential problems of implementing high-stakes testing and increased standardization, it is necessary to effect change from the bottom up—with students, teachers, and researchers, who blur the line between researcher and activist.

CONTRIBUTIONS OF LITERACY RESEARCH

We are interested in teasing out the features, dilemmas, and processes researchers have developed to address how racial differences shape learning, development, and classroom relations in their studies of literacy processes. Through analysis of the profiles of research projects presented in this volume, we hope to answer questions raised about this type of research, such as: How do researchers manage the ethical and social dimensions of this work? And, most importantly, What can be learned about literacy processes and achievement by focusing on race?

I. Developing Local Knowledge of Teaching and Learning Practices

The first objective in this volume is to foreground the experiences of students of color, their learning contexts, and the teachers who work with them, as these are still too rarely represented in literacy studies. As Daiute and Jones (this volume) point out, understanding racial and ethnic conflict has been a national preoccupation in the United States for many years, yet whether and how children engage in discussions about race and ethnicity has only recently become a focus. Issues of identity, social development, and the ongoing need to foster positive relationships in schools warrant further inquiry into children's racial and ethnic understandings as they occur in daily discourse. The researchers in this volume have each sought to address issues of race directly in providing accounts of students who do not respond to current forms of literacy instruction (cf., Delpit, 1995; Nieto, 1999).

Unfortunately, much literacy research in the past has tended to erase students' racial backgrounds. When literacy research has focused on race, it is often in general terms. Ignoring the particulars of different cultural and ethnic groups, researchers have obscured the real racial tensions dividing literacy classrooms and our understanding of social experience.

II. Theorizing Our Own Racial Positions

The second objective is to make explicit research processes, including choices in negotiating representation issues, the role that racial identity plays in the research process, and the sociopolitical contexts and consequences of literacy research on race. We believe that this is an important move in research because the tendency in literacy research has been to focus on "social constructs of difference in terms of 'other' without fully considering the implications of theorizing our own racial positions" (Goodburn, 1999, p. 68). Indeed, we need to consider the privileged position of our discourses, acknowledging our own investments and considering the consequences of what we write beyond mere confession (Goodburn, 1999; Keating, 1995, p. 904).

III. Considering the Ethics and Consequences of Our Research

Our third objective is to argue that researchers examining race need to be reflexive in their attempts to understand identity. The reflexivity we each strive to achieve in the chapters that follow has important ethical implications. After all, the ways that we construct our research agendas, carry out these projects, and disseminate the results of these projects "directly raise questions about who has the power to define whom, and when, and how" (McCarthy & Crichlow, 1993, p. xvi). But this reflexivity should not prevent us from doing our research. Without our efforts, students' and teachers' voices may never be heard unless we investigate the complexities of literacy learning in urban settings.

The type of reflexivity we have in mind entails reflecting on the source of our knowledge and the discursive practices from which we look at ourselves and others (Goodburn, 1999). Thus, the authors in this volume not only provide accounts of students, but reflect upon their own stances as researchers. For example, we have each attempted to answer the following questions:

- How are we reading our students?
- How do we decide what is significant and how do we determine how to describe this significance?
- Why do we use language and literacy as we do in our professional and private lives?
- What roles do language and literacy play in our construction of identity, as well as in the identities of those whom we believe are different from us inside and outside the classroom (Moss & Walters, 1993, p. 135)?
- What are the consequences of our research for the students we observe and for ourselves?

IV. Detailing the Value of the Research Process for Change

Our fourth objective is to reveal the consequences of research that not only details the experiences of students but the outcomes and value of the actual research process itself: coming to terms with our multiple purposes, audiences, and responsibilities as potential agents of change as we discuss the value of this type of research in addressing issues of racial inequality in school literacy achievement.

WAYS OF SEEING THE INVISIBLE

Researchers in this volume demonstrate that race can be made more visible in literacy research as they foreground the following questions through examining students' and teachers' work in literacy instructional contexts: What is being represented, and why? What is missing? What values about literacy achievement are accepted? Which literacy processes make the most sense to me? Why do others not make sense? What role might race be playing in my interpretations? To make these aspects of racism in literacy research more visible, more questionable, we discovered that we needed to reflect on our view of epistemology—the experiences and realities that are accepted as the foundation of knowledge—and on the best forms of research that allowed us to think through race, power, and privilege.

When working in interpretive research traditions, the epistemology of the researchers is a part of the "data set." As Geertz (1983) reminds us, we can't represent what informants see but only what we see through our interpretive lens based on our experience. As qualitative researchers, we accept this perspective on the importance of the "I" of the researchers in the evolution of our research projects. The uniqueness of the researchers in this volume rests in their attempts to make visible their racial identities—how they understand how race circumscribes and informs understandings of self and others and works to privilege one perspective over another—as a part of the research process itself that must be theorized and interrogated along with other data.

RACIAL EPISTEMOLOGY IN LITERACY RESEARCH

As researchers representing the literate practices of the students we observe, we have sought to work what Fine (1994) has called the "hyphen" at which point the self and other "both separates and merges personal identities with our inventions of Others" (p. 70). To work the hyphen means using our personal stories and reflections to explore the ways we can represent others responsibly—not to engage in "simple reflexivity"—and transcend an either-or epistemology of self and other. The assumption motivating such an approach to research underscores an epistemological concern about the source of knowing. On the one hand, traditional views of knowledge insist that the individual mind is the source of knowledge, a way of knowing. On the other, critical race theory calls attention to the intersubjective and contingent nature of knowledge (e.g., Ladson-Billings & Tate, 1995; Delgado, 1995). Knowledge depends on relationships with others. Seen in this way, "epistemology is a system of knowing" (Ladson-Billings, 2000, p. 257) or worldview through which we see the world. A worldview serves as a lens or frame, determining how knowledge is produced and distributed, what is of value or legitimate and what is not, who can speak, and who cannot (Foucault, 1972). One cannot ignore the differential relations of power that come into play when a more dominant worldview comes into conflict with a more subordinate one, as is the case when the focus is on the legitimacy of African American vernacular or Spanish in schools. At the heart of this tension are such questions as, "Whose story is true?" and "What story will be considered legitimate enough to reach the public?"

Of particular concern is that the way in which the dominant European American worldview constructs race may come into conflict with the traditions of a subordinate group's own constructions. Specifically, Ladson-Billings (2001) points out that "notions of double consciousness (Du Bois, 1903/1953), *mestiza* consciousness (Anzaldua, 1987), and 'tribal secrets' (Warrior, 1995) discovered and uncovered by scholars of color explicate the ways that discursive, social, and institutional structures have created a sense of 'otherness' for those outside the dominant paradigm" (p. 258). These are perspectives from which educators might better understand multiple consciousness, constructions of race, positions of inclusion and exclusion, and potential liberation from the tyranny of oppression, each challenging "unitary notions" of identity (Ladson-Billings, 2001, pp. 259–262). Equally important, these perspectives not only underscore how race "works to inform one's relationship to knowledge and its production" (p. 266), but affirms an epistemology that recognizes the value of multiple and equally valid standpoints.

Racial epistemology is developed in critical conversation with the forces that shape our work as qualitative researchers. Delgado Bernal (1998) offers one such example, drawing on Corbin and Strauss's (1990) construct of "theoretical sensitivity"—the attributes of the researcher that enable him or her to give meaning to data. In turn, she describes four sources of "theoretical sensitivity": one's personal experience, one's reading of the existing literature, one's professional experience, and what is learned or discovered about one's personal identity in the analytic research process itself.

Who we are and what we have come to know as being right or true or of value is based on the raced text of our life story. First, personal experience as part of "theoretical sensitivity" is what is learned through past life experiences that help the researcher to "understand certain situations and why and what might happen in a particular setting under certain conditions" (1998, p. 564). Delgado Bernal claims it is culturally informed because it reaches "past the individual" and into "community memory" and history (p. 564). Drawing upon her past, she describes how her family experience of conquest, labor market stratification, and resistance and the storytelling of her community and family have shaped the types of research she has taken on, the kinds of questions she asks, and the kinds of data she believes to be important. Second, what we know is also based on what we have read. Delgado Bernal points out that what she has read both in the research and popular press has been related to who she is and had an effect on what she was "sensitive to look for in my data" (p. 565). Third, her professional experiences as a bilingual teacher and in community education in Latino communities have allowed her to "move into the educational environment and gain insight into the lives of Chicana students more quickly than someone who has never worked in a school setting with Chicana students" (p. 566). Fourth, the more interactions she has with her data, the more insight she has (Straus & Corbin, 1990). Delgado Bernal developed a "focus group strategy" that allowed her interpretations to be fed by the participants in her study and established an interactive process that fed her theoretical construction of her data. Finally, she closes her story by pointing to the continuous development of understanding of one-self culturally and racially as part of the process of doing research.

Delgado Bernal's illustration of how these categories of sources of personal knowledge helped her analyze the way "who she is" informed her research provides a framework for reflection on how race informs research generally. Delgado Bernal's work has led us to define what we are working toward in developing a sense of our own racialized epistemology as we guide our projects.

Although it has become readily accepted that researchers are never really absent from their work, it is equally clear that we must find ways to "write the self" in our research (Weis, Fine, Weseen, & Wong, 2000), working the hyphen in order to understand how our race influences our actions and interpretations. It is exactly this process toward understanding that we feel is so valuable and that Behar (1993), a cultural anthropologist, underscores when she explains that, "We ask for revelations of others, but we reveal little or nothing of ourselves; we make others vulnerable, but we ourselves remain invulnerable" (p. 273). Thus, we make ourselves vulnerable in the stories that we tell. These are stories that illustrate the value of revisiting our representations of others, at times demonstrating the ways that we can unknowingly distort the realties of the students to whom we are most committed.

KEY FEATURES OF LITERACY RESEARCH
FOR RACIAL UNDERSTANDING

Given this notion of an "achieved" racialized epistemology, we have developed a set of research assumptions that provide the context for us to recognize our "blind vision" (Cochran-Smith, 2000). "Blind vision" entails making the most of our commitment to uncovering racism while at once recognizing our limitations in being able to do so. These assumptions include: (1) accepting that in any single piece of research, we can only offer partial and tentative conclusions; (2) accepting that we will fail to produce fully the kinds of representations of students, teachers, and their work that we believe are possible but lie outside of our current knowledge and experience; (3) accepting conflict and incongruencies in our data because we know that this will feed productive interpretation; and finally (4) valuing the analytic power of framing and reframing our data. Working with these assumptions about research allows us to create a space from which to view the "invisible" nature of racism in our work.

To demonstrate our commitment to uncovering racism in classroom literacy communities and in instructional practices, we found ourselves gravitating toward certain forms of research projects. Because we wanted to keep the conversation focused on race, we found we needed to develop projects that allowed us to do the following well. We needed research constructs that allowed us to portray current realities without claiming anything as a final or conclusive reality. In other words, we wanted our representations to be viewed as partial and in dialogue with other possible representations. We wanted our research processes to reflect what we believe is necessary to teach in racially cognizant ways—as a scrutiny of interpretations. We wanted to resist representations that suggested "best practices" or located racism in individual acts by teachers or students. Finally, we wanted to highlight the value of stabilizing the partial explanations of our experiences in literacy classrooms (in the form of research reports or texts), demonstrating the consequences in terms of developing our perspective on our work of unpacking what is accessible to us while simultaneously raising questions about what we were missing.

Below we outline features of the research projects in this volume that enable "blind vision" (Cochran-Smith, 2000) about race in literacy research:

- *Contextualized.* Although all good research values the importance of careful, in-depth description and analysis of context in researching about race, we include our own purposes for doing this work as part of the context. In other words, we know that the commitments and intentions we bring to our projects will shape what we see as context and that it is important to describe these commitments.

- *Long-Term.* Many of the projects in this volume are part of long-term commitments to teachers and students. We portray and represent our work in these classrooms and with these teachers in a number of different "reports" over time. As a consequence, we might frame the ways that we represent teachers and students in one instance, but reframe our understanding when we revisit our earlier representations. This is especially true when we try to understand motives and actions through one or more theoretical lenses.
- *Self-Reflexive.* In order to stay vigilant in our focus on how racism is at work in our projects, we need continually to seek out contradictions, to force ourselves to describe that which is hard to explain, the response that didn't fit our expectations. We seek out conflict, engage in negotiation, and represent a reconciliation of our beliefs with our findings. In some projects, this takes the shape of trying out multiple theories as lenses for understanding. In other projects, this takes the shape of looking at the same data by asking multiple questions. And, in still others, interpretation is informed by engaging in collaborative interpretations with multiple readers of the data.

ORGANIZATION OF THE BOOK

The Historical View

In her preface to this collection, Gloria Ladson-Billings reminds us of the extent to which literacy has always been a site of struggle in the United States, implicitly addressing Enciso's concern about why "the story has to be told again." In fact, despite our leaders' unyielding faith in education as the "great equalizer" in forming common schools in the mid-19th century, neither Thomas Jefferson nor Horace Mann had envisioned a place for students of color (or women) in publicly funded schools. Yet, historically, African Americans have always understood the importance of education, as we discussed earlier. Benjamin Roberts, an activist in Boston, struggled to integrate schools that culminated in *Roberts v. Boston* (1849) but his plea was denied in the court's ruling; adolescent girls of African descent hid their books (or contraband) beneath their embroidery in what were ostensibly sewing schools, despite attempts by plantation owners to keep these girls (and all African Americans) illiterate; and Frederick Douglass's (1992) powerful words associating education, liberty, and struggle echo in *Zelman v. Simmons-Harris* (2002), a case supporting school choice in

Cleveland. Douglass wrote over a hundred years earlier that "[e]ducation means . . . emancipation. It means light and liberty. It means the uplifting of the soul of man into glorious light of truth, the light by which men can only be made free."

Yet the end of struggle that the *Brown v. Board of Education* (1954) appeared to signify nearly 50 years ago has been all too evanescent. As Prendergast (2002) has argued recently, the decision enforcing the Fourteenth amendment (equal protection under the law) was perhaps more rhetorical than real. This is all too evident given the recent dismantling of desegregation. In fact, Pamela Grundy's (2002) interviews with former students at the all-Black Second Ward High School in Charlotte, North Carolina, bring into focus the process of resegregation and what that means despite a century and a half of struggle for equity in education. The schools in Charlotte are "more segregated than they have been in twenty-five years," Grundy explains. Despite this fact, a federal judge freed Charlotte schools from the mandate of *Brown*, thus giving the district unitary status. Essentially, this is the legal term used in determining that "no present racial inequities were the result of *deliberate* (editors' emphasis) segregation" (Grundy, 2002, p. 34). This decision in Charlotte brought the end of busing. Similarly, David Halbfinger's (2002) *New York Times* account of James Meredith's legacy 40 years after he integrated the University of Mississippi reminds us of a struggle that many college-age students are too young to know about. Halbfinger recalls that Meredith gained entrance to Ole Miss "backed by 300 federal marshals and 30,000 troops as thousands of white students and outsiders ran riot over the campus. Two men were left dead and at least 300 wounded." The ghosts of this time will never really be put to rest.

Given this historical backdrop that Ladson-Billings implicitly points to, the value of the studies presented in this collection may be seen in the researchers' sustained attempts to examine the multiple and conflicting ways in which both teachers and students understand race in school and the potential for both teachers and researchers to reinscribe structures of inequality. In making this point, Ladson-Billings tells her own story of how scholars reacted to her initial attempts to articulate critical race theory, a lens that many of the authors have adopted in telling their own stories. One reviewer of her work felt that the central tenets of critical race theory were "divisive and destructive," that such an approach to investigating literacy "had no place" in education. Insisting on the permanence of race in the classroom and our lives and the equities that privilege those who are already advantaged runs a similar risk—one that makes us vulnerable as we seek to "work the hypen" of researcher/researched, insider/outsider, self/other, and researcher/activist. Thus, the volume is filled with uneasy tensions that, as Ladson-Billings points out, "revolve around subject matter and social matters. And, they revolve around theory, practice, and praxis" (this volume).

The danger of critique is that we are often left with unanswered questions. For example, Ladson-Billings asks:

- What do practitioners and policy makers know (or know better) as a result of the studies presented in this volume?
- What are the ways that will enable us to consider race and its various permutations?
- What new methodologies will allow us to consider a variety of persistent social injustices and inequities?
- What is the next step?

Ultimately, Ladson-Billings believes that the "charge falls to a broad and diverse range of scholars, some who are actively engaged in working against racial understanding and a much larger contingent who sits on the sidelines content to ignore and diminish the issue" (this volume). It is not only time to talk directly about race—even when such talk makes us uncomfortable—but it is time to act.

Part I: The Value of Stories

In Part I of this volume, "Recognizing Teacher and Student Racial Identities," we begin with the stories that teachers and students tell in constructing race in their daily interactions and the effects that these narratives have on the tellers. The value of stories is a hallmark of critical race theory in that storytelling is a means for "analyz[ing] the myths, presuppositions, and received wisdoms that make up the common culture about race that invariably render blacks and other minorities one down" (Delgado, 1995, p. xiv). Ladson-Billings (2000) builds on this view, explaining the value of storytelling to the qualitative researcher: "that it can be used to demonstrate how the same phenomenon can be told in different and multiple ways depending on the story-tellers" (p. 268).

In Chapter 1, Cazden underscores the powerful stories that teacher practitioners tell, stories that, in keeping with Cochran-Smith's sense of what enables "blind vision" in literacy research focusing on race, are contextual, self-reflexive, and reframed over time. In turn, Cazden argues that the experiences of teacher practitioners serve as an important complement to the researchers whose perspectives are distinctly more distant from the contexts that these teacher practitioners negotiate every day through their interactions with students and their parents. In matters concerning race, both the "insider" perspectives of teachers and the "outsider" perspectives of researchers are necessary and legitimate means for understanding literacy and race—particularly the issues that Cazden takes up in this first chapter: teachers' expectations of students and the place of language variation in schools. Of course, the distinctions between insider and outsider blur, as many of the authors in this volume demonstrate when they assume the role of both teacher and researcher (such as Willis, Appleman, and Enciso in this volume).

As Cazden points out, few educators (or researchers) reflect on the possible biases that influence their own teaching, which is why the stories she recounts are so powerful. This is particularly true when she describes Michelle Fine's struggle to "detrack" a ninth grade classroom. Based on her field notes, Fine reflects upon her lowered expectations for students who appeared "disengaged" or the ways she may have contributed to perpetuating the dynamics of stratification in the classroom (Fine, Anand, Jordan, & Sherman, 2000). Similarly, Cazden details Cynthia Ballenger's (1999) and Vivian Paley's (1979, 1995) stories of vulnerability. Both reveal their attempts as White teachers to teach students of color, each raising questions about what they understood initially, but also what they were missing in what they thought and wrote. This is the type of self-reflexivity that we think is so necessary in creating the conditions for change. Specifically, Ballenger writes that, "I began with these children expecting deficits, not because they or their background were deficient—I was definitely against such a view—but because I did not know how to see their strengths" (p. 3). Thus she turned to what others had written and to a teacher-researcher cooperative to understand how she could better understand students' strengths. For Cazden, Ballenger represents "a powerful, self-initiated, on-going professional growth." Similarly, Paley's (1979) writing over 20 years ago in *White Teacher* included very public statements about race and racism. At that time, she wrote: "My uncertainties about labeling behavior and intelligence in general have been exposed by my dilemmas concerning black children" (p. xvii). Paley has since revisited her experiences in a new preface to *White Teacher*.

Cazden also underscores a fundamental tension between goals of equity in American education and the lack of resources that prevent minority and poor children from receiving a quality education. Inequalities in school financing clearly affect the quality of teacher preparation and the availability of materials to which teachers and students have access. Within schools, tracking, or what Darling-Hammond (1995) calls "the rationing of curriculum," also insures that some students will have access to the kind of knowledge they will need to succeed; others will not. Not until we have a "total picture" of schools, Cazden argues, will we be in a position to change conditions of inequity.

Ultimately, Cazden helps to frame the chapters that follow because she affirms an epistemology or worldview by recognizing the value of multiple and equally legitimate perspectives. This is an argument that finds its source in feminist and critical race theory and serves as a unifying theme in this collection.

In Chapter 2, Willis helps to build upon Cazden's argument for the complementarity of insider and outsider perspectives in literacy research. Studying her own classroom, Willis offers the duel perspective of both teacher and researcher in describing the challenges of teaching preservice teachers the skills, attitudes, and behaviors they need to acquire in order to teach children from culturally and linguistically diverse backgrounds. The question guiding her research is how students either addressed or simply ignored issues of race in their journals and oral responses to classroom activities and approaches to teaching and learning about multicultural literature.

To illustrate students' responses, she used excerpts from the writings and conversations of two students, one male Latino and one European American female, enrolled in the same course. Their responses typified other students' reactions to what teaching about race means. The male student welcomed Willis's interest in focusing on race and White privilege in a preservice course. In fact, each of the students of color called attention to their identity with cultural/ethnic, gender, and social class groups. But he also asked in his journal, "Why do we seem to always skirt around issues concerning racism and bigotry?" In contrast, the female student reflected on her unfamiliarity with people of other races, not her own cultural background. At the same time, she expressed interest in examining issues that would enable her to teach multicultural literature. However, with each new reading and accompanying activities, the minority students' responses expressed both anger and exposure—at least as understood through the lens of her Latino student's journal. White students appeared to strengthen their resolve to remain silent around issues of race by failing to address issues of race and privilege altogether. One way to explain this anger is to see the extent to which minority students carry the burden of discussing race. This is in large part because White students resist seeing White as a race or the relevance of race to teaching or to their own lives. In Willis's own words:

> The diversity of the students in the class, especially the students
> of color whose lives were affected by the inequalities described in our

readings, made it difficult for some White students to continue to ignore the reality of inequity, prejudice, and discrimination. It authorized their fellow classmates to voice their opposition to institutionalized racism. The course, and the manner in which it was constructed, legitimated their voices, experiences, literature, and ways of knowing. (this volume)

But we also learn that White students, in general, used silence in the classroom as a "weapon" for resistance, choosing not to address issues of race and privilege in discussion or in their journals. Insulted by exercises and handouts that seemed to be calling them racists, they conveyed in classroom discussion the sense that literacy learning and teaching is a racially neutral process.

In telling this story, Willis draws upon critical race theory's emphasis on narrative as a means for contextualizing events and the importance of acknowledging racism as ever present and normal in American society. In turn, Willis details the challenges of negotiating her mostly White students' resistance to conversations about race or the multiple ways in which White privilege has shaped their thinking and provided advantages in their lives. Thus, this is the story of a class she taught that, in her words, "was less than successful." At the same time, Willis tells a story of personal transformation, or "parallax," that finds its source in her attempts to locate her students' resistance to racialized discourse. Like the teachers upon whom Cazden focuses in Chapter 1, Willis positions herself in ways that change how she reflects upon and introduces issues of race in her teaching. This is a chapter that is as much about her as it is her students. Willis comes away with a profound understanding of what is involved in challenging institutional discourses about race. Viewing the experience 2 years after she taught the class, she realized that she focused primarily on her White students in an effort to guide them through issues that were foreign to them. The cost was high, however, because she also now sees that she disregarded the needs of her students of color, who believed that concepts of race and multiculturalism were not given the emphasis they believed was necessary.

Willis and Cazden emphasize the complementarity of insider and outsider perspectives in literacy research, particularly self-reflexive accounts that complicate our understanding of how teaching affects students and ourselves. Even our most well-meaning attempts can perpetuate the very structures of inequity that we try to disrupt. In Chapter 3, Appleman, like Willis, blurs the line between teacher and researcher. But Appleman adds another layer of complexity to what Willis observes. In studying the dynamics of teaching and learning in a multicultural literature class, Appleman provides a reflexive account of how she constructs images of the students about whom she writes. In doing so, she addresses a number of overarching questions that pertain to all of the studies presented in this volume:

- Do teacher narratives and ethnographies risk the foibles of storytelling: exaggeration, privileging of perspective, selection of details for effect, interpretations of "truth"?
- Does crossing racial lines necessarily compromise a researcher's reliability?
- Can we avoid "othering" students of color?

In her analyses, she interrogates some of her basic assumptions about her stance as teacher and researcher and the insidious nature of White privilege. In turn, she provides specific critiques that revolve around how the students, especially the students of color she portrays, point out nuances of word choice and the presence of some unconsciously racist assumptions about the lives of the students and their families.

Appleman brings into focus the ways that power, representation, and invention came into play as she seeks to understand adolescence and disrupt racist practices that place minority students at distinct educational disadvantages. Especially poignant are her analyses and reframing of her own published studies. Here she reflects upon the extent to which she has reinscribed power and structural inequities in portraying students whose writing she held up for examination and illustration in the past. Memories haunt her as she asks us to consider whether she might have misconstrued her students' words, perhaps even silencing her students or making them speak the way she wanted them to. Most central for the purposes of this volume, she asks researchers to consider the extent to which narratives and ethnographies risk the foibles of storytelling: namely, exaggeration, privileging of perspective, selection of details for effect, interpretations of "truth." What unsuspected and unpredictable tensions might arise between researchers and research participants? Can we write about our students without objectifying them? Finally, how are the issues raised in all these questions exacerbated by racial differences between researchers and subjects?

Part II: Making Race Visible

In Part II, "Working Against 'Color Blind' Practices and Contexts," the authors build on the themes raised in Part I, particularly the focus on research that is contextual, long-term, and self-reflexive (Cochran-Smith,

2000). In doing so, Larson and Sternglass address in their respective chapters the ways in which race and racism appear in the situations they describe. In keeping with critical race theory, the authors acknowledge that racism is always present and that it is our role to make it as visible and open to scrutiny as possible. Racism in these studies manifests itself in teachers' low expectations for students of color (Chapter 4) and the stereotypes that serve as racial barriers to opportunity in New York City where the trustees of the City University of New York have sought to eliminate remediation programs (Chapter 5). These are types of barriers that prevent poor and working-class students of all racial and ethnic groups from receiving the kind of educational support they deserved. In each case, the researchers "work the hyphen" between self and other as they become participants in students' struggles to achieve an equal chance at education in schools that deny them the resources they need to succeed. These resources include financing, quality of teacher preparation, and the availability of programs to support student learning.

In Chapter 4, Larson examines the ways that discourse positions both teachers and students, finding that traditional IRE (initiate, respond, evaluate) structures of classroom interaction tend to limit student participation and even silence students of color. Drawing upon the work of Goffman, Bakhtin, Foucault, the New London Group, and others, she underscores the power relations that determine what counts in classrooms and who speaks. Most strikingly, her accounts of classroom discourse reveal the ways in which teachers use "literacy pedagogy" as a tool for surveillance, regulation, and discipline. In turn, she also argues that the nature of classroom interaction can be attributed to what she observes is "teachers' racialized beliefs about students' abilities."

Reflecting upon the consequences of her research on race, Larson considers the extent to which she might be complicit in sustaining structures of inequality in schools. This is particularly true when Larson was unable to change a teacher she observed who described her students as "animals" and invoked a "longstanding deficit model of cultural deprivation" (this volume). Not to challenge negative assumptions may suggest complicity, but Larson also points out that the data she collected for the study she describes in this volume goes a long way toward exposing "insidious" practices in school. Thus we see in her work her attempt to negotiate her role as a researcher writing about race.

In a 6-year longitudinal study of writing and learning, Marilyn Sternglass details in Chapter 5 the experiences of two Latino students at the City University of New York. Specifically, their experiences at this urban university provide evidence that recognition of stereotyping served as a strong impetus to disabuse others of characterizing them as members of a group with only negative traits. In addition to having to confront harmful stereotypes, one of the students, who had learned English as a second language, found her writing frequently evaluated by individuals who had little knowledge of language development issues. More motivated than hampered by these problems, the students described in this chapter overcame these prejudices and lack of expertise to achieve both their educational and personal goals and enhance their pride in their own backgrounds, cultures, and personal identities. They came to see that writing gave them an opportunity to incorporate their worldviews into serious analyses of social issues.

Set in the context of institutional discourse about race and equal opportunity, Sternglass underscores the need for institutional reform. She points out that higher education needs to acknowledge and respect the importance of developmental learning. Such an approach can offer students of all backgrounds adequate time and opportunity to demonstrate that they not only have the capability to succeed, but that they have the ability to bring fresh perspectives to significant questions and issues.

Part III: Interpretive Frames of Research

In Part III, "Making Visible Power and Discrimination," the authors bring us inside classrooms to understand the ways in which classroom instruction has the potential to reinscribe the very power relations that we try to disrupt in our research. This is a salient perspective that emerges when the focus is turned on student-teacher relationships in low-track classrooms comprised of students of color who also happen to be poor. Thus we see the ways that classroom discourse can reinforce the kind of stratification that studies of tracking have demonstrated (e.g., Oakes, 1985; Oakes & Guiton, 1995; Yonezawa, Wells, & Serna, 2002). In their respective chapters, Enciso and Daiute and Jones also reveal students' interpretations of race in students' writing, with students confronting racial tensions in their own lives. Overall, each of the authors in this final section urge us to interrogate the interpretive frames through which we construct categories of race, class, ethnicity, and gender.

In Chapter 6, Sperling seeks to uncover some of the invisible forces that work upon students and teachers within "classroom moments of interaction," and the ways in which such moments shape identities, skills, knowledge, and values. In one classroom she studies, Sperling describes the pressures that exert themselves upon students studying literature in what she terms an evolving "social community" or what Bakhtin would describe as a "multivoiced" classroom. Students don't have paper on which to write, there are far more shelves in the library than books, and students meet a stream of substitute teachers who will never really know them. These are the conditions that motivate Sperling's literacy research in an urban community where she identifies a fundamental tension between politics and sound pedagogy, a tension that is often overlooked and that brings the parent she meets to tears because her daughter isn't learning White middle-class values. These are the conditions that exist in stark contrast to the second classroom Sperling describes, one set in suburbia, where most of the students—most of whom are White—are readying themselves for college. Ultimately, she maintains that identities, skills, knowledge, and values are mediated by culture, race, and class.

In Chapter 7, Enciso draws upon antiracist and poststructuralist theories to help her make sense of her work as a teacher, reader, and researcher in the midst of social inequities and daily, local constructions of discrimination. Her interest in working with a mixed-raced class of fourth and fifth grade readers was to understand how she (or anyone) could teach reading while attending closely to the social, cultural, and political discourses that often separated children from one another as friends and readers. In turn, Enciso argues that by attending to social discourses about discrimination within the context of reading education, a culturally relevant content and pedagogy can be enacted that fosters interest in and understanding of the multiple dimensions of our ways of interpreting ourselves and others as readers, social members of a class, and cultural members of a society.

Daiute and Jones in Chapter 8 also describe the extent to which researchers' points of view are significant in constructing race and ethnicity in their study of children's writing. As in Enciso's study, Daiute and Jones's investigation provides readers with students' understanding of race in a curriculum analyzing discrimination conflicts. The research they discuss is part of a larger study in two public schools—a Chapter One school with over 50% of the families it serves qualifying for financial assistance, and a non-Chapter One school serving children from a slightly broader range of economic backgrounds. Students wrote stories about a group of African American children who must transfer to a White school when the only middle school in their community closes, literary works depicting peer conflicts ("What happened? How did the people involved feel? How did it all turn out?"). Their narratives about personal experiences described a range of conflicts from fights about toys, to debates about fairness in jump rope games, to emotional appeals about exclusivity in friendships, and intense reflections on physical and psychological bias.

In their analyses of student writing, Daiute and Jones found differences in how African American, Latino and White children portrayed the instigators of conflict, represented conflict itself, or described their roles and responsibilities in negotiating conflict. At the same time that Daiute and

Jones recognize the relative impossibility of separating the political and the subjective from their own representations, they provide a methodology for reading student writing in ways that can help "objectify" readings of student writing. Their approach grows out of the personal transformations that occurred as the result of writing up their study. As Daiute and Jones point out, this means moving beyond our own expectations of how students treat race in their writing, and our own experiences, which can color our understanding of differences among students of color. Indeed, as the researchers observe, "Children's discussion of racial and ethnic issues is not always explicit; understandings of race and ethnicity can appear in more subtle or implicit forms and not all ethnic or racial minority children are politicized around these issues." Thus, Daiute and Jones urge readers to avoid essentializing students. After all, racial and ethnic group dynamics are mediated by socioeconomic and gender factors, which are reshaped and readjusted in different ways in different contexts. In this, they emphasize the role of perspective taking that underscores an epistemological concern about the source of knowing: Can we write about our students without objectifying them? And how are the issues raised in all these questions exacerbated by racial differences between researchers and subjects?

IMPLICATIONS OF STUDYING RACE IN
THE CONTEXT OF LITERACY RESEARCH

To summarize, we have underscored four objectives we think should inform literacy research that seeks to change the current inequities in schooling that affect poor, minority students. These objectives entail developing local knowledge of teaching and learning practices to insure that students' and teachers' voices are heard; theorizing our own racial positions and privilege in order to cast doubt on the concept that decision making is ever "race-neutral" or that "we accept seemingly neutral criteria . . . at face value" (Flagg, 1998, p. 4); considering the ethics of our research agendas and consequences of what we find in order to understand the extent to which, as researchers, we reinscribe traditional categories of race and power; and, finally, detailing the value of the research process in order to position ourselves and readers for change. In attempting to meet these four objectives, we hope to provide direction for policy and school reform.

With Pat Enciso (Chapter 7), we understand the difficulty of describing the experience of teaching "at the center of the shifting relations and status associated with cultural identity, cultural affiliations and their meaning in a racist society." As she points out, "The difficulty stems, in part, from recognizing that [each of us is] one of many people over the decades who have tried to tell [the] same story, to indicate to others that it is almost unbearable at times to see children sinking or drifting away because 'who they are' is so frequently and persistently discounted. [We] have to wonder why the story has to be told again, and if it is me who should be telling it."

NOTE

1. This heading is inspired by a first exploration of the notion of social construction in teachers' racial identities in Abt-Perkins, D. (1995). Are you calling her a racist? Language, context, and the struggle to better understand conflicts concerning race. *Women and Language, 18*(1), 25–30.

ACKNOWLEDGMENT

We would like to thank all of our colleagues at the Assembly for Research, part of the National Council of Teachers of English. The Assembly has created a community for experienced as well as emerging researchers in literacy and eduction to meet and support one another. In today's research climate, organizations such as the Assembly provide safe havens for research that is innovative and that challenges accepted belief systems. We are also grateful for the insight and support of Carol Collins. Without her tenacity, her belief in the importance of our subject, and her confidence in our work, this project would have never been brought to fruition. Carol has a steadfast commitment to supporting literacy research that meaningfully addresses racial and social issues. Her dedication to this project is evidence of this commitment.

REFERENCES

Anderson, J. (1988). *The education of blacks in the south, 1860–1935.* Chapel Hill: University of North Carolina Press.

Anzaldua, G. (1987). *Borderlands/La Frontera: The new mestiza.* San Francisco: Aunt Lute.

Ball, A. (1996). Expository writing patterns of African American students. *English Journal, 85*(1), 27–36.

Ballenger, C. (1999). *Teaching other people's children: Literacy and learning in a bilingual classroom.* New York: Teachers College Press.

Behar, R. (1993). *Translated woman: Crossing the border with Esperanza's story.* Boston: Beacon Press.

Bell, D. (1992). *Faces at the bottom of the well*. New York: Basic Books.

Cazden, C. (1994). What is sharing time for? In A. Dyson & C. Genishi (Eds.), *The need for story: Cultural diversity in classroom and community* (pp. 72–79). Urbana, IL: National Council of Teachers of English.

Cochran-Smith, M. (2000). Blind Vision: Unlearning racism in teacher education. *Harvard Educational Review, 70*(2), 157–190.

Corbin, J., & Strauss, A. (1990). *Basics of qualitative research: Grounded theory procedures and techniques*. Thousand Oaks, CA: Sage Publications.

Correspondents of the *New York Times*. (2001). *How race is lived in America: Pulling Together, Pulling Apart*. New York: Henry Holt.

Darling-Hammond, L. (1995). Inequality and access to knowledge. In J. A. Banks & C. A. Banks (Eds.), *Handbook of research on multicultural education* (pp. 465–483). New York: Macmillan.

De La Luz Reyes, M. (Ed.). (2000). *The best for our children: Critical perspectives on literacy for Latino students*. New York: Teachers College Press.

Delgado, R. (1995). *Critical race theory: The cutting edge*. Philadelphia: Temple University Press.

Delgado Bernal, D. (1998). Using a Chicana feminist epistemology in educational research. *Harvard Educational Review, 68*(4), 555–579.

Delpit, L. (1995). *Other people's children: Cultural conflict in the classroom*. New York: New Press.

Dillard, C. B. (1997, April). *The substance of things hoped for, the evidence of things not seen: Toward an endarkened feminist ideology in research*. Paper presented at the annual meeting of the American Educational Research Association, Chicago, IL.

Douglass, F. (1992). The blessings of liberty and education: An Address delivered in Manassas, Virginia, on 3 September 1894. In J. Blassingame and J. McKivigan (Eds.), *5 The Frederick Douglass Papers*. Quoted in *Zelman v. Simmons-Harris*, 122 S. Ct. 2460, 2480 (Thomas, J., concurring, 2002).

Du Bois, W. E. B. (1953). *The souls of black folk*. New York: Fawcett. (Original work published in 1903)

duCille, A. (1996). *Skin trade*. Cambridge, MA: Harvard University Press.

Dyson, A. (1997). *What difference does difference make? Teacher reflections on diversity, literacy and the urban primary school*. Urbana, IL: National Council of Teachers of English.

Ferguson, R. (1998). Teachers' perceptions and expectations and the black-white test score gap. In C. Jencks, & M. Phillips (Eds.), *The black-white test score gap* (pp. 273–317). Washington, DC: The Brookings Institute.

Fine, M. (1994). Working the hyphens: Reinventing self and other in qualitative research. In N. R. Denzin & W. S. Lincoln (Eds.), *Handbook of qualitative research* (pp. 70–82). Thousand Oaks, CA: Sage.

Fine, M., Anand, B., Jordan, C., & Sherman, D. (2000). Before the bleach gets us all. In M. Fine & L. Weiss (Eds.), *Construction sites: Excavating race, class, and gender among urban youth* (pp. 161–179). New York: Teachers College Press.

Fine, M., Weiss, L., & Powell, L. (1997). Communities of difference: A critical look at desegregated spaces created for and by youth. *Harvard Educational Review, 67,* 247–284.

Flagg, B. (1998). *Was blind but now I see: White race consciousness & the law.* New York: New York University Press.

Foucault, M. (1972). *The archaeology of knowledge.* New York: Pantheon.

Freedman, S., Simons, E., Kalnin, J., Casareno, A., & The M-Class Teams. (1999). *Inside city schools: Investigating literacy in multicultural classrooms.* New York: Teachers College Press.

Gay, G. (2000). *Culturally responsive teaching: Theory, research, and practice.* New York: Teachers College Press.

Geertz, C. (1983). *Local knowledge: Further essays in interpretive anthropology.* New York: Basic Books.

Goodburn, A. (1999). Racing (erasing) white privilege in teacher/research writing about race. In K. Gilyard (Ed.), *Race, rhetoric, and composition* (pp. 67–86). Urbana, IL: National Council of Teachers of English.

Grundy, P. (2002, September 15). Testimony: Segregation revisited. *New York Times Magazine,* 34–36.

Gutierrez, K. (1992). A comparison of instructional contexts in writing process classrooms with Latino children. *Education and Urban Society, 24,* 244–262.

Halbfinger, D. (2002). 40 years later, Ole Miss asks when the past will be past. *nytimes.com.*

Heath, S. B. (1983). *Ways with words: Language, life, and work in communities and classrooms.* Cambridge, UK: Cambridge University Press.

Jencks, C., & Phillips, M. (Eds.). (1998). *The black-white test score gap.* Washington, DC: The Brookings Institute.

Kaestle, C. (1983/1999). *Pillars of the republic: Common schools and American society.* New York: Hill and Wang.

Keating, A. (1995). Interrogating "whiteness," (de)constructing "race." *College English, 57,* 901–918.

Kincheloe, J., Steinberg, S. R., Rodriguez, N. M., & Chennualt, R. E. (Eds.). (2000). *White reign: Deploying whiteness in America.* New York: St. Martin's Press.

Ladson-Billings, G. (1994). *The dreamkeepers: Successful teachers of African American children.* SF: Josey-Bass Publishers.

Ladson-Billings, G. (1999). Preparing teachers for diverse student populations: A critical race theory perspective. In A. Iran-Nejad & P. David Pearson (Eds.), *Review of Research in Education, 24,* 211–247.

Ladson-Billings, G. (2000). Racialized discourses and ethnic epistemologies. In N. Denzin & Y. Lincoln (Eds.), *Handbook of qualitative research* (2nd ed.) (pp. 257–277). Thousand Oaks, CA: Sage Publications.

Ladson-Billings, G. (2001). Racialized discourses and ethnic epistemologies. In N. Denzin & Y. S. Lincoln (Eds.), *Handbook of qualitative research* (pp. 259–277). Thousand Oaks, CA: Sage Publications.

Ladson-Billings, G., & Tate, W. F. (1995). Toward a critical race theory of education. *Teachers College Record, 97*(1), 47–68.

Landsman, J. (2001). *A white teacher talks about race.* Lanham, Maryland: The Scarecrow Press.

Lee, C. (1993). *Signifying as a scaffold for literary interpretation: The pedagogical implication of an African American discourse genre.* NCTE research report. Urbana, IL: National Council of Teachers of English.

Lee, C. (1994). *Signifying as a scaffold for literacy interpretation: The pedagogical implication of an African-American discourse genre.* NCTE research report. Urbana, IL: National Council of Teachers of English.

Lewis, S. A., & Jonsberg, S. D. (2001, March 30). *Color-Blindness in the classroom: Can black and White students talk meaningfully across the barrier of race?* Paper presented at the National Council of Teachers of English Conference, Birmingham, AL.

Lopez, G. (2001). Re-visiting white racism in educational research: Critical race theory and the problem of method. *Educational Researcher, 30*(1), 29–33.

Lopez, I. (1995). The social construction of race. In R. Delgado (Ed.), *Critical race theory: The cutting edge* (p. 203). Philadelphia: Temple University Press.

McCarthy, C., & Crichlow, W. (1993). *Race identity and representation in education.* London: Routledge.

Michaels, S. (1991). Hearing the connections in children's oral and written discourse. In C. Mitchell & K. Weiler (Eds.), *Rewriting literacy: Culture and the discourse of the other* (pp. 103–122). New York: Bergen & Garvey.

Moss, B., & Walters, K. (1993). Rethinking diversity: Axes of difference in the writing classroom. In L. Odell (Ed.), *Theory and practice in the teaching of writing: Rethinking the discipline* (pp. 132–185). Carbondale: Southern Illinois University Press.

Natriello, G., & Pallas, A. (2001). The development and impact of high-stakes testing. In G. Orfield & M. Kornhaber (Eds.), *Raising standards or raising barriers? Inequality and high stakes testing in public education* (pp. 19–38). New York: The Century Foundation Press.

Nieto, S. (1999). *The light in their eyes: Creating multicultural learning communities.* New York: Teachers College Press.

Oakes, J. (1985). *Keeping Track: How schools structure inequality.* New Haven, CT: Yale University Press.

Oakes, J. (1986). *Keeping Track: How schools structure inequality.* New Haven, CT: Yale University Press.

Oakes, J., & Guiton, G. (1995). Matchmaking: The dynamics of high school tracking decisions. *American Educational Research Journal, 32,* 3–34.

Omi, M., & Winant, H. (1994). *Racial formation in the United States: From the 1960s to the 1990s.* London: Routledge.

Orfield, G., Eaton, S., & The Harvard Project on School Desegregation (1996). *Dismantling desegregation: The quiet reversal of Brown v. Board of Education.* New York: The New Press.

Orfield, G., & Gordon, N. (2001). (Eds.). *Schools more separate: Consequences of a decade of resegregation.* Cambridge, MA: The Civil Rights Project, Harvard University.

Orfield, G., & Kornhaber, M. (Eds.). (2001). *Raising standards or raising barriers? Inequality and high stakes testing in public education*. Washington, DC: Century Foundation Press.

Paley, V. (1979). *White teacher*. Cambridge, MA: Harvard University Press.

Paley, V. (1995). *Kwanzaa and me*. Cambridge, MA: Harvard University Press.

Prendergast, C. (2002). The economy of literacy: How the supreme court stalled the civil rights movement. *Harvard Educational Review, 72*, 206–229.

Santow, M. (2002). *Whiteness and progress: Saul Alinsky and the politics of racial geography in Chicago, 1959–1965*. Unpublished manuscript, Gonzaga University, Spokane, WA.

Schaafsma, D. (1993). *Eating on the street: Teaching literacy in a multicultural society*. Pittsburgh: University of Pittsburgh Press.

Straus, A., & Corbin, J. (1990). *Basics of qualitative research: Grounded theory procedures and techniques*. Newbury Park, CA: Sage.

Tatum, B. D. (1997). *"Why are all the black kids sitting together in the cafeteria?" and other conversations about race*. New York: Basic Books.

Tyack, D. (1974). *The one best system: A history of American urban education*. Cambridge, MA: Harvard University Press.

Warrior, R. (1995). *Tribal secrets: Recovering American Indian intellectual traditions*. Minneapolis: University of Minnesota Press.

Weis, L., Fine, M., Weseen, S., & Wong, M. (2000). Qualitative research, representations, and social responsibilities. In L. Weis & M. Fine (Eds.), *Speed bumps: A student-friendly guide to qualitative research* (pp. 32–66). New York: Teachers College Press.

Yonezawa, S., Wells, A., & Serna, I. (2002). Choosing tracks: Freedom of choice in detracking schools. *American Educational Research Journal, 39*, 37–68.

PART I

Recognizing Teacher and Student Racial Identities

Teacher and Student Attitudes on Racial Issues: The Complementarity of Practitioner Research and Outsider Research

Courtney B. Cazden

Anna Deveare Smith is an actor, teacher, and playwright, best known for her two one-woman plays based on her interviews with diverse voices from communities at critical moments of violent interracial encounters: *Fires in the Mirror* (1993), about Crown Heights, Brooklyn; and *Twilight Los Angeles* (1994). Her thoughts about race have resonance for educators:

> Race as a concern, as "matter," is like fog in our country, or like floating anxiety. One moment we rest on our laurels—that things are better—after all, people aren't still being chased by dogs as they try to go to school. The next moment it's the most "serious problem our nation has to face."
>
> Unlike academia, where people can "study" blacks or other ethnicities, and never actually talk about race, in the theater we must embody the material. In academia, professors can glide over the students' complicated feelings or their own complicated feelings about the subject with the excuse that they have to "cover the material." In the theater we can't simply "cover the material"; we "become the material." (Smith, 2000, p. 96)

I begin with these words from Smith's (2000) autobiographical reflections on her research strategies and problems, *Talk to Me: Listening between the Lines*, because of similarities between her concern about race in the theater and ours in education.[1] Teachers, like actors, "embody the material" and, again like actors, cannot "glide over the students' complicated feelings or their own." So when teachers do research on matters of equity, those always present and powerfully influential "complicated feelings" are more apt to be acknowledged and voiced than in research by classroom outsiders that contribute analyses of more extensive data about the same concerns but inherently from more distanced positions.

The limitations of such distanced positions were vividly shown in two articles in the April 1999 issue of *Education Week*. A front-page article (Olson, 1999a) announced that "The National Research Council last week mapped out an ambitious, 15-year strategy for increasing the usefulness of education research" (p. 1). The article went on to explain that "The idea for developing a national, strategic program for education research came from an unlikely source: highway research . . . [that resulted in] the use of tougher asphalt for paving and the development of longer-lasting concrete" (p. 16).[2] Unlikely, indeed! Could any domain of human life be further from the densely interpersonal world of classrooms than the materials of highway construction?

Closer to the classroom world is a second article (Olson, 1999b) in a special "research section" of the same *Education Week* issue. It begins, "If whole-school reforms practiced truth-in-advertising, even the best would carry a warning like this, 'Works if implemented. Implementation variable'" (pp. 28–29). One wonders whether implementing newer standards for asphalt and concrete, like the implementation of educational programs, requires the generation and integration of local knowledge. One wonders also if Lynn Olson, the author of both articles, was aware of the dissonance between them, dissonance so severe that the argument in the second seems to negate the prestigious National Research Council's research model in the first.

There is no mention of the potential value of practitioner research in the second article. I am adding the argument that research by those who have to enact the implementation of any new program, nationally certified or more locally legislated, can contribute to successful implementation and effective school change. As one teacher researcher, Magda Enriquez-Beitler (2000), put it, one source of questions for such research is any discrepancy between "what is intended" and "what actually occurs." A practitioner's "discrepancy" is a within-classroom analogue of larger-scale "variable implementation."

I will give examples of the complementarity of research by outsiders and insiders in two specific matters of "race" where there is a clear discrepancy between the goal of equitable opportunities to learn and classroom realities: first, the influence of teacher expectations; second, the importance of teacher and student attitudes toward language variation.

A FEW DEFINITIONS

Before turning to these examples, some definitions are in order.

Insider Research and Outsider Research

First, I am drawing the dividing line between kinds of research according to the position of the researcher, the same line that Smith draws between academics and actors. In education, the distinction is between those insiders (teachers and other practitioners, even students) who enact what they then document and analyze, and those outsiders (usually based in a university) who observe and analyze situations in which they have not participated. The more accurate category labels would be *insider research* and *outsider research*, but I will use interchangeably the more common terms, *practitioner* research and *university research*, respectively.

The practitioner-university boundary, like most category boundaries, becomes blurred in its particulars, sometimes to an especially rich effect. Smith is both outsider (and a Stanford University professor) when she interviews and edits the words of others and insider practitioner when she later enacts each of her interviewees in her one-person performances. In a reverse crossover, two university professors, Magdalene Lampert and Deborah Ball, are insiders as they teach daily mathematics lessons in a local elementary school but then revert to a more traditional university role as they analyze videotapes and write about those lessons. I use purer categories here only for the sake of argument about their complementarity.

"Race" and "Racism"

Another definitional issue surrounds the terms *race* and *racism*. It would probably be less jarring to readers to write about "ethnicity" or "differential treatment based on color," but I have adopted the usage of researcher/actress Smith on race and of psychologist Tatum (1997) on racism. Tatum defines racism as a "system of advantage based on race":

> This definition of racism is useful because it allows us to see that racism, like other forms of oppression, is not only a personal ideology based on racial prejudice, but a *system* involving cultural messages and institutional policies and practices as well as the beliefs and actions of individuals. (p. 173)

In writing about race and racism, I am naming only this particular source of differential treatment (in contrast to other sources such as social class, gender, or sexual orientation). I am *not* trying to reify labels that are increasingly dysfunctional. (Cf., reports on data from the 2000 census in which persons could list multiple ethnic and racial identities for the first time; frequent articles in our daily newspapers about individuals who identify themselves with multiple labels; and analyses such as Heath [1995]).

Attitudes

Finally, I am using the word *attitudes* in a non-technical way to include the cluster of values and beliefs that generate behavior. This is what I understand Vygotsky (1987) to be describing metaphorically and lyrically in the last chapter of *Thought and Language*:

> Thought has its origins in the motivating sphere of consciousness, a sphere that includes our inclinations and needs, our interests and impulses, and our affect and emotion. The affective and volitional tendency stands behind thought. Only here do we find the answer to the final "why" in the analysis of thinking. We have compared thought to a hovering cloud that gushes a shower of words. To extend this analogy, we must compare the motivation of thought to the wind that puts the thought in motion. (p. 282)

I would add that the "wind" also puts into motion actions as well as words—of speaking in one way or another, learning or refusing to learn—and may be part of conscious awareness or not. "Racism" as defined by Tatum applies to effect, not intent.

RESEARCH ON TEACHER EXPECTATIONS OF MINORITY STUDENTS' ACHIEVEMENT

In her chapter on "Inequality and access to knowledge" in the *Handbook of Research on Multicultural Education*, Linda Darling-Hammond (1995) synthesizes outsider research on many levels of differential treatment. Outside the schoolhouse door, there are inequalities in school financing, among states and among districts within them, that significantly affect the quality of teacher preparation and the availability of materials such that fewer and lower-quality resources are available for the poor and students of color. Within schools but still outside classrooms, there are inequalities due to within-school tracking that Darling-Hammond calls "the rationing of curriculum," especially in middle school and high school, that further decrease opportunities to learn for the same students.

The total picture of these all-too-common structures of inequalities suggests that they may be the default option, how the educational system works unless special effort is made to change it. We can then understand why Edmund Gordon (1999), the distinguished psychologist who was the first director of research for Head Start when it was founded in 1965 and recently codirector of the College Board's National Task Force on Minority High Achievement, writes, "Being at risk may be an iatrogenic condition"

(p. 35)—in medicine, an illness caused by medical institutions' own actions.

Not included in Darling-Hammond's sources of inequality is the more controversial influence of teachers' differential expectations. But this source receives focal attention in another compilation of research reviews on *The Black-White Test Score Gap* (Jencks & Phillips, 1998). One chapter is on "Teacher perceptions and expectations and the black-white test score gap" (Ferguson, 1998). At the end of a 40-page analysis of this difficult research area, Ferguson concludes:

> My bottom line conclusion is that teachers' perceptions, expectations, and behaviors probably do help to sustain, and perhaps even to expand, the black-white test score gap. The magnitude of the effect is uncertain, but it may be quite substantial if effects accumulate from kindergarten through high school. The full story is quite complicated and parts of it currently hang by thin threads of evidence. Much remains on this research agenda. (p. 313)

Even more significantly, Ferguson's chapter is singled out by William Julius Wilson in his "Commentary" on the entire volume. Emphasizing the crucial importance of research not on individual-level analyses but on "the impact of the *social structure of inequality* on racial group outcomes, including the impact of relational, organizational, and collective processes," (1998, p. 503, emphasis in the original), Wilson states that "only Ferguson's chapter 8 on the effect of teacher perceptions and expectations of black youngsters represents the latter" (p. 507). In Wilson's straightforward summary of Ferguson's review, "Teachers' lack of faith in black children's potential, even when it is not based on racial bias per se but on the children's past behavior, can adversely affect these children's future test scores" (p. 504). Quoting Charles Tilly, Wilson (1998) argues that "The crucial causal mechanisms behind categorical inequality operate in the domain of collective experience and social interaction" (p. 508).

Those conducting research on "collective experience and social interaction," whether outsiders or insiders, rarely admit publicly to possible biases in their own perceptions and expectations of the students they study or teach (cf., Peshkin, 2000). Courageous exceptions in the reports of one outsider and two teachers call our attention to the more general silence.

In collaborative outsider and insider research, outsider Michelle Fine joined English department chair Bernadette Anand and teachers Carlton Jordan and Dana Sherman to document their struggle to successfully detrack ninth grade English in Montclair, New Jersey (2000). "Drawn from Michelle's participant observation and grounded in interactions in and beyond Carlton's and Dana's classrooms, we collectively write a biography of a public space for intentional interruption, a space for rigorous democracy, grown among youth and adults across 'differences'" (p. 164).

Relevant here is one event involving observer Michelle's expectations. As part of their detracking work, the two teachers created peer discussion groups "balanced" by race, gender, and achievement. But in discussions of *The Odyssey*, a troublesome trend persisted. In the following quotations from an earlier draft of Fine et al. (2000), the "I" is Michelle Fine (Fine, Anand, Jordan, Sherman, n.d.), from her seat at the back of the room:

> In a set of 22 groups, in just over half of them (13), black male members seem to disengage, heads on desk, quiet . . . I take note and, in retrospect, admit with embarrassment that I have thought often, far too often, they hadn't completed the reading or the assignment. And then during one of those wonderful moments of professional development among Dana, Carlton, and me—at Starbucks of course—we pondered what would happen if the youths were allowed to sit first with their friends, and then were distributed into discussion groups (p. 33).

The next day, Carlton tries out the new participation structure:

> The invitation to sit with friends produced spontaneously . . . an all-black male, animated study group. In that group, the boys were working through the text. No heads down, flipping through papers, looking at sneakers, drawing comics. What had previously looked like black-boy-disengagement was instead a contextual effect in which African American boys in mixed-race groups didn't, couldn't, wouldn't or weren't feeling invited to engage. They weren't expected to be/trusting that they would be heard. This cannot be mistaken for the absence of preparation. I had been fooled by my own racialized read of their disengagement. Once the big switch was introduced, students counted off by four and "integrated." Animation and participation were not always but much more evenly distributed. (pp. 33–34)

Michelle concludes:

> As I watched the original "balanced" groups, I witnessed the simple, painful replay of broader dynamics of stratification. So much for teacher "neutrality." If all we do is to create "equal access," then unequal outcomes will "naturally" occur. (p. 34)

Similar public acknowledgments of problems in their expectations for their students are given by teacher researchers Cynthia Ballenger and Vivian Paley. Ballenger (1999) was the only non-Haitian adult in a day-care center in the Boston Haitian community. Although she could speak Haitian Creole, she knew she was an outsider to her children's culture. Looking back on that experience in the beginning of her book-length account, *Teaching Other Peoples' Children*, she remembers:

> I began with these children expecting deficits, not because they or their background were deficient—I was definitely against such a view—but because I did not know how to see their strengths. This is the story of how I came to see them. (p. 3)

Ballenger was familiar with Shirley Brice Heath's now classic outsider ethnographic research, *Ways with Words* (1983), but engaging in that kind of multiyear community ethnography was out of the question. So she found ways to adapt some of Heath's ways of learning to her own situation.

Ballenger's resources became careful observational records of her children when they were with her and with Haitian adults or playing with their peers, and her reflections on those observations in two separate discourse worlds outside her classroom. One was the world of the Haitian social service agency of which the center was a part and the class on Child Development she conducted for Haitian adults who hoped to get jobs in early childhood education. Here she could consult, in Creole when necessary, with Haitian parents and colleagues. The other discourse world was the teacher research group in which she has been a long-term member (Gallas et al., 1996).

In these adult worlds, Ballenger was not working alone. Conversations in the center connected her more closely to her children and, beyond them, to Haitian culture. Conversations in the seminar connected her to related research literature, including Heath's, and gave her a place to discuss the changes she was trying out in her classroom—changes in classroom discipline and control, and changes in ways of teaching the heart of her curriculum, story books and the ABCs. Together, observations and conversations added up to powerful, self-initiated, ongoing professional growth.

Vivian Paley, also a teacher of young children, has recounted her changing understandings of what it takes to make a classroom successful for all its children in two of her many books about her early childhood classroom in an independent school in Chicago: *White Teacher* (1979) and *Kwanzaa and Me* (1995), written 16 years apart.

White Teacher is Paley's first book. The preface to the original edition opens with a question:

> "Why do you talk so much about the black children?" The question comes from Elaine, who is a student teacher in my kindergarten class . . . "I'll bet you comment three times as often about black children in this class, even though there are only ten blacks to twenty whites." [S]he thinks I feel less certain in my judgments of black children.

She is only half-right. My uncertainties about labeling behavior and intelligence in general have been exposed by my dilemmas concerning black children. (1979, xvii)

The book is devoted to Paley's self-reflections on what it means to be
a White teacher of Black children in an integrated school. She considers
analogies to her own childhood experience as a Jewish outsider in Chicago
and New Orleans. She learns eagerly from Janet, a Black student teacher,
until Janet leaves, because, "I'm not cut out to be the company 'black.' I
belong in the inner-city schools teaching black children" (p. 44). Paley
admits that "I had seen myself as the catalyst for change in my classes. But
it was the black children who were showing the way" (p. 76). At the end,
she agonizes over why she so often speaks of "the black girls" but "never
needed a collective 'white' to help me identify characteristics that individual
white children shared," and asks, "Had I made no progress then in five
years?" (p. 130).

Sixteen years and six books later, just as self-reflectively, Paley returns
to these issues in *Kwanzaa and Me*. This time the catalyst is a visitor, Sonya
Carter—"Hey, white teacher, it's me, Ayana"—one of the Black girls in
the *White Teacher* kindergarten. "Now I needed her to be Ayana again, to
inspire me as she did long ago . . . I want her to tell me that this is still a
good place for Ayana, this integrated classroom, because a lot of people
are sure it isn't. And that it probably never was" (pp. 1–2). But Ayana
cannot provide such reassurance, and bluntly confirms racist criticisms of
the school. This time Paley turns for help to her Black parents, and especially to a Black teacher colleague, Lorraine. Taking in their criticisms and
suggestions, Paley learns to acknowledge differences and even describe and
explain them to her young students—differences in skin color and names,
hair texture and care, and holidays like Kwanzaa.

Paley's self-reflectiveness takes one more public step. In a new preface
to the 2000 reprinting of *White Teacher*, she recounts a school faculty
meeting in 1973, 2 years before the book was first published but not included in it:

Why, I have often wondered, did I deliberately keep it out?
   The year is 1973. A unique event is taking place at our bimonthly faculty
meeting. Six African-American parents have come to talk about their children's experiences in our school . . . We expect to be told, by this panel of
black men and women, how well we are doing.
   The story that emerges is entirely different. If six boys are running in the
hall, says one father, the black boy will be singled out. Another parent is even
more specific: I have watched teachers make so much of what a white child

says, then barely acknowledge the opinion of a black child. It has happened to my own daughter. And so it goes around the table . . .

You're wrong, a teacher says. There's absolutely no color line here. All the children are treated the same.

My colleagues and I become silent. The meeting ends without further discussion . . . Later it is discovered that someone neglected to turn on the tape recorder. The meeting is never referred to again. (xiii-xiv)

For Paley, this incident, 27 years before and never made public, became the impetus for her teacher research on race and racism reported in both books.[3]

For us, reading it now, the incident is all too contemporary. Couldn't such a meeting still happen in many schools? Don't the parents' complaints about bias in discipline and bias in whose classroom voice is valued bear an unsettling resemblance to "racial profiling"? Doesn't the faculty silence fit the perception of a British observer that "Race is the issue that dare not speak its name in America"?

In contrast to that silent faculty, Ballenger and Paley became aware of the "discrepancy" between their ideal and their practice and report their struggles to overcome it. But what about teachers who do not share their initial awareness? How can they change (or be changed)? In their editors' introduction to *The Black-White Test Score Gap*, Jencks and Phillips (1998) repeat Ferguson's final conclusion:

Exhorting teachers to have more faith in black children's potential is unlikely to change their expectations. But professional development programs in which teachers actually see disadvantaged black children performing at a high level can make a difference. (p. 30)

In other words, when people are not able to think themselves into new ways of acting, maybe they can be "acted into new ways of thinking." If teachers somehow come to change their ways of teaching, maybe their expectations will be increased by the audible and visible evidence of their students' increased learning.

University researchers Lea Hubbard and Hugh Mehan (1999) analyze one failure of that professional development strategy. They were studying the nationwide implementation of the AVID program exported from its initial success in San Diego. AVID (Advancement via Individual Determination) is an untracked high school elective course teaching study skills and building students' social capital support that had been proven effective in San Diego in increasing the proportion of low-income and minority students attending college (Mehan et al., 1996). Among Hubbard and Mehan's (1999) objectives in the dissemination study was understanding how local "cultural beliefs about race and intelligence become structural constraints impinging on educational reform" (p. 214).

One of the sites that adopted AVID was "Oakwood," a North Carolina community proud of its two high schools' overall academic success despite the very small percentage of African American students who went on to 4-year colleges. Concerned educators and parents hoped that AVID could help. In a rich account of local educational and political history as well as observations and interviews, Hubbard and Mehan conclude:

> After four years, an average of [only] 120 students per year are enrolled in AVID and affiliated college preparatory classes at OHS and East Oakwood High School . . . The deep-seated beliefs about race and intelligence and teachers' attempts to protect the tracking system we have detailed in this article account in large part for the relatively small size of AVID's program in Oakwood and elsewhere. This study has shown that if the reasons for the success or failure of educational reform are to be fully understood, it is essential to deconstruct the corrupting racist practices that shape our nation's educational system at its core. (1999, pp. 224–225)

"Deconstructing the corrupting racist practices" requires the participation of insiders to each local site. In Oakwood, that would require participants other than individual teachers—educators like Oakwood High School principal Lou Paulson or Gifted and Talented supervisor Tim Grant, who both wanted AVID to succeed and whose accounts, from their perspectives, of the "discrepancies" between plan and realization could help explain in more intensive detail why it didn't.

RESEARCH ON ATTITUDES TOWARD
LANGUAGE VARIATION AND BLACK ENGLISH

For reasons that have to do with controversies over race and racism rather than linguistic differences themselves, the most discussed United States dialect is African American Vernacular English (AAVE). Over the past 30 years, controversies have erupted into public consciousness three times over differences in forms, functions, and social status between AAVE and Standard English (SE) (which is, after all, simply another dialect of our common language) and the possible influence of such differences on African Americans' lowered academic achievement.[4]

The first time was during the late 1960s in the context of President Johnson's War on Poverty. In the most militant of the local Head Start programs, the Child Development Group of Mississippi (CDGM), books were proudly created using the children's language:

If a toad *hop* up on you and *wet* on you he *make* a big blister on your feet (italics added to identify AAVE verb forms).

When southern senators attacked CDGM, really for its militancy, quotes from such books became justifications for their congressional arguments against budget appropriations.

A decade later, in 1979, what came to be called the "Black English" court case was brought in Ann Arbor, Michigan on behalf of Black students who were failing in school. The judge's decision in favor of the plaintiffs ordered the school system to take dialect differences into account in their reading instruction. Most recently, in the late 1990s, the "Ebonics" controversy erupted over attempts by the Oakland, California school board to help African Americans learn Standard English.

Two research studies by outsiders during the first and last of these controversies surveyed the language attitudes of groups of African American adults and students. In the late 1960s, two Black Harvard graduate students, Betty Bryant and Melissa Tillman, and I conducted a study of attitudes in the Boston area. In what would now be called focus groups, Bryant and Tillman interviewed community leaders, parents, and teachers from two preschools selected for their contrasting influence of Black Power ideology (remember this study's late 1960s date). We entitled our report, "Making it and Going Home" (Cazden, Bryant, & Tillman, 1970), adopting a quote from one of our informants, and that title still seems to capture the understandably conflicting attitudes reported then and now.

Whether the parents rejected Black English because they believed its origins came from slave experience, or appreciated it for its expressive power, they felt it had no place in school. They acknowledged that "Most of us have two faces," but held that since children learn to speak Black English at home, school—even preschool—should teach in, and teach, Standard English. Teachers expressed more conflict about language than parents. Understanding that survival is the main thing, and "Lots of times your mouth can help you," they wondered if it's an illusion that survival in relationships with the White community requires Standard English. Community leaders were the most positive in their evaluation of Black English and more openly resentful that it is always Black people who have to change.

In the wake of the recent Ebonics controversy, John Ogbu (1999), a Nigerian American Berkeley anthropologist who lives in Oakland and sent his children to Oakland schools, wrote up a study he had conducted in 1988–1990 about language attitudes in one Oakland neighborhood. In his observations and extensive interviews with students and adults, Ogbu found evidence of what he calls "incompatible beliefs," and he criticizes sociolin-

guistic studies that "have remained classroom discourse analysis" and ignore the "historical, societal and cultural factors outside school that shape
the social perceptions and interpretations of students and teachers in the
classroom" (p. 149).

Another outside researcher, Signithia Fordham, has conducted an intensive analysis of student ways of speaking and acting in one school,
"Capitol High," an all-Black high school in Washington, D.C. Like Ogbu,
Fordham (1999) argues against a narrow linguistic focus on differences in
syntax (such as verb forms) and pronunciation (such as "dat" for *that* and
"aks" for *ask*) and includes students' preferred speech volume and non-
mainstream semantic codes, and their attitudes toward expectations of visibility (AAVE) and passivity (SE). She describes the students' "weapons of
the weak" and their "rhetoric of resistance," especially to the English curriculum requirement that they learn to communicate in SE:

> Their resistance to this state-approved curriculum requirement is their way of
> "dissin'" or disrespecting this dialect. Thus dissin' the standard is at the core
> of the guerilla warfare at the school and is fundamentally revealed in both
> the students' refusal to discontinue their use of Ebonics as the language of
> communication while at or in school, and their wholesale avoidance of the
> standard dialect in most other contexts. (p. 273)

In the end, Fordham urges teachers to understand the meanings of
their students' language practices, to avoid conveying disdain for discourse
markers of Black identity and implying that academic success requires "a
flight from the Black self" (p. 280). But she acknowledges that "Obviously,
I do not have complete answers" (p. 287). More "complete answers" have
to come from teachers' insider reports of what happens when they try to
cope with the discrepancy between a curriculum objective and students'
complex attitudes toward it.

Bob Fecho (2000) provides one such report. In contrast to Ballenger
and Paley, both teachers in early childhood, Fecho, now teaching at the
University of Georgia, was at the time of this research a high school English
teacher with a class of all African or Caribbean American students, mixed
in prior achievement and 9–12 grade levels.[5] Committed to an inquiry curriculum, his overall literacy question for this particular year was, "How
does learning about language connect you to your world?" (pp. 374–375).
One incident stimulated the students into engaged and personal inquiries.

Controversy over dialect use erupted when Kenya gave an engaging
presentation in a "natural" style. When she finished, one peer commented
that Kenya needed to switch from Black English to standard usage when

she presented for a final evaluation. When Fecho added this comment to the class chart, another peer came back with the crucial question, "Why is Black English under the 'Needs Improvement' category?" Fecho guided the ensuing controversy into inquiries into language use. Instead of smoothing over the student controversy or taking sides in it [as either radical social critic or mainstream moralizer], he welcomed it as stimulus for more motivated student work. Presenting three case study students in this journal article, Fecho (2000) concludes about changes in their perspectives on language:

> For these students and others like them, it is not a matter of *if* they are able to speak and write in the mainstream codes—they could and did at various times in my classroom—but is more a matter of figuring out why they would feel disposed to do so. A key factor is motivation. The students were deepening their awareness of the role language played in their lives. In doing so they were confronting whatever reluctance and reservation they might have had for more consistent use of the mainstream codes of power. Inquiry became a means, then, through which students began to enlarge their locus of control. (pp. 386–387)

THE ARGUMENT FOR COMPLEMENTARITY BETWEEN INSIDER AND OUTSIDER RESEARCH ON RACIAL ISSUES

In these examples of research on teacher expectations and on attitudes toward language variation, outsider research and insider research both make essential contributions. My point here is that those contributions are both different and complementary. First, while outsider research can collect a more extensive set of data from a larger sample of people and sites, practitioners' insider research can collect a more intensive set of data on a smaller number of people. Second, while outside researchers can analyze their data in more varied and sophisticated ways than practitioners usually have time or expertise to do, insiders, especially teachers, can bring to their analyses insights about affective as well as cognitive aspects of students' lives gleaned from hours of living together (1,000 hours in elementary school).

By the very nature of the densely human nature of classrooms, and the role of the teacher in somehow marshalling all that human energy for given educational goals, teachers can't ignore affective currents and crosscurrents. In research on such affect-loaded issues as race and racism, the inclusion of these affective influences—even when not part of the original research plan—becomes especially important.

NOTES

1. This chapter began as a keynote address at the NCTE Research Conference in Chicago in February 1999. I am especially grateful to past and present colleagues on the Spencer Practitioner Research, Communication, and Mentoring Committee: Marty Rutherford, Dixie Goswami, Diane Waff, Judy Buchanan, Renee Moore, Jacqueline Royster, and Cindy Ballenger. Special thanks to Michele Foster for comments on an earlier draft.

2. Thanks to Vermont teacher researcher Robert Baroz for calling these articles to my attention.

3. An important research study of silence about racial issues among high school teachers (Pollock, 2001) was published too late to be discussed in this chapter.

4. See Wolfram et al. (1999) for an overview of language variation; Perry and Delpit (1998) and Adger et al. (1999) specifically about African American Vernacular English. Baugh (1997) explains that the term "Ebonics" was coined in 1973 by a group of Black scholars combining *ebony* (Black) and *phonics* (speech sounds).

5. In fairness to busy teachers who have a major problem of finding time for the additional role of researcher, I need to say that both Ballenger and Fecho began this research as doctoral theses, and Paley's independent school may have made fewer bureaucratic demands on her non-teaching time.

REFERENCES

Adger, C. T., Christian, D., & Taylor, O. (Eds.). (1999). *Making the connection: Language and academic achievement among African American students.* McHenry, IL: Delta Systems.

Ballenger, C. (1999). *Teaching other people's children: Literacy and learning in a bilingual classroom.* New York: Teachers College Press.

Baugh, J. (1997). What's in a name? That by which we call the linguistic consequences of the African slave trade. *The Quarterly, 19*(1), 9.

Cazden, C., Bryant, B. H., & Tillman, M. A. (1970). Making it and going home: The attitudes of Black people toward language education. *Harvard Graduate School of Education Association Bulletin, 14*(3), 3–9. Expanded version in *The second and third Lincoln Conference on Dialectology* (pp. 307–325), J. Griffeth & L. E. Miner (Eds.). University, AL: University of Alabama Press.

Darling-Hammond, L. (1995). Inequality and access to knowledge. In J. A. Banks & C. A. Banks (Eds.), *Handbook of research on multicultural education* (pp. 465–483). New York: Macmillan.

Enriquez-Beitler, M. (2000, December 1). *From inquiry to understanding—Be a PRO, leave a mark.* Keynote address to the Spencer foundation Practitioner Research Communication and Mentoring Grant Program Meeting of the Grantees, Albuquerque, NM.

Fecho, B. (2000). Critical inquiries into language in an urban classroom. *Research in the Teaching of English, 34*, 368–395.

Fine, M., Anand, B., Jordan, C., & Sherman, D. (2000). Before the bleach gets us all. In M. Fine & L. Weiss (Eds.), *Construction sites: Excavating race, class, and gender among urban youth* (pp. 161–179). New York: Teachers College Press.

Fine, M., Anand, B., Jordan, C., & Sherman, D. (n.d.). Before the bleach gets us all. [Unpublished version of chapter included in Fine et al., 2000.]

Fordham, S. (1999). Dissin' "the standard": Ebonics as guerrilla warfare at Capital High. *Anthropology and Education Quarterly, 30*(3), 277–293.

Ferguson, R. F. (1998). Teachers' perceptions and expectations and the black-white test score gap. In C. Jencks & M. Phillips (Eds.), *The black-white test score gap* (pp. 273–317). Washington, DC: Brookings Institution Press.

Gallas, K., Anton-Oldenburg, M., Ballenger, C., Beseler, C., Griffin, S., Pappenheimer, R., & Swain, J. (1996). Talking the talk and walking the walk: Researching oral language in the classroom. *Language Arts, 73*, 608–617.

Gordon, E. W. (1999). *Education and justice: A view from the back of the bus.* New York: Teachers College Press.

Heath, S. B. (1983). *Ways with words: Language, life, and work in communities and classrooms.* Cambridge, UK: Cambridge University Press.

Heath, S. B. (1995). Race, ethnicity, and the defiance of categories. In W. D. Hawley & A. W. Jackson (Eds.), *Toward a common destiny: Improving race and ethnic relations in America* (pp. 39–70). San Francisco: Josey-Bass.

Hubbard, L., & Mehan, H. (1999). Race and reform: Educational "niche picking" in a hostile environment. *Journal of Negro Education, 68*(2), 213–226.

Jencks, C., & Phillips, M. (1998). *The black-white test score gap.* Washington, DC: Brookings Institution Press.

Mehan, H., Villanueva, I., Hubbard, L., & Lintz, A. (1996). *Constructing school success: The consequences of untracking low-achieving students.* New York: Cambridge University Press.

Ogbu, J. U. (1999). Beyond language: Ebonics, proper English, and identity in a Black-American speech community. *American Educational Research Journal, 36*, 147–184.

Olson, L. (1999a, April 14). NRC seeks new agenda for research: Proposal calls for year-long dialogue. *Education Week, XVIII 31*, 1, 16.

Olson, L. (1999b, April 14). Following the plan: Success in whole-school reform, researchers say, depends on how well schools implement the designs. *Education Week, XVIII 31*, 28–29, 32.

Paley, V. (1979). *White teacher.* Cambridge: Harvard University Press.

Paley, V. (1995). *Kwanzaa and me.* Cambridge: Harvard University Press.

Perry, T., & Delpit, L. (1998). *The real Ebonics debate: Power, language, and the education of African American children.* Boston: Beacon Press.

Peshkin, A. (2000). The nature of interpretation in qualitative research. *Educational Researcher, 29*(9), 5–9.

Pollock, M. (2001). How the question we ask most about race in education is the very question we most suppress. *Educational Researcher, 30*(9), 2–12.

Smith, A. D. (1993). *Fires in the mirror: Crown Heights, Brooklyn, and other iden-tities*. New York: Anchor Books/Doubleday.

Smith, A. D. (1994). *Twilight—Los Angeles, 1992 on the road: A search for Ameri-can character*. New York: Anchor Books.

Smith, A. D. (2000). *Talk to me: Listening between the lines*. New York: Random House.

Tatum, B. D. (1997). *"Why are all the black kids sitting together in the cafeteria?" and other conversations about race*. New York: Basic Books.

Wilson, W. J. (1998). The role of the environment in the black-white test score gap. In C. Jencks & M. Phillips (Eds.), *The black-white test score gap* (pp. 501–510). Washington, DC: Brookings Institution Press

Wilson, W. J. (2000). The role of the environment in the black-white test score gap. In C. Jencks & M. Phillips (Eds.), *The black-white test score gap* (pp. 501–510). Washington, DC: Brookings Institution Press.

Wolfram, W., Adger, C. T., & Christian, D. (1999). *Dialects in schools and com-munities*. Mahwah, NJ: Erlbaum.

CHAPTER 2

Parallax: Addressing Race in Preservice Literacy Education

Arlette Ingram Willis

Within the field of education there is a clear pattern of wanting to deny, or at least marginalize, race as an important and ever-present factor. Issues of diversity, ranging from ethnic studies in the 1960s to multiculturalism in the 1980s and antiracist/antibias studies in the 1990s have made very little inroads into the thinking of many preservice and in-service teachers. Despite nearly 40 years of research that specifically targets the attitudes, behaviors, and skills needed by white preservice teachers to teach children from culturally and linguistically diverse backgrounds, little has changed. For example, during the past decade, we have read the data on preservice teachers, which acknowledges that 92% are White, female, monolingual, and from middle-income homes, whether suburbia or in rural areas. Despite national, state, and institutional charges for change, little real action has occurred. Similarly, the NCES report, *Teacher Quality—A report on the preparation and qualifications of public school teachers* (Lewis et al., 1999) states that 80% of new teachers are not comfortable with their knowledge of cultural and linguistic differences in their student population.

Like these national norms, the majority of students in my preservice class are White, female, upper to middle class, monolingual English speakers. Their life and school experiences reflect their homogenous home and school lives. In fact, prior to attending college they seldom have had experiences interacting with students or instructors of color. Further, few have engaged in public conversations about race or acknowledged the multiple ways in which White privilege has shaped their thinking or provided advantages in their lives. More often than not, they argue in support of a meritocracy—that they have worked hard for everything they have achieved.

For most of my White students, race is a problem for people of color, not their problem, or at least, not a problem for which they can bring about change. Unfortunately, such a perspective actually makes them complicit in creating structural inequalities. As Spina and Tai (1998) have argued, "Not seeing race is predicated on not seeing White as a race and in denying Whiteness as a focus of critique and analysis. Ignoring the racial construction of Whiteness reinscribes its centrality and reinforces its privilege and oppressive position as normative" (p. 37). In my classes I make a diligent effort to center issues of race, so that students can begin to see themselves as agents of change.

To understand students' evolving understanding of race, I have undertaken a self-study of my teaching of an undergraduate preservice English methods course, one that is informed by critical pedagogy. Following the work of Freire, Henry Giroux, Donaldo Macedo, and Ira Shor, I seek to create an atmosphere and climate through shared experiences where we can use a common language, reach understandings, develop dispositions, and hone skills to teach in a diverse society. I have always thought of my classes as providing a "homogeneity of experience," to quote Audre Lorde (1984, p. 285), for all of the students in my classes. Usually, this process goes well; that is, until my class during the fall semester of 1998.

Although I have learned a great deal from the "successful" classes, I also learned from the class that was less than successful. The class's lack of positive response to the readings I gave them motivated me to locate the source of their resistance. My experiences with this class created for me a parallax—a change in how I reflect upon and position issues of race in the course. Of importance to me in this chapter is understanding how students either addressed or simply ignored issues of race in their written and oral responses to classroom activities and approaches to teaching and learning about multicultural literature.

To illustrate students' responses, I use excerpts from the writings and conversations of two students, one Latino and one European American female, enrolled in the same course. What follows rests largely on my use of a critical race theory lens to reflect upon my teaching of this particular literacy methods course.

CRITICAL RACE THEORY

Critical race theory emerged out of the field of law during the late 1970s as an alternative way of understanding the changes in political, legal, and social policies affecting people of color. Researchers began to look more closely at how concepts once thought to be supportive of socially just and democratic ideas (like color blindness, legal equality, merit, integration) instead "reflected, created, and perpetuated institutional racial power" (Roithmayer, 1999, p. 2). Critical race theory also calls into question the way in which "the colorblind perspective represses and renders irrelevant the ways in which race shapes social relationships" (p. 2). It is a relatively new framework for the analysis of educational phenomenon (Ladson-Billings & Tate, 1995). In the field of literacy, where becoming literate is an intensely social process, critical race theory legitimizes a focus on racial issues as a means of understanding the interconnectedness and influences of race in literacy learning and teaching.

I draw upon two key aspects of critical race theory to help shape my work: (1) the importance of acknowledging racism as ever present and normal in American society, and (2) the use of narratives as a means of contextualizing events (Roithmayer, 1999). To that end, this chapter includes descriptions of selective classroom activities designed to encourage students to make visible racial inequities within our society. In addition, this chapter includes student-written narratives because students were encouraged to construct their own narratives as a way to reflect upon their lives and experiences, the course, and their future plans as teachers. Further, critical race theorists advocate the use of narratives to help authorize a discourse of knowing, experiences, understandings, and social values not permitted otherwise (Delgado, 1989). This chapter is also a narrative that reveals my shift in perspective, or a parallax.

I interweave the reflective thoughts and experiences of two students, Samuel and Caitlyn (pseudonyms), to create my narrative of how they chose to address issues of race. I selected these two students because their work helps to illustrate the vast differences in how activities and discussions about race were understood and received. In addition, the two students are broadly representative of students from different racial, class, and gender categories that reflect the backgrounds and the experiences of other students in the class. Finally, I conclude this chapter by raising questions about the institutional silencing that projects literacy learning and teaching as a racially neutral process.

A NARRATIVE OF THE COURSE: PUBLIC VOICES

As with most classes, the first day sets the stage for the rest of the semester. One of the most important features of this day is to make clear the ground rules for discussions on issues of race and ethnicity, culture, class, gender, and sexual orientation. Equally important, I want to make sure that everyone feels comfortable sharing her or his opinions. Class begins with a series of activities, with each student presenting orally information to their classmates. Next, I share with the class the syllabus, which includes an extensive list of required readings written by people of color, one of the more subtle ways to signal the importance of talking about race. I also describe for the class my philosophical stance, ending the first day by asking students to write a response to the following question [used with the permission of Nancy Hansen-Krening (1992)]: "How does your cultural perspective affect the students you teach?"

Students' Written Responses to the Question of Race

The response of my 21 students (16 white females, 3 white males, 1 African American female, and 1 Latino) in the fall of 1998 were typical of years past. First, most European American students do not identify themselves by using cultural/ethnic or linguistic terms. Second, European American students generally located themselves and issues of diversity outside of their realm of experience. They suggest that their parents and teachers are at fault for their limited understandings and knowledge of diverse groups. In addition, most point to attending the university as the first time in their lives that they have connections and relationships with anyone who is not White. An excerpt from Caitlyn's response to the question that illustrates this point: "In the spectrum of cultural education I would say I fit somewhere in the middle. I had a limited cultural perspective before coming to the U of I due in part to geographic location and also due in part to the limited cultural perspectives my teachers had."

By way of contrast, students of color responded to Hansen-Krening's question by identifying themselves as members of cultural/ethnic, gender, and social class groups. These students also articulate how their perspectives and commitment to these issues are likely to affect their teaching. An excerpt from Samuel's response clarifies this point: "For students of Latino backgrounds I think the experience will be positive for the most part. For those that are not (Latino) especially European Americans, there may be a great deal of negativity, but I hope to work out my issues long before my teaching experience." Samuel appeared to understand that his status as a Latino within a racialized society may be a source of comfort for his future Latino students and one that may bias his work with non-Latinos. Yet he plans to make a conscious effort not to discriminate among his students.

Students' Autobiographical Writings on Culture and Ethnicity

Students shared excerpts from their autobiographies in the next class, describing their cultural and ethnic heritage. Caitlyn identified her Irish, Italian, and Catholic roots and revealed that she had studied abroad for a semester. She saw herself as undistinguishable from most of the other students in her class. She also communicated that although the notion of "fitting in" had comforted her earlier in her life, she realized that "Up until this point I lived in my fairy-tale land, sheltered from the evils of life . . . I was suffocating in the tiny box that my parents had so kindly and carefully created for me." Hence, she sought to gain a greater understanding of her cultural heritage and global diversity.

Samuel also began his autobiography with a description of his heritage. He identified himself as Puerto Rican. Samuel portrayed his father's side of the family as wealthy with Spanish and Puerto Rican bloodlines and his mother's side of the family as lower middle class with Arawak (Indian), African, and Puerto Rican bloodlines. All of Samuel's great grandparents and grandparents had lived on the island of Puerto Rico. He also detailed how difficult life was after his parents divorced. An intellectually gifted student, Samuel explained how he was placed in a school for gifted and talented children, but often got into fistfights with his wealthy classmates. In high school, Samuel sought information about his people and their history and culture, only to be discouraged by some of his teachers. He portrayed himself as conflicted about being a Puerto Rican American because "my Spanish is of the street, my skin is pale, which transforms my features into what many believe to be that of a Caucasian, and I have lived in the United States all of my life." Samuel described his college days as a life that was centered around one goal: "to become a full person; one that understands his place in this world and is not afraid to assert oneself as a young Latino."

I characterize the initial writings by these two students, as well as their in-class participation, both verbal and non-verbal, as part of their "public voices." That is, students tend to respond in ways they believe are non-offensive or tolerant early in the semester. Generally, as their understandings about the classroom climate, interpretive community, and basic student-to-student and student-to- instructor trust grows so does their ability to share more comfortably and confidently. Further, I use their responses as a beginning point for understanding where they might fit on Janice Helm's (1992) continuum of racial identity formation (ranging from contact attitudes to autonomy) and Beverly Tatum's (1992) application of Helm's continuum to preservice teacher educators. Tatum uses racial identity development theory to help students in her classes understand race in society. I use racial identity development theory to understand my students better as people who are beginning to acknowledge their own racial identity. At this point in the semester, it would be premature to make a definitive decision. However, my reflection on their work begins a process that allows me a way to begin to understand how, or whether, they see themselves as racialized beings in a racialized society. (I use the term to describe a society that is consumed by race.)

Deconstructing Social Inequalities and Power

For most students, this is the first course that requires them to use their hearts and their heads. It is a course that moves beyond intellectualizing about issues of race and ethnicity, class, gender, and sexual orientation, and also to deconstruct social inequalities and power and privilege. It is also a course that asks students to address these issues within their own lives and within the lives of the characters in the literature we read. Moreover, the course is not based on the ideas, values, beliefs, experiences, language, lives, or literature of European Americans. In point of fact, some European American students are confronted with a new and alternative set of cultural and linguistic referents. For those students who have believed in the universality of the European American experience, "steeped in an educational experience in which sexist, racist, classist, homophobic and other ideological messages have supported their positions as right and proper" (Higginbotham, 1996, p. 203), this is an unsettling time.

Understandably, this is a course that causes some European American students great anxiety. European Americans are not a monolithic group; while some students expressed angst, others expressed delight to be in a class that openly and frankly discussed institutional and social inequalities, and one that used theory and literature written by scholars and authors of color. Likewise, the students of color are not a monolithic group, but they revealed their comfort and pleasure with the opportunity to discuss institutional and social inequalities and to have required theory and literature by authors of color that were not available in most of their other courses.

Nevertheless, I sensed a growing uneasiness within the class when issues of race and ethnicity, class, gender, and sexual orientation were discussed. Tension was indeed palpable when we addressed power and privilege. It was as if somehow private conversations were becoming part of a public discourse and some students were uncomfortable with the space in which the conversation occurred. For example, in previous classes at this point in the semester the use of the language of superiority hidden in the "us" and "them" dichotomy was beginning to diminish. In this class, some students remained completely oblivious to its use and the sense of privilege and "othering" that it suggests. The diversity of cultures within the class and the race and gender of the instructor, however, made it difficult to ignore that we were not all alike.

To either confirm or disconfirm my initial impressions of individuals' understanding and acknowledgement of institutional and social inequalities, I use the Horatio Alger exercise. It is a vicarious experience that illustrates that the disingenuousness media images of structural and social inequalities are personal, individual, or minority group failures and short-comings. The Horatio Alger exercise has five objectives:

1. To illustrate that a person's race contributes to the privileges and disadvantages he or she encounters growing up in society;
2. To demonstrate that the "playing field" is not level;
3. To illustrate some of the advantages and disadvantages we experience in our lives and the effects these play on our opportunities and "successes";
4. To recognize that we often regard oppression and prejudice that affects us personally as the most important and to see this as prejudice as well; and
5. To acknowledge that we may often "compete" to be the most oppressed and to understand why and how this affects us (Canto, 1993).

I do this activity outside of our classroom because it requires an unobstructed space to complete. Throughout the exercise no talking is allowed, yet students are encouraged to note mentally their feelings and emotions. Students begin by holding hands in a horizontal line; then, in response to a series of questions that focus on race and class inequities, they are required to either step forward or backward from that line. The exercise helps to demonstrate that inequalities result from birth (race, class, and gender), and do not reflect intelligence or individual effort.

I watch as students step forward, backward, and as they look around for their classmates. Interestingly, only a handful of affluent White students were moving forward, and all others were somewhere in the back. One of the White male students stopped participating: he definitely stood less than 10 feet in front of me, crossed his arms over his chest, and glared at me angrily as I continued to read the statements. Clearly, I had hit a nerve with him as his behavior expressed overt and active resistance to the exercise. Other students also began to resist, much more passively, as they began to take smaller steps forward and larger steps backward. Their behavior suggested a passive resistance to the task, while giving the illusion of compliance.

When the exercise ended, I repeated the directions to remain silent and to return to class. After students had taken their seats I asked students to describe their feelings. No one spoke. I waited several minutes as I looked at a sea of downcast faces and distant eyes. A wall of silence, like an invisible forcefield had begun to erect itself within our classroom.

At this point it was clear to me that the class was not ready for an open discussion. I shifted gears and suggested that students write their response to the activity. Caitlyn explained her feelings in this way: "The exercise we did outside made me embarrassed of my own personal advantages . . . a White, middle class, college student . . . it exposed me to my peers. I felt ashamed to be standing in the front of the group." Like the White male who stopped participating, she felt angry, exposed, and guilty.

Samuel's response was also passionate and expressed some of his immediate feelings of anger and exposure. However, his feelings caught me completely off-guard as he wrote:

> I hated every moment of it [the exercise] as I was forced to critically analyze how unfair life is. . . . I know where I came from, but for the most part it is a secret; hoping never to return, but where I am from is always in me; it will never leave . . . My mind is preset to channel zero . . . "being better" is a "dream deferred." . . . I don't want to be pitied.

Later, Samuel shared with me that many of his classmates expressed their pity for him and his life circumstances, without acknowledging how their life circumstances had created opportunities and privileges that he did not have, and they did not earn.

From this exercise students began to see more clearly the importance of situating conversations about educational achievement and attainment within conversations about race. As Cornel West (1993) has argued, "race matters" in every facet of American society, including education. What this particular exercise makes clear is that White privilege exists and is not earned. For some students the exercise dispossesses them of their fantasy that everyone plays on a level playing field—that everyone has equal opportunities to be successful. After completing this exercise, students know that their accomplishments can no longer be summed up neatly as merely a reward for their hard work and individual effort alone. Now they will also need to acknowledge that inherent within our educational system are unearned White privileges.

STUDENT NARRATIVES: REFLECTIVE JOURNALS

A review of students' journals offers a more intimate portrait of each individual and their evolving sense of racial identity. Caitlyn, like a small group of other European American students, remained silent in class, but clearly expressed herself in her journal. In the excerpt that follows, she acknowledges some of her feelings on issues of race and the reason for her silence.

> I must admit that I was very intimidated coming into this course. I'm painfully aware that I am (in) the majority; one of the ninety percentile that make up secondary English educators. For me, intimidation breeds silence. I sat and watched the first two classes planning out in my head what I would say to each question posed, yet never opening my mouth out of fear that my ignorance to issues at hand would be exposed.

Caitlyn's honesty and her fear of the class, me, and reading and talking about race surprised me. The readings had been selected because they were mild, more positive versions of the "in-your-face" and blame the oppressor alternatives. Her response also indicated that the readings that I believed to be mild and non-threatening opportunities for discussions of race were seen as threatening and an attack on the self-worth of some students who were unfamiliar with the literature.

Samuel's journal also revealed that he felt a level of discomfort with the direction of the course, focusing his concerns on his classmates' reactions to the readings and the Horatio Alger exercise. He expressed his feelings in his journal as follows:

> Reading Jonathan Kozol's *Savage Inequalities* reminded me of the schools I attended while in grade school, and those that I was fortunate enough not to attend. What struck me most about this book is not so much its content, but the reactions after we read the book, by my classmates. These reactions were precisely what I expected as many of them all of a sudden became advocates of the poor, while an equal amount decide to keep quiet about the issue mentioned, . . . worse yet, I could tell some answers were manufactured.
>
> The Horatio Alger exercise was something different about this class. After it was done I had ten new friends who cared about my family's welfare—to be truthful they could care less. They speak to me like I am a child or poor soul that needs comforting—I don't need their pity, in fact; they need me more than I need them.

Samuel's journal helped me to clarify how the Horatio Alger exercise could affect students of color. It was obvious that he resented what he perceived as his new status in the eyes of his classmates, "a poor minority who needed their help." He also resented his new role as cultural translator and ambassador for his White classmates. He seemed to understand the cultural racism that fueled their misunderstandings of his life.

Tatum's (1999) definition of *cultural racism* helps to foreground some key issues that came up in students' journals, especially Samuel's. By *cul-*

tural racism, Tatum means the "cultural images and messages affirming the assumed superiority of whites and the assumed inferiority of people of color—it is like smog in the air—sometimes so thick it is visible, other times less apparent, but always, day in and day out, we breathe it in" (p. 2). Samuel could see through the fog and he did not appreciate the view. I began to notice a change in the manner in which Samuel interacted with his classmates following this series of events. He remained outspoken, but now he expressed his opinions more cautiously than before. Some of the passion and fervor he had before the Horatio Alger exercise seemed to dissipate.

ADDRESSING STUDENTS' SILENCE BY PUSHING THE ENVELOPE

It became increasing apparent that some students were using silence "as a weapon" (Ladson-Billings, 1996) to forestall further discussions of race. Nevertheless, I continued to nudge students to think and discuss publicly their ideas on issues of race, power, and privilege as they affect literacy learning and teaching. For me, teaching about race means "continually challenging institutional discourses" (Anzaldua, 1990, p. xxv), even when it is difficult for students to address these issues.

To challenge further students' assumptions about race I distributed Delpit's (1989) article "The Silenced Dialogue," instructing them to read it in class and discuss it in small groups, before we had a whole class discussion. When the small groups reflected on the article, they refused to connect the text to their own lives. Surprisingly, no one mentioned this activity in their reflective journals. This article generally spawns emotional responses ranging from anger to outrage among most White students, but with this class, there was not so much as a blink of recognition.

I nudged a little more forcefully by requiring the students to respond in a paired written conversation activity to Peggy McIntosh's (1988) article entitled "White Privilege." I outlined points in the article where they were to stop, write, and reply to their partner. Again, they performed the task dutifully. Following this activity, however, several students responded in their journals that the activity was helpful for them to think, write, and share their feelings about race and privilege. Caitlyn wrote to her partner that the McIntosh article, along with other articles we had read and the Horatio Alger exercise, "has culminated awareness of the privileges afforded to me, but I am left with one question, 'What do I do about it?'" Her partner did not answer her question. Instead he shifted the conversation's focus to gender.

Similarly, Samuel and his partner had a stilted shared written conversation as Samuel questioned his classmates' willingness to respond more openly and opinionatedly to the article by McIntosh. Specifically, he asked his partner why it seems that "some . . . person, who happens to be White, speaks and legitimizes a person of color's claim." His partner chose not to respond to his query and shifted the focus of the exchange in her reply.

I perceived the class's response to these two readings and accompanying activities as means of strengthening their resolve to remain silent around issues of race. In a further effort to extend in-class conversations about race during the writer's workshop, I wrote a letter to the class about how displeased I was with their lukewarm response to issues of race, class, gender, power, and privilege. Further, I expressed my frustration with their silence as well as their resistant and immature attitudes. Then, I read aloud the letter to them. There was still silence. Obviously, I was working too hard with a group of students who could not imagine themselves as holding racist attitudes, or what Joyce King (1991) has identified as *dysconscious racism*. King defines *dysconsciousness* as "an uncritical habit of mind that justifies inequity and exploitation by accepting the existing order of things as given" (p. 135). My nudging and input seemed counterproductive.

MASKING DISCONTENT IN ADDRESSING ISSUES OF RACE

Caitlyn never became a vocal member of the class; she hid behind the public wall of silence as she continued to write insightful journals. I was concerned that she and others might be refusing to learn the material, turning off the course content, materials, discussions, students of color, instructor, and all that I desired to teach them. Herbert Kohl (1994) describes this phenomenon as "not-learning." Specifically, he writes that

> learning how to not-learn is an intellectual and social challenge; sometimes you have to work very hard at it. It consists of an active, often ingenious, willful rejection of even the most compassionate and well-designed teaching. Not-learning tends to take place when someone has to deal with unavoidable challenges to her or his personal and family loyalties, integrity, and identity. (p. 134)

Fortunately, Caitlyn's journals revealed a more vibrant and thoughtful side of her evolving sense of self and racial identity as well as the fact that she was learning. In one entry, she communicates her understanding of her evolution:

> This class has taught me that though I will be assuming a new title next semester, I will forever be a student, a learner . . . This class has

also taught me that ignorance and oppression are synonymous. I was offended by the first few exercises that taught me that I was in the role of oppressor. I was insulted by exercises and handouts that seemed to be calling me a racist. I claimed ignorance as my scape-goat, but ignorance in turn breeds oppression. Because I knew nothing about the minority cultures that the class was based on I kept quiet.

Samuel's views on the class, and on issues of race also continued to evolve. He sent me an e-mail message one afternoon when he was feeling particularly frustrated about how issues of race were being dealt with in class. His comments are a definite contrast to Caitlyn's. In part, here's what he wrote:

> I have some questions concerning the class, most notably, "Why do we seem to always skirt around issues concerning racism and bigotry?" It is my belief that it is these things we must first work through in order to achieve some real understanding of what multi-culturalism really is . . . Anyone can say they believe this or that, but when push comes to shove theory goes out the door. Many of the students in the class seem to be empathetic and understanding toward the plight of minorities in America, but as I have seen and heard many of them before—they are no more than hypocrites at best. . . . How do I express what I feel without having them hate all minori-ties, or damaging their ever so sensitive egos?

Samuel's reflections helped me to understand how unconsciously I had be-gun to focus on helping the White students deconstruct their Whiteness, adjust to notions of White privilege, and work through scholarship about race that was foreign to them. I was working very hard at making the classroom comfortable for these students, while I was also unknowingly disregarding the effects of this focus on the students of color. For Samuel, it seemed that the concepts of race and multiculturalism were being short changed within a course and context designed to address them. He also felt pressure to inform his classmates, a role he did not embrace with plea-sure, but one he nonetheless decided to assume.

Other students mirrored and echoed the sentiments both Caitlyn and Samuel expressed. For example, anonymous midterm course evaluations revealed that several students thought the course overemphasized issues of race and ethnicity, class, gender, sexual orientation, and power and privi-lege while shortchanging more "important" information they needed to become effective literacy teachers. Others acknowledged that attempts to delve below the surface of issues of race, class, and linguistic differences were important, but had indeed been met by silence among their classmates. However, generally students believed that it was time to move on with information on how to teach English/Language Arts.

Paramount among the concerns listed was how English content (grammar, writing, literature, reading, listening, speaking, and drama) were missing from the course, although it is a course on pedagogy. Some students mentioned that a gentle sprinkling of multicultural literature was sufficient to address issues of difference and the ongoing discussions were unnecessary. These students were not making a connection between knowing about their own racial understandings and preparing to become an effective teacher for all students.

IDENTIFYING SOME SOURCES OF STUDENTS' RESISTANCE TO TALKING, WRITING, AND DISCUSSING RACE

Tatum's (1992) research has identified three major sources of students' resistance to discussions about racism:

1. Race is considered a taboo topic for discussion, especially in racially mixed settings.
2. Many students, regardless of racial-group membership, have been socialized to think of the United States as a just society.
3. Many students, particularly White students, initially deny any personal prejudice, recognizing the impact of racism on other people's lives, but failing to acknowledge its impact on their own. (p. 5)

Tatum's list of resistant behaviors sufficiently sums up many of the behaviors I observed in my class. Similarly, Chan and Treacy's (1996) identification of active and passive forms of resistance by students in multicultural education courses was helpful in understanding the processes that my students were undergoing. The researchers note that active resistance, the least common form, results in behaviors that overtly challenge the course, content, ideas, and materials used in the course. Students who are active resistors also may verbally challenge the instructor and classmates. Passive resistance, the most common form, is revealed through silence; limited cooperation, participation, and engagement; and absence or tardiness to class. In this class students exhibited both active and passive resistance.

STUDENT NARRATIVES: TEACHING MULTICULTURAL LITERATURE

Following the midpoint of the semester, I introduce several multicultural novels to accomplish three goals. First, the novels extend conversations about race and its place in the curriculum. Second, I use them as models to help students understand, read, learn, and teach about various subcultures within the United States and to debunk canonical notions of the universality of select literature. Third, these novels extend the literature choices of future teachers by focusing on literature written by authors of color. Eight of the 10 titles to be read are written by authors who are people of color. Moreover, the literature legitimizes multicultural literature's place in secondary classrooms. In this setting, multicultural literature can offer opportunities for students to engage in conversations about literature and race, culture, gender, class, sexual orientation, and power and privilege.

Several European American students in this class expressed their fears about teaching multicultural literature. Class conversations and discussions of multicultural literature often lacked the depth I desired as students' comments tended to oversimplify notions about race, class, gender, and culture. Specifically, students mentioned "not ever being able to know enough about all cultures" and "offending some culture by not addressing their literature" as their two overriding fears. A possible reason for the fears expressed by some White students was reflected in Caitlyn's journal:

> In the past, I've seemed to candy coat multiculturalism and multicultural education. Somewhere along the way I adopted the view that as long as I taught a few Maya Angelou poems, did a unit on Leslie Marmon Silko's *Tracks*, and spent some time analyzing *The Joy Luck Club*, I would provide a multicultural base for my students. Yet I was looking at multicultural education as what I could teach my students, not what they could teach me. In the past month I have learned that (adopting) a multicultural perspective is not something that you learn from reading Asian American, Native American, or African American authors.

Samuel's response to multicultural literature surfaced one day, quite unexpectedly, during a discussion of the novel *American Knees*, a book written by Asian American author Shawn Wong. Samuel, with uncanny insight, responded to his classmates' lack of sensitivity to the novel by highlighting their avoidance of racial issues within the text. He acknowledged their liberal stance but called them to task for their lack of respect for the author's viewpoint. By far, it was a breakthrough moment for the class as Samuel displayed his ability to move beyond the text and his willingness to address the context of our classroom. He encouraged his peers to remove their "rose-colored glasses" and accept the variance within the "American" experience. His message was met with silence, although one student responded in her journal to his comments as follows:

> Samuel brought up an important point in class tonight; he observed that our class is still afraid to have an in-depth, emotional discussion about issues of race and culture. I agree that we tend to distance ourselves from the topic by approaching it in a more "academic" than personable manner, but I'm not sure I know how to change this . . . I realize that, by keeping quiet, I am assuming a passive role in learning more about different cultures. Expecting others to educate me . . . is an irresponsible way to address issues of race and culture. And I hope that many of my classmates will come upon the same realization.

From that day forward, Samuel's contributions to class discussions appeared to be rekindled with his former passion and fervor. With each new text, he openly challenged his classmates to reconsider their positions on issues of race, class, gender, and power as these issues related to the teaching of literature.

Caitlyn's and Samuel's reflective writings represent a distinctive difference in their experiences, understandings, and growth throughout the semester. Their writings illustrate dramatically different responses to issues of race, class, and gender by students of color and White students. For example, many White students were comfortable intellectualizing about racism privately, but found it difficult to acknowledge that they had benefited from White privilege and institutional racism. Generally, the students of color were comfortable publicly discussing social inequities, institutional racism, and describing their life experiences.

However, once racial and class differences were no longer private matters, both groups grew uncomfortable with their new knowledge. Further, many White students resisted learning cultural constructions of knowledge and theoretical positions, and multicultural literature, especially when called upon to deconstruct racism. By way of contrast, the students of color were not only comfortable discussing cultural constructions of knowledge and theoretical positions as espoused by scholars of color; they welcomed opportunities to discuss issues of race and privilege in the fictionalized lives of characters in novels written by authors of color. They spoke openly in small and large whole-group sessions and made attempts to connect their growing understandings and conversations to real life. Furthermore, students of color redirected attempts to universalize experiences, preferring to understand issues within the multiple contexts in which they were presented.

After class one evening, the students of color spoke with me. They shared their concerns about the silence of their White classmates as well as conversations held with their classmates outside of our class. It was then that I realized that in all my teachings about race, power, and privilege I had not fully considered the position(s) or the emotional and psychological toll the course was having on my students of color. I had not realized how hard it must be for them to take classes each day and converse with their resistant classmates as they also attempted to work along with me to make our class a meaningful, if not life-changing, experience. Along with me, these students of color had assumed the responsibility of informing their resistant classmates about the often invisible and intangible effects of racism and privilege within their personal lives as well as within the lives of the characters in the literature we read. I had not asked the students of color to assume this responsibility; it was something they seemed to sense was needed, and they stepped up and took charge.

IMPLICATIONS: THE CHALLENGES OF ADDRESSING RACE AND PRIVILEGE IN A PRESERVICE METHODS CLASS

I am several years removed from this experience, yet even now as I reflect upon this rather hellish semester I still struggle with understanding why this class responded so differently. One explanation is that the class was largely European American females from middle-class and upper-middle-class to suburban environments with limited experiences and interest in race and literature written by authors of color. Caitlyn's journal captured the gist of the thinking of several other students who also expressed how they felt intimidated by a class that openly addressed issues of race, class, gender, sexual orientation, and power as well as focused on the writings of scholars and authors of color.

Second, the course was required, but there was only one section. Thus students had little choice of instructors. Higginbotham (1996) suggests that "students can behave very differently depending on whether a course is an elective, required as part of the core curriculum, or required for their major" (pp. 206–207). My race, gender, class, and ideological positioning may have affected some students' willingness to participate in the class. Third, requiring students to record and to reflect upon issues of race and privilege in a mixed-race, public setting may cause some students heightened levels of discomfort.

If literacy educators truly believe that they are preparing preservice teachers for all children, these explanations seem overly simplistic. The explanations do not address more fundamental questions regarding the importance of race, class, gender, language, sexual orientation, power, and privilege in preservice literacy courses. Speaking of race, Toni Morrison (1992) notes that, "race has become metaphorical—a way of referring to and disguising forces, events, classes, and expression of social decay and economic division far more threatening to the body politic than biological 'race' ever was" (p. 63). While issues of race took center stage in this course and in this narrative, it is important to point out there was also a clear subtext of intersection of race and social class.

In this course, students were encouraged to move beyond academic and intellectual arguments and beyond empathetic and sympathetic feelings toward deconstructing individual and institutional racism. This idea challenged many students to become change agents in their new roles as teachers. The diversity of the students in the class, especially the students of color whose lives were affected by the inequalities described in our readings, made it difficult for some White students to continue to ignore the reality of inequity, prejudice, and discrimination. It authorized their fellow classmates to voice their opposition to institutionalized racism. The course, and the manner in which it was constructed, legitimated their voices, experiences, literature, and ways of knowing.

After examining student work, and countless hours of reflection and writing about the course, I became aware of my shifting position, or my parallax. I believe that Audre Lorde (1984) rightly claimed "there are very real differences between us of race, age, and sex. But it is not those differences between us that are separating us. It is rather our refusal to recognize those differences, and to examine the distortions that result from our misnaming them and their effects upon human behavior and expectations" (p. 285). My work is not the first to describe or discuss notions of resistance by preservice teachers to issues of race. There have been similar observations and studies that illustrate how other instructors of color have met silence and resistance from White students. Ladson-Billings (1996) articulates that "student silence can be used as a weapon. Rather than feeling unable to use one's voice in a forceful way to provoke dialogue, silence can be used as a means of resistance that shuts down dialogic processes in the classroom" (p. 85).

In my review of all the students' responses, I found that not all White students were silent, although none appeared to openly embrace race and difference. Among the White students, there was a small group who did not address issues of race, class, gender, and power and privilege in any of their writings for the course. This small group of students also never mentioned the tension in the classroom or their complicity in the upkeep of the wall of silence in their writings or class discussion groups. Yet their unannounced collective unity, which underscores their Whiteness and privilege in a racialized society, affected the climate and interpretive community of the class. It also limited in very real ways their ability to open up their thinking to new knowledge, learn from scholars of color, and read a rich bevy of literature written by authors of color.

By way of contrast, the reactions of students of color to discussions of issues of race, class, gender, language, sexual orientation, power, and privilege have not been sufficiently addressed in the literature on teacher education or literacy. In my class, the views of students of color were similar to those expressed by Samuel. Recall that some of the activities caused Samuel to relive and reexperience very painful moments in his life and caused his classmates to offer what he perceived as disingenuous concerns for his life experiences. Samuel's willingness to take the risk of offending some of his peers caused me to review the responses of other students of color more carefully as a viable and valued source of information on how they were evolving within a course designed to address issues of race and privilege.

As I reflect on my teaching about race within this literacy course, I note that my viewpoints have shifted, and I see my role much differently. After deconstructing my own teaching, I noted that in my zeal to inform White students of past and current inequities, I had recentered Whiteness in discussions of people of color, leading some Whites to affirm stereotypical notions of difference as deviant. Much of my effort to inform students centered on informing White students about their Whiteness and privileged status, thus centering their Whiteness in the course. In addition, unknowingly I had exacted a toll on Samuel and some other students of color in the class. Samuel's response and reflective writings made clear to me that while it is important to help White students learn to address issues of race and privilege, it should not occur at the psychological or emotional expense of students of color. I realize now, as never before, how much I depended on the students of color to help inform their White classmates about inequity and social injustice. I also realize how unaware I was that positioning the students of color as central to class discussions permitted Whites to view discussions of the oppression and subordination as inconsequential to their daily lives. Students of color were ready participants in discussions of oppression, or experiences of discriminatory practices, which pushed some Whites away from participating.

Given my new understandings and viewpoints, I also reflected on the literature in the field and what it has to say about race and literacy education. What I found is while there are many well-intentioned folks, and countless calls for reconceptualization, the research and literature on preservice literacy teacher education and issues of race and privilege continues to offer an excessive publication of, and an overindulgence in, helping

European American students understand their Whiteness, the marginalization of the needs of the students of color, and a superficial attention to the intersection of race, class, gender, and power in pedagogy and content. In the future, it is advised that narratives written by scholars and teachers of color, as authentic voices of our experiences, be included in all courses to balance viewpoints of the "other." A number of books are available on preservice education that address race, inequity, and the like, but most of them are written by Whites about people of color and what they feel, believe, and value. I submit that reading about issues of race and inequities brought about by race are best found in those who have experienced it firsthand.

Further, I argue that it is imperative to acknowledge and promote discussions of the intersection of race and literacy, as part of the "new literacies." These discussions should occur collaboratively with scholars of color as cocreators whose voices, experiences, languages, and knowledges are fundamental to addressing race. By knowledges, I mean the different ways one knows or understands the world. It is more complex than knowledge in the singular, which often refers to cognition. To actively reinvent knowledges "means continually challenging institutionalized discourses. It means being suspicious of the dominant culture's interpretation of 'our' experience, of the way they 'read' us" (Anzaldua 1990, p. xxv). The field, at large, must redirect their vision to centralize issues of race and privilege within discussions of literacy research and education from the works of all scholars.

REFERENCES

Anzaldua, G. (Ed.). (1990). *Making face, making soul. Haciendo Caras. Creative and Critical perspectives by Feminists of Color.* San Francisco, CA: Aunt Lute Books.

Berry, W. (1997). Personal politics: American autobiography. *The Virginia Quarterly, 73,* 609–626.

Canto, M. (1993). *Unlearning Prejudice. Celebrating diversity: Trainer's Manuel.* Oakland, CA: University of California Agricultural Extension.

Chan, C., & Treacy, M. (1996). Resistance in multicultural courses: Student, faculty, and classroom dynamics. *American Behavioral Scientist, 40*(2), 212–222.

Delgado, R. (1989). Storytelling for oppositionists and Others: A plea for narrative. *Michigan Law Review, 87,* 24111–24112.

Delpit, L. (1989). The silenced dialogue: Power and pedagogy in educating other people's children. *Harvard Educational Review, 56,* 280–298.

Hansen-Krening, N. (1992). Authors of color: A multicultural perspective. *Journal of Reading, 36*(2), 124–129.

Helm, J. (1992). *A race is a nice thing to have: A guide to being a white person or understanding the white person in your life.* Topeka, KS: Content Communications.

Higginbotham, E. (1996). Getting all students to listen: Analyzing and coping with student resistance. *American Behavioral Scientist, 40*(2), 230–239.

King, J. (1991). Dyconscious racism: Ideology, identity, and the miseducation of teachers. *Journal of Negro Education, 60*(2), 133–146.

Kohl, H. (1994). "I won't learn from you": Confronting student resistance. *Rethinking our classrooms: Teaching for equity and social justice* (pp. 134–135). Milwaukee: Rethinking Our Schools.

Ladson-Billings, G. (1996). Silences as weapons: Challenges of a Black professor teaching white students. *Theory into Practice, 35*(2), 79–85.

Ladson-Billings, G., & Tate, W. (1995). Toward a critical race theory of education. *Teachers College Record, 97*(1), 47–68.

Lewis, L., Parsad, B., Carey, N., Bartfai, N., Farris, E., Smerdon, B., & Greene, B. (1999). *Teacher quality: A report on the preparation and qualifications of public school teachers.* National Center of Educational Statistics. Publication Number 1999080. NCES: Washington, DC. Available on-line: http://nces.ed.gov/pubsearch/pubsinfo.asp?pubid=1999080.

Lorde, A. (1984). *Age, race, class, and sex: Women redefining difference, Sister Outsider.* Trumansburg, NY: Crossing Press.

McIntosh, P. (1988). White privilege: Unpacking the invisible knapsack. *Peace & Freedom,* 10–12.

McLaren, P., & Munoz, J. (2000). Contesting whiteness: Critical perspectives on the struggle for social justice. In C. Ovando & P. McLaren (Eds.), *The politics of multiculturalism and bilingual education: Students and teachers caught in the cross fire* (pp. 23–49). Boston: McGraw-Hill Higher Education.

Morrison, T. (1992). *Playing in the dark: Whiteness and the literary imagination.* Cambridge, MA: Harvard University Press.

Roithmayer, D. (1999). Introduction. In L. Parker, D. Deyhle, & S. Villenas (Eds.), *Race is . . . race isn't: Critical race theory and qualitative studies in education* (pp. 1–6). Boulder, CO: Westview Press.

Sleeter, C. (1994). White racism. *Multicultural Education, 1,* 5–39.

Spina, S., & Tai, R. (1998). The politics of racial identity: A pedagogy of invisibility. *Educational Researcher, 27,* 36–40, 48.

Tatum, B. (1992). *Why are all the Black kids sitting together in the cafeteria? and other conversations about race: A psychologist explains the development of racial identity.* New York: Basic Books.

Tatum, B. (1997). *"Why are all the black kids sitting together in the cafeteria?" And other conversations about race.* New York: Basic Books.

Tatum, B. (1999). When you're called a racist. *The Education Digest, 65*(1), 29–32.

West, C. (1993). *Race matters.* Boston, MA: Beacon Press.

CHAPTER 3

"Are You Makin' Me Famous or Makin' Me a Fool?" Responsibility and Respect in Representation

Deborah Appleman

It's the end of a particularly trying second hour Multicultural Literature class in an urban high school in Minneapolis where I have returned to high school teaching after a 10-year absence. The 31 students in the class, 9th through 12th graders—White, Black, Latino, and Native American—bustle out of my classroom into the overcrowded hallway to join their friends. Darwin dawdles, dropping books and papers and rearranging his overflowing backpack. We've had some good after-class chats of late. I call out to him.

"Darwin, hey, how's it going?"

"OK, I guess."

"You know, Darwin, your writing in this class is really good. I was wondering . . . I'm going to a conference in a few months and I want to use some of the papers you've written for our class. Is it okay if I show them to folks? Can I give you a piece of paper to get your permission and your parents'?"

"You want *my* papers? You're kiddin', right?"

"No, Darwin, I'm not kidding."

"My folks don't care and they ain't home to sign nothin' anyway. Well, I guess it all depends on what you are going to say to those people about me. Will you be makin' me famous or making me a fool?"

I turn away, hoping Darwin doesn't notice my guilty blush. What *was* I going to do?

THE PROBLEM OF REPRESENTATION

Through vivid description, case study analysis, and other methods of qualitative inquiry, many researchers have created powerful images of urban adolescents. Michelle Fine and her colleagues (Weis & Fine, 2000), for example, bring to light issues of class and invisibility, especially in the lives of students of color and female students. Similarly, Heath and McLaughlin (1993), among others, have documented the complexities faced by urban youth as they come of age at home, at work, and at school. Yet even the most carefully conceived and scrupulously executed qualitative research raises issues of power, representation, and perhaps even invention.

In *Adolescence: A Farewell to Childhood*, Louise Kaplan (1986) writes,

> Every human society endeavors to preserve itself by inventing the adolescence it requires. Yes, to put it another way, we could say that every society invents the adolescence it deserves and then regards that invention as monstrous, saintly, or heroic. (p. 49)

Qualitative researchers who seek to understand adolescence and disrupt negative school practice may also be guilty of this kind of perpetuation. When this "monstrous" portrayal occurs along racial lines, it can veer into objectification and stereotype.

Does this kind of research really move us to any kind of enhanced understanding of how to serve better the educational needs of the young people we choose as our focal subjects in qualitative research? Skelton and Valentine (1998) assert that "young people have not been particularly en-franchised by the research conducted on their lives" (p. 21). In fact, youth cultural studies may have reified the politics of cultural difference, meeting the needs of privileged academic researchers but not benefiting the lives of the often-disadvantaged young people under scrutiny. In these fast-changing times, the globalization of popular culture threatens to homogenize youth culture and reify the age-demarcated group status (e.g., Yon, 2000) that we have created for them.

Contemporary scholarship on urban youth has begun to acknowledge the degree to which school practices, cultural constructions, and even research methodology conspire to create a status category of "youth or adolescents" that may perpetrate power relations. This oppression through categorization restricts the ability of youth to be perceived as individuals and perpetuates a kind of status purgatory between childhood and adulthood. This oppression, as we will see in the examples I offer from my own work, affects the portrayals of all adolescents but is even more problematic when the portrayals cut across racial lines.

Recently, researchers have applied a Foucaultian perspective in examining the relations of power within literacy research, specifically, as Rabinow notes (1994/1997), "a relationship in which one person tries to control the conduct of the other" (p. 292). Taking up Fine's (1994) perceptive cautions, other researchers have been addressing the degree to which power relations play out in the context of literacy research, especially given the degree to which race, class, gender, and age are implicated in the relations of power in a research context. To explore this perspective, I revisit data and publications from previous and ongoing work with urban adolescents (Appleman, 1999, 2000a and b; Hynds & Appleman, 1997).

I conduct research on the experiences of urban adolescents, both in and out of the classroom, to help identify ways in which their school experiences might be reconstructed to serve better their needs. In the tradition of qualitative research, I have presented individual cases that allow the experiences of the focal students to inform our understanding of the adolescent experience. In retrospect, as the print of published articles has dried and the students have grown, for better or worse, into adults, captured forever as the adolescents they once were or that I made them out to be, I wonder if my portrayal of them served only my scholarly needs, and not theirs at all. In fact, I wonder if my research not only failed to benefit them, but was, in some ways, actually harmful.

QUESTIONS FOR OUR CONSIDERATION

And I really hope no white person ever has cause to write about me because they never understand Black love is Black wealth and they'll probably talk about my hard childhood and never understand that all the while I was quite happy.

—from "Nikki-Rosa" by Nikki Giovanni

Even as I write this essay, 5 years after Darwin left my classroom for the last time, his query haunts me. I certainly didn't make him famous. But did I make him a fool? Should I have corrected his non-standard English, misquoting him as I relate our conversation? If I change his words, I am projecting my mainstream speech on him, changing his words into mine in a distasteful show of power. I can silence him and make him speak the way I want him to. If I transcribe his words verbatim, I might be (and have been) accused of caricature. Is my willingness to leave his speech and writing "uncorrected" part of the liberal but misguided undereducation of students of color that Lisa Delpit (1995) describes? Should I decide I have no right to write about Darwin and his fellow classmates of color at all, even if I write in the hope of advancing his literacy and the literacy education of other students in urban schools?

Does a well-motivated gesture of research turn at best, into an unintended betrayal, and, at worst, an act of racist objectification? Is Nikki Giovanni right in asserting that White people fundamentally don't understand enough about Black people to write about them? If so, what implications does that have for White qualitative researchers who write about young people of color?

Through a critical reexamination of my own research methodology and selected publications, I hope, with the clarity of hindsight, to evaluate whether the research I conducted contributed to the marginal status of the young people I purported to help. In addition, by examining my own work, I hope to raise more general questions about the nature of qualitative research with youth—questions that guide my own analysis and that may serve as useful checkpoints for other researchers as well. For example, do researcher narratives and ethnographies risk the foibles of storytelling: exaggeration, privileging of perspective, selection of details for effect, interpretations of "truth"? What unsuspected and unpredictable tensions might arise between researchers and research participants? *Can* we write about our students without objectifying them? Finally, and perhaps most centrally for the purposes of this volume, how are the issues raised in all these questions exacerbated by racial differences between researchers and subjects? In order to examine these questions, I revisit data that features urban adolescents from communities of color and working-class communities.

CONTEXT OF THE REPRESENTATIONS

The research I revisit is drawn from two different studies. The first study took place in an urban classroom in Minneapolis, Minnesota. This study examined the intersections of race, class, gender, and reading responses to a range of multicultural texts (Hynds & Appleman, 1997). I was the full-time teacher for the duration of the 12-week trimester. The class was a Language Arts elective entitled Multicultural Literature. There were 31 students enrolled in the class, ranging from grades 9 through 12. Fifteen students were White; 16 were students of color. Of these, one was Native American, four were Latino, three were Asian American, and eight were African American. Darwin was a member of that class.

The second study was conducted at that same urban school, with two high school seniors, one female (Alice) and one male (Matt), both White and lower middle class. The students were "underachieving" in school, skipping classes and not completing assignments. In interviews for a previous study (Appleman, 1999), they had indicated that they found the atmosphere of their large urban school to be uninspiring and stifling. Thus, the purpose of the study was to attempt to create a learning context in which the students might be more motivated. With the students' help, we designed a course with weekly assignments in reading and writing poetry. I met weekly with the students in a variety of locations—libraries, restaurants, coffeehouses, and bookstores. What resulted was a 12-week independent study in poetry.

Some Representations for Consideration

What follows are some representations generated from those studies, from my own published work and work in progress—written descriptions, narratives, and student work. I aim to reconsider those representations in light of considerations of power relations, race, and issues of representation. Not long ago, at a workshop on multicultural literature in California, I shared some of these data—the students' own work, some anecdotes, and my description of them. After the workshop, two participants approached me with accusations of misrepresentation and racism. Why had I picked these students? Wasn't I perpetuating stereotypes of Black males as criminals and White females as vulnerable do-gooders? Didn't I see that I was using the students to stand in for an entire population? Didn't I realize I was contributing to our cultural knowledge of such students by reifying these attributes through my representations of them? At the time, I didn't think they were right. I defended myself by saying I had presented them as they were, not as they wanted them to be or as I saw them. Yet my naive portrayal was far from raceless and was in dire need of what Michael Apple (1993) calls "a critical interruption."

As a White researcher describing and representing students of color, I am "constructing the other" (Apple, 1993). Apple points out that the vision of "the Other" (his caps) symbolizes an immense set of fears—fears that can be perpetuated by social production unless there is some kind of critical interruption. Rereading these descriptions with a Foucaultian eye to the traces of hegemony therein have caused me to second-guess my motivations, methodology, and the resulting representations. Here are two such representations for further consideration. They are of three adolescents, drawn from the studies described above: Alice, Darwin, and LaKeisha.

Alice

This story will surprise those who believe that if literary theory were to be taught to secondary students, it would be most appropriate with college preparatory students. I met Alice during her sophomore year when I was teaching a class on multicultural literature at her high school. In previous work I described Alice in the following way:

Alice is the middle child and only daughter in a split-apart family of five. She idolizes her two older brothers, both of whom are still remembered by teachers at her urban Minneapolis high school as being "brilliant" but troubled. Alice's oldest brother is a recovering heroin addict. She lives at home with her two younger brothers and her single mother, a full-time graduate student.

Alice favors the look of studied castoff casualness sported by the "alternative" crowd. Her hair changes colors frequently (though always with a wash and not a dye). Alice has an offbeat kind of fashion flair; she can make Doc Martens work with a dress. Lavender is her favorite color and she sports silver rings on most of her fingers, including her thumbs. As a present to herself, Alice got her tongue pierced on her 18th birthday; a decision met with horror by her mother who considered it a defiling of Alice's natural and honest beauty.

Alice was a remarkably unremarkable student. She moved uncritically through her required reading, wrote nearly illegible essays, hated her journal and perfected the pout of the reluctant learner. Her classroom participation was regular and sometimes brave, but hardly ever fully engaged. Between independent studies and college classes at the local university, Alice generally manages to never spend an entire day in school (Hynds & Appleman, 1997, p. 283).

During her junior year, long after our time together in class was over, Alice asked me if we could do an independent study project as an alternative way of earning her English credits. She said she simply couldn't find any English classes she could tolerate. She seemed restless, unsatisfied, hungry for something not on the school menu. When asked what she wanted to study with me, she replied, "Women's studies. I'm not sure what it is, but I think I'd like it."

Looking back, I can recognize that power relations of class and status are clearly evident in this description. Alice hated the traditional power relations between teacher and student, and I promised her I would change it to help her learn. We worked together to create a non-hierarchical learning structure. Together, we tried to reshape the power relationship of teacher and student by changing our locations of learning—pancake restaurants, coffee shops, bookstores, Alice's living room—and by engaging in non-school-sanctioned behaviors.

However, as I wrote about her, my work created another set of troubling issues between researchers and the people they research. For example, at Alice's high school graduation party, her mother introduced me as Alice's mentor, but did I do her family justice in my portrayal of them? Were

Alice's parents' marital status and her brother's drug addiction really essential details to include? Did I have the right to include them, knowing that I was using them to help readers infer certain aspects of Alice and her mother? Yes, both Alice and her mother read the descriptions, but their tacit approval doesn't absolve me of the responsibility I bear in drawing a permanent portrait of her and her family that is not entirely flattering and not at all useful to anyone but me.

Darwin and LaKeisha

Around that marked circle sat Darwin and his response to "We Real Cool"; next to him, staring across the circle at her White classmates and White teacher, was LaKeisha, a strong and proud young woman who, on being given a handout entitled "Cultural Background Activity," pointedly queried, "May I ask, ma'am, for what purpose, for what possible purpose, are we doing these activities?" It's one thing to ask a homogeneous group of students to describe their cultural background; it's another for LaKeisha, whose cultural background has been not only a source of pride but a source of social oppression and racial prejudice. For LaKeisha, there is no such thing as an innocent discussion about race, especially in a classroom as clearly socially segregated as ours naturally seemed to be. As Vivian Paley (1989, 1995) and Lisa Delpit (1995) have so poignantly observed, my role as a White teacher is fraught with implications of power, position, and pain that, at the moment, LaKeisha understood far better than I did. I mumbled something to LaKeisha about understanding what it is that we each bring to the texts we read, and that the reading of multicultural texts may require us to consider how our own cultural background affects our reading of those texts. LaKeisha slowly shook her head and stared me down.

Some colleagues have pointed out that even these brief descriptions of Darwin and LaKeisha are "raced." In previous versions of the article (Hynds & Appleman, 1997), I had included descriptions of LaKeisha's hair, jewelry, and painted fingernails, which I had edited out. I thought my description was fair, even neutral. Yet let us consider the last sentence of the description: "Lakeisha slowly shook her head and stared me down." There is really nothing neutral about this description; it paints LaKeisha as petulant and problematic, as I attempt to animate a particular representation of a resistant student of color. Similarly, I count on the words *strong* and *proud* to evoke a set of characteristics that may be too broadly drawn. Without admitting to it, I am using LaKeisha to stand in for all young

African American women. By describing her in a particular way, I encourage my readers to evoke a specific category of a female African American urban adolescent. When, I wonder, does descriptive representation veer into stereotype?

Similarly, my representation of Darwin may serve to perpetuate the image of young Black men as gangbangers. There were other African American males in the class about whom I did not write. I chose to tell Darwin's story partly because of how compelling I found him to be. He seemed to be walking a tightrope between his "associates" and his schoolmates. At the time, I thought he had an equal chance of going to jail or going to college. My role, I thought, was to improve the odds of the latter through good teaching and empathetic mentorship, to the degree that it was possible. But regardless of his own progress I perpetuated the very stereotypes that we were fighting against. By using Darwin's journal, I used his own words as building bricks of a negative and all-too-familiar social construction of African American males as marginal, even criminal. By selecting particular details of his life and school experiences, I unnecessarily exposed his vulnerability and perpetuated another stereotype. This, I've learned, is the danger of invoking the general through the particular.

Reconsideration of Representation in Retrospect

As both a teacher and a researcher, I worked with these students who were "on the margins." As a teacher, I treated them with respect, and I was deeply committed to helping them learn. But I was also a researcher, writing up my observations across class and racial lines. I worry that the good work I did as a teacher interested in "empowering" her students was undone by the truthful work I did as a researcher. Am I guilty of intellectual oppression and insensitivity, made particularly ironic by the critical theory that frames my work? Did I, for example, exert unjustified power over my students by inscribing my impressions in a permanent representation, imprisoning them in a sometimes unflattering image of their adolescent selves in order to make a theoretical point?

This problem of interpretation has been raised in recent scholarship about qualitative research—what Peshkin (2000) calls "metanarrative reflections." Peshkin encourages qualitative researchers to uncover the "problematics" in their journeys of interpretation in order to "show the way a researcher's self, or identity in a situation intertwines with his or her understanding of the object of the investigation . . ." (p. 5). After all, Peshkin explains, "the researcher's orientation and the definition of the situation cannot help but have ramifications for the way people are treated or thought of" (p. 5).

Therefore, I need to consider the degree to which the categories I held prior to my interaction with Darwin, LaKeisha, and Alice might have led me to interpret them the way I expected them to be, not necessarily the way they were. Only through a scrupulous reexamination of my own expectations can I begin to separate the "reality" of my subjects from my portrayal of them. As my interpretations cross racial lines, my interpretations can become dangerously close to the presuppositions that constitute racism.

OBJECTIFICATION THROUGH NARRATION

It is not just through description that young people can be marginalized or objectified in our work; we can also oppress them through our narratives, a kind of qualitative researchers' version of a master narrative. Peshkin (2000) points out the danger of interpretation in creating narratives when he writes that "interpretation is an act of imagination and logic. It entails perceiving importance, order, and form in what one is learning that relates to the argument, story, narrative that is continually undergoing creation" (p. 8).

Two Incidents for Consideration

What follows are two narratives that also require the kind of poststudy reflection that Peshkin (2000) advocates. The narratives spring from the second study featuring Alice, whom you've already met, and Matt. Alice and Matt were both underachieving high school students from working-class families. They were struggling in their large urban high school with bad attendance and poor grades. At Alice's suggestion, we created an independent study designed to free them from the oppressive controls of school and its attempts to standardize them into a particular kind of acquiescent adolescence. What resulted was a positive learning experience for both Alice and Matt. I sometimes wish I would have left our lessons private and unproclaimed. But I have spoken and written about them frequently and, as I've stated earlier, I've begun to second-guess my own methodology.

Incident 1: Discussing Conceptions of Beauty with a Pierced Tongue

Alice, Matt, and I meet in a coffee shop on Franklin Avenue in Minneapolis, a marginal area of town. I barely beat them to the place. I still am not used to the fact that although they were both notoriously tardy at school they are invariably on time for our appointments. Alice reads a poem she wrote about the blue room of her childhood. We can't understand a word she says. Last night was her eighteenth birthday and she got her tongue pierced. It's swollen.

Matt wonders aloud why she did it. I mutter something about contemporary theories of women resisting American standards of beauty. Alice says that's crap; she just wanted to do it because it seemed like an eighteen-year-old thing to do. Matt agrees with me, and asks Alice what beauty is. She asks him the same question back. He says, "I think we should try to answer it by writing poems. Isn't that why people write them in the first place?"

I think, *This could never, ever happen within the walls of that school.*

Incident 2: A Little Bit of Ginsburg

We're in a coffee shop that serves as a favorite hangout for students and faculty from a nearby liberal arts college. We have just been at the bookstore next door, where Alice and Matt spent two hours on the floor reading poetry. I had told them I would buy them each a volume of their choice. Alice chooses *WomanTongue*, a collection of performances by spoken-word artists. Matt chooses an anthology of beat poets called *On the Street*.

We're all drinking cappuccino. Matt and Alice light up cigarettes and we begin the part of our session together where we each read a poem. Matt begins with an Allen Ginsburg poem, "A Supermarket in California."

The middle-aged man next to us who had previously been scowling begins reciting the poem as Matt reads it. Matt is delighted; Alice is slightly annoyed. The man turns his chair toward us and tells Matt he's surprised that someone his age can "dig" Ginsburg. Matt replies, "Of course, man. There's a little bit of Ginsburg in every poem I write."

Reconsideration of Narration

Every word above is true, but when it happened in real time, the students were unaware that the incidents would be frozen in time as part of a research study. I wonder if I have a right to make these private and precious events public? I worry that the public telling of our time together betrays Matt and Alice. And, even if I haven't hurt them, I do doubt the degree to which my writing about them contributed to any larger understanding of educational processes.

Perhaps I should have let them speak for themselves. Valentine, Skelton, and Chambers (1998), for example, argue for a "more youth-centered research methodology" (p. 24) in which young people might tell their own stories. Moreover, Alderson (1995) reminds us of the importance of allowing our research subjects some choice in how they are presented in academic areas, especially after personal and regular contact with the researcher has lapsed. In these portrayals, do I risk making them vulnerable to criticism and perhaps even ridicule in order to make a point, hoisting their fragile adolescent psyches on my own methodological petard?

Matt and Alice are White; Darwin and LaKeisha are African American. Although issues of problematic representation are clearly evident in the portrayals of Matt and Alice, those issues become more salient, it seems, with Darwin and LaKeisha. Why? Perhaps, as Cornell West (1993) so succinctly summarizes, it is simply because, in our society of unequal access and privilege, "race matters." In workshops across the country, I have shared Darwin's journal entries, filled with dreams of college, references to "dead homies," philosophical ruminations on women and racism and descriptions of casual drug use. I have constructed him as "other," feeding into stereotypes and assumptions about young Black men.

Although qualitative researchers may not necessarily align themselves with the political conservatives most likely, in Apple's (1993) view, to do the "othering," constructing images of "the other" can be a dangerous enterprise, animating cultural misunderstandings, and as Nikki Rosa reminds us, completely misapprehending the subject due to racial ignorance. Such ignorance can lead to the kind of shorthand portrayals that border on racism. As Bill Ayers (1997) reminds us, "Racism, again, is more than bias or prejudice, more than a few bad ideas floating around aimlessly—it includes the structures of privilege and oppression linked to race and backed up by force, powerful structures that are the roots of prejudice" (p. 133).

TOWARD A NEW METHODOLOGY

Given that our research contributes to the social construction of youth, we need to rethink how young people might play a part "in the discussion of the research findings and, where possible, the dissemination of this material" (Valentine, Skelton, & Chambers, 1998, p. 23). Researchers might rely more on transcription and other ways of making their research more multivocal. A clearer picture of Darwin, for example, might emerge from the following interview that was conducted with him by an African American college student:

AMINAH: What were your ideas of what multicultural literature was before you began the class and how that's transcended to the end of the class, if you still feel the same way about what you thought it was or if that's kind of changed.

DARWIN: First, I just signed up for the class just to get it. But I didn't really understand what was the concept of the class at first. But I sat there and she was telling us and showing us the different books she was going to read and all that. I started to like it after a while.

AMINAH: So how would you define it? What would you say multicultural literature is?

DARWIN: I would say it is for multicultural kids, so they can learn more about their culture and stuff like that. I'd say on a scale of one to ten, I give it nine. I really liked the class.

AMINAH: And when you say it's for multicultural kids, do you think White kids can get anything out of it?

DARWIN: Yah, they need to be in there, too. Because a lot of their people put us in the situation that we're in. So they need to get better history and understanding of where we're coming from, from the minority perspective. So they can see the problems that we went through.

AMINAH: How do you think the dynamics went in the class? Because your class seems fairly mixed. But did you feel uncomfortable speaking out with this topic more than you might in a more traditional English where you maybe would read more White literature?

DARWIN: Well, I'm outspoken myself anyway. It don't matter to me. I don't really care what other people think about me or anything like that. So, I say what I feel at that moment.

AMINAH: Did you feel included in the literature? That your own voice was there? Echoed?

DARWIN: Yes.

AMINAH: Had you felt that way before?

DARWIN: No, never. I went to a predominantly White school, so it was like really different.

AMINAH: Was even a class like that offered there?

DARWIN: No, no.

AMINAH: If you were to talk to another student who is a peer of yours and who had not been in the class, how would you kind of sell the class to them? It sounds like you really liked it. What would you tell them are some of the benefits that we get from reading multicultural literature?

DARWIN: That it goes back to like your cultural backgrounds and stuff. It helps you learn about who you are and that you should never take a backseat. You know, you should always strive for the best in anything you do, as a minority.

In the above excerpt, Darwin is able to express himself fully and his perspective seems more contextualized than any excerpts might be. My researcher's interpretation is not mediating his presence. Additionally, my interpretation doesn't guide the questions themselves or even my presentation of the resulting interview. The subject is free from my interpretation and the reader can draw his or her own conclusion. In some ways I am showing rather than telling. Though clearly research stories can not be told entirely through the use of transcripts, including them in the results can provide a check for the researcher's own interpretation, which guides selection and presentation. Additionally, because the interviewer is both young and African American, the conversation takes place with someone with whom the power differential is less evident. Peshkin (2000) claims that it is the duality between the researcher and the researched that adds to the danger of reading into the data what I expect to be there. As an insider, Aminah doesn't animate those "othering" kinds of expectations.

CONCLUSION

In order to interrupt the power relations that too frequently undermine the value of qualitative research, Lutrell (2000) argues for a "good enough" methodology, one that recognizes the impossibility of eradicating power relations but does name them and trace the degree to which those tensions and imbalances inform both the process of investigation and the resulting research.

In one of his last published essays, the late Alan Peshkin (2000) writes candidly about the process of interpretation in qualitative research. As he considers his data on Pueblo Indian schoolchildren, Peshkin wonders "if I was so hellbent on pursuing duality that I made it into a template within which everything else had to fit" (p. 7). While Peshkin's template may be useful in explaining certain elements of learning practice and school attitudes among Pueblo Indians (p. 7), he also realizes the danger of reifying assumptions of cultural difference into research findings. Peshkin ruminates on the nature of interpretation and concludes the following:

Finally, interpretation has to do with a perspectival accounting for what I have learned, or the shaping of the meanings and understandings of what has gone on from some point of view, an issue of crisis in representation for some observers (see Gubrium and Holstein, 1997). It is inconceivable to me that I can conduct any aspect of my research except from some point of view, which is to say that other interpretations, other meanings and understandings, are imaginable. Indeed, they may offer sturdy competition to my own. For everyone's work, however, there is a court, not of last resort, but of public discourse. It comes into session when our work is published. (p. 9)

All of us who cross cultures when we write and research, all of us who interpret and inscribe the lives of young people in our work, need to be mindful to call that court of public discourse "into session," a session convened by this very volume. Peshkin urges us "to be forthcoming and honest about how we work as researcher" and to develop "a reflective awareness" that "contributes to enhancing the quality of our interpretive acts" (p. 9). To do so is important for the efficacy of all qualitative work; for work that is situated at the borders of class and racial divides it is even more critical, given how costly and dangerous reckless interpretations can be to our subjects and their communities. Our methodology will never be perfect, but through careful reflection it might become "good enough."

In all likelihood, none of our subjects will become famous. But let us be certain that we make none of them fools.

REFERENCES

Alderson, P. (1995). *Listening to children: Children, ethics and social research.* Ilford: Barnardo's.

Apple, M. (1993). Constructing the other. In C. McCarthy & W. Crichlow (Eds.), *Race identity and representation in education* (pp. 24–40). New York: Routledge.

Appleman, D. (1999). Alice, Lolita, and me: Learning to read "feminist" with a tenth-grade urban adolescent. In L. Alvine & L. Cullum (Eds.), *Breaking the cycle* (pp. 71–89). Portsmouth, NH: Heinemann.

Appleman, D. (2000a, November). *Talking, Reading, Writing, and Race: Contributions of Literacy Research to Racial Understanding.* Paper presented at the National Council of Teachers of English Annual Convention, Milwaukee, WI.

Appleman, D. (2000b, December). *Unintended betrayal: Dilemmas of representation in research with youth.* National Reading Conference Annual Meeting, Scottsdale, AZ.

Ayers, W. (1997). Racing in America. In M. Fine, M. L. Weis, L. Powell, & L. Wong (Eds.), *Offwhite: Readings on race, power, and society* (pp. 129–137). New York: Routledge.

Delpit, L. (1995). *Other people's children: Cultural conflict in the classroom.* New York: The New Press.

Fine, M. (1994). Working the hyphens: Reinventing self and other in qualitative research. In N. Denizin & Y. Lincoln (Eds.), *Handbook of qualitative research* (pp. 70–82). Thousand Oaks, CA: Sage.

Heath, S., & McLaughlin, M. (1993). *Identity and inner-city youth: Beyond ethnicity and gender.* New York: Teachers College Press.

Hynds, S., & Appleman, D. (1997). Walking our talk: Between response and responsibility in the literature classroom. *English Education, 29,* 272–293.

Kaplan, L. (1986). *Adolescence: The farewell to childhood.* Northvale, NJ: Jason Aronson.

Lutrell, W. (2000). "Good enough" methods for ethnographic research. *Harvard Educational Review, 70,* 499–523.

Paley, V. (1989). *White teacher.* Cambridge: Harvard University Press.

Paley, V. (1995). *Kwannza and me.* Cambridge: Harvard University Press.

Peshkin, A. (2000). The nature of interpretation in qualitative research. *Educational Researcher, 29,* 5–10.

Rabinow, P. (Ed.). (1997). *Michel Foucault: Ethics, subjectivity, and truth.* (R. Hurley, Trans.). New York: The New Press. (Original work published 1994)

Skelton, T., & Valentine, G. (Eds.). (1998). *Cool places: Geographies of youth cultures.* London: Routledge.

Valentine, G., Skelton, T., & Chambers, D. (1998). Cool places: An introduction to youth and youth cultures. In T. Skelton & G. Valentine (Eds.), *Cool places: Geographies of youth cultures* (pp. 1–35). London: Routledge.

Weis, L., & Fine, M. (Eds.). (2000). *Construction sites: Excavating race, class, and gender among urban youth.* New York: Teachers College Press.

West, C. (1993). *Race matters.* Boston: Beacon Press.

Yon, D. (2000). *Elusive culture: Schooling, race, and identity in global times.* Albany, NY: State University of New York Press.

PART II

Working Against "Color Blind" Practices and Contexts

Negotiating Race in Classroom Research: Tensions and Possibilities

Joanne Larson

As a qualitative researcher, my role as a participant observer in research projects is always a complicated, socially constructed activity. This chapter will enable me to articulate the tensions and possibilities I encounter as I conduct research in urban schools. I will discuss how I negotiate my identity as a White, middle-class female researcher in a mid-sized, high-poverty urban school district, articulating specifically the ethical and political dilemmas I face. Race, in particular, plays a central role in the studies I describe in this chapter. I will argue that race—mine and that of the teachers and students with whom I worked—surfaced as a key point of tension in my analyses that had specific consequences on access to data and public revelations of findings.

Race is central to my identity as a researcher for personal as well as professional reasons. Both my personal and professional lives focus on fighting for social justice and equity on multiple levels. Personally, as a wife of an African American man and a mother of a biracial son with a serious neurological disorder, I am committed to fighting against racist and other discriminatory practices in schools and society and for my husband and son's equal access to participation in both. My commitment to fighting institutionalized discrimination on multiple levels did not begin with my marriage or the birth of my son. I grew up in a British and Austrian aristocratic family structure in which girls and women were positioned as unimportant and trivial. This experience framed and radicalized my worldview and informs my present political commitments. I am appalled at the ways in which our society blindly supports the systematic exclusion of underrepresented groups from just and equal education.

Professionally, my passion for justice and equity has led me to the field of education with a mission to fight for social justice through school reform. An idealistic goal, perhaps, but it is nonetheless a driving force behind my research and teaching. Central to my understanding of equity is the notion of participation. Equal participation is a necessary, while perhaps not sufficient, prerequisite to a just society. I have focused my research on understanding participation on both societal and interpersonal levels through analysis of classroom interaction. My research on participation in classroom "literacy events" (Heath, 1983), in particular, has grown out of this desire to understand the nature of participation in classrooms and the ways in which access to participation is facilitated or inhibited in classroom discourse processes.

To understand participation, my analyses focus on how interaction is constructed in classroom participation frameworks. Specifically, I draw on Goffman's (1981) conception of the participation framework as a linguistic structure that organizes and is organized by talk and interaction in activity. Through analysis of the ways in which the teacher and students position each other in participation frameworks, I am able to document shifts in positions, or footings (Goffman, 1981), and the consequences of these shifts or a lack thereof on access to participation (Larson, 1999, 2001; Larson & Maier, 2000). Access to participation is also mediated by whether students are positioned as objects or subjects of literacy pedagogy (Edelsky, 1996; Freebody, Luke, & Gilbert, 1991). Students as objects perform literacy exercises, whereas students as subjects read or write meaningful texts for meaningful purposes. Classroom participation frameworks help to uncover the available positions in literacy events.

In the analysis of the participation frameworks in the classrooms discussed in this chapter, I found that the lack of opportunity to shift roles (e.g., restricting students to objects of instruction) limited students' participation to mere observation of the dominant literacy practices (Street, 1995) that were presented by teachers. In conducting the literacy research described here, race has emerged as a key construct in the analysis and has infused the research process itself.

HOW LANGUAGE PRACTICES POSITION STUDENTS AND MEDIATE ACCESS

My analyses are grounded in a view of literacy as a social practice that is linked to cultural and linguistic practices and power relationships in specific contexts (Lankshear & Knobel, 2002; New London Group, 1996; Street, 1995). As a social practice, literacy learning is mediated by language use in face-to-face interaction in specific contexts, for specific audiences and purposes (Duranti, 1997; Dyson, 1993; Gee, 2001; Gutierrez, 2001; Lee, 2001). Literacy learning is accomplished in a context in which social actors position, and are positioned by, each other in verbal, non-verbal, and textual interaction (Heath, 1983/1996; Luke, 1994).

Because classroom interaction carries powerful messages about what counts as literacy (Luke, 1994) and about the relationship of power, knowledge, and identity, it is important to investigate how language practices position students as objects or subjects in relation to text construction and how that relationship to text mediates access to participation in literacy activities. The ways in which power relations underlying this positioning deny access to participation necessitates an analysis of the consequences of being an object or a subject of literacy pedagogy in classrooms. Analysis of discourse is a key tool in understanding these relations of power and their role in constructing what counts as literacy knowledge in classrooms (Gee, 1996, 1999; Luke, 1992).

Teaching as a Form of Surveillance

In my analyses of urban classrooms, teachers used literacy pedagogy as a form of surveillance, regulation, and discipline in which students were positioned as consumers (e.g., objects) of teachers' literacy (Foucault, 1979; Lankshear & Knobel, 2002; Luke, 1992). Classroom discursive practices position social actors in interaction and, through that positioning, contribute to the construction of students' social identities (Davies & Harré, 1990). The social meaning of utterances depends upon the positioning of speakers within the participation framework as it is locally constructed in moment-to-moment interaction. Thus, language arts instruction may be used as a panoptical practice (Foucault, 1979) that constructs students as objects to be disciplined in ways that exclude meaningful participation in literacy events. In other words, teachers in the classrooms I observed used literacy pedagogical practices to monitor students' minds and bodies (Luke, 1992) rather than to provide opportunities to actually read or write meaningful texts.

I found that students' attempts to question the ways in which teachers positioned them in classroom interaction were thwarted by institutionalized disciplinary discourse practices. Consequently, students were excluded from meaningful participation in literacy events as teaching literacy remained focused on classroom management. The focus on classroom management issues was rooted in teachers' racialized beliefs (Goldberg, 1993) about students' abilities.

The Construction of Participation Roles and Power Relations through Indexicality

Indexicality is a useful framework for understanding how language use in classrooms contributed to the construction of participation roles and power relations. Observing the organization of talk and interaction in classroom participation frameworks reveals how contextually situated language practices position teachers and students in various roles and how shifts in those roles mediate access to participation in literacy events (Duranti, 1997; Goffman, 1981; Goodwin, C., 1996; Goodwin, M., 1990). In the studies discussed in this chapter, I found that teachers index students' language, race, and social class as sources of learning problems and position students according to assumptions related to these identity markers. *Index* is defined here as the relationship of properties of speech to cultural contexts (Ochs, 1992). I have argued elsewhere that the discourse practices (indexical field) in the classrooms I observed mark non-White students as "other"—that is, different than teachers, school administrators, and district officials—which results in reciprocal distancing (Larson & Irvine, 1999).

In a classroom there are multiple indexical meanings where coparticipants agree to participate; however, urban contexts systematically exclude the students' indexical meanings in everyday language practices thereby limiting legitimized knowledge to dominant language and literacy practices. Understanding how students' indexical meanings are excluded in face-to-face interaction may illustrate how the racialized indexing of institutions such as schools marginalize the consciousness (Du Bois, 1903/1989) of African American and other underrepresented groups. Teachers and students in the classrooms I observed constructed a shared indexical context around school-based literacy that typically excluded non-White students' language and literacy practices. As I will illustrate in this chapter, we can see this exclusionary process when students attempt to bring in their own knowledge and practices to classroom activities.

Teacher Talk and Relations of Power

Using this theoretical framework, I argue that power relations in the wider world are evident in teachers' discourse and in reading instruction through a process termed *reciprocal distancing* (Larson & Irvine, 1999). Reciprocal distancing is a discourse process in which teachers and students invoke sociohistorical and political distances between their communities in classroom interaction (Larson & Irvine, 1999). Reciprocal distancing occurs when there is a devaluing of students' linguistic and sociocultural knowledge and resources. My research has shown that this distancing is linguistically marked in interactions in which teachers and students have struggled over whose cultural practices would serve as resources in the classroom.

THE RESEARCH: STUDIES OF LANGUAGE ARTS TEXTBOOKS AND LITERACY PEDAGOGY IN TWO URBAN CLASSROOMS

I will describe two areas of research; the first is a qualitative study of three Language Arts textbook series that were piloted in Northeast City School

District (a pseudonym). I served on the district's advisory committee, observed and interviewed teachers throughout the district, and provided a comprehensive research report to district administration. The second area of research is part of a larger ethnographic study of two local elementary teachers funded by the Spencer Foundation. My focus for this chapter is on literacy pedagogy and the instantiation of what one of the teachers in the study, an urban kindergarten teacher, described as *whole-language-based teaching*. This teacher articulated that her literacy curriculum integrated both whole language and skills-based pedagogies to adequately prepare her students for "school-based literacy" (Street, 1995).

Both studies I describe here were conducted in the Northeast City School District (NCSD). This district struggles with high poverty levels and low reading scores. African American and Latino students make up 80% of the student population, while 79% of the teachers are European American and do not live in their schools' neighborhoods. The administrative staff of the district is 61% European American and 39% African American, Latino, or what the district calls "other." Poverty rates (as measured by the percentage of students receiving free lunch) are high, up to 98% in some schools. The annual publication of students' test scores on the new state Fourth Grade English Language Arts (ELA) test, brings renewed concern about poor performance. In 1999, the year in which I conducted the research described here, only 24% of NCSD students met the state standard.

Constructing Academic Disadvantage

Early in the analysis of the data from the textbook project, I met with a high-level central office administrator to discuss my findings. One of the most salient features of my preliminary analysis was the clear deficit model ideology that teachers, both African American and White, held when referencing their predominantly African American students. Teachers in the textbook study described their students as being without language, as not having appropriate background experiences to prepare them for school, and as being so far behind as to need extensive remediation to catch up to grade level. Similarly, the kindergarten teacher and her peers described students as culturally deprived.

The school district had been cited by the federal government for civil rights violations due to the overrepresentation of non-White students in Special Education classes. My findings about teachers' racialized ideologies made this White female administrator uneasy because she directed me to submit only one copy of my report to her and to mark it "Confidential: Not for Distribution." I was also asked to write an "executive summary" of the study in which she directed me to report only on the uses of the textbook and not to mention teachers' comments about students. My report was suppressed at central office and the superintendent never saw it. District office insiders told me that the report simply disappeared.

After my service for the district was completed, I continued to analyze the classroom observation and interview data more thoroughly with my colleague Patricia Irvine. Throughout the more than 24 hours of interviews and comprehensive field notes, we found that teachers' literacy practices were influenced by beliefs that their students' abilities and background were deficient. Teachers overwhelmingly located failure in the students, not the curriculum, instructional practices, or institutional constraints. Moreover, they described their students as incompetent English speakers, attributing their reading difficulties to a lack of "language" and to their "backgrounds." The enacted curriculum was reduced to what they believed "these students" could handle and resulted in a basic-skills pedagogy that limited students' access to literacy learning by positioning them as pedagogical objects. We observed no activities in which students were reading and writing texts; rather, they completed exercises focused on isolated skills such as recognizing letter-sound correspondence and making lists of consonant clusters.

Specifically, when we asked teachers about what factors contribute to learning to read, they revealed racialized beliefs about the students' cultural and language practices (Goldberg, 1993). All of the teachers, both African American and White, attributed students' poor literacy skills to their background experiences and home environments. They mentioned museum trips and being read to as examples of the kinds of experiences they believe are necessary for school literacy, experiences Heath (1983) has documented are characteristic of White middle-class language socialization.

We argued that teacher comments about "urban kids," "these children," and "inner-city students" are terms that index the non-White majority of students in this district. My experience on other long-term ethnographic research projects both in the city and area suburbs and as a teacher educator in this and nearby areas has demonstrated that teachers and administrators believe that Northeast's academic achievement problems are due to its large, poor, non-White student population. Thus, racialized indexing is a common discourse practice used to make sense of poor academic achievement in this district by focusing on the racial, ethnic, and social class characteristics of the students and their community.

An Example of Racialized Indexing

The following excerpts from the interview and observation of one White third grade teacher's lesson on subject-verb agreement provides one example of racialized indexing processes from among many I observed.[1] In the following interview, the teacher is describing a "verb conjugation" lesson that she would conduct later in her classroom. On this particular day she had 23 students in class: 17 who were African American and 6 who were White.

> This [lesson] is a conjugation of the verb "be," which is an interesting idea in itself considering all the Ebonics (laughter) controversy of things. Because I have kids that won't conjugate. I mean they'll use wrong conjugations, ya know, they'll say "he is" or "we is" so this should be interesting today (heh heh) because it's not it's not natural for some of them to conjugate. So it will be interesting, ya know, to get them to use the correct conjugations of the verb "be."

Elsewhere, I have observed (Larson & Irvine, 1999) that this teacher marked the students' language, "Ebonics," as the reason for their incorrect or "wrong conjugations." The students were, in fact, conjugating verbs in African American Vernacular English (AAVE) (Smitherman, 1977/1986, 2000). Her beliefs about students' lack of "natural" language ability reflect social and institutional beliefs about nonstandard language. Such beliefs have exclusionary consequences for literacy learning when put into practice. For example, this teacher's beliefs about her African American students' language abilities influenced her decision to limit her lesson to a grammar worksheet.

The teacher's sporadic laughter in her interview may indicate a colluding stance with the interviewer. I have found that White teachers reveal their ideologies in specific ways to interviewers who are also White. This air of collusion, indexed in her "in-joke" tonal semantics and "you know what I mean" laughter and gestures, may indicate the teacher's assumption of a shared indexical field (Hanks, 1990) with me because I am White, that I would know what her joking tone meant. The idea of collusion poses an ethical dilemma for me. Do I participate in this collusion to get the data? Or do I point out the potentially racist implications of her comments in the moment? In this study, I chose to let the teachers talk and to take the work of revealing these beliefs to other teachers, both locally and nationally, and to the research community through workshops, presentations, and publications.

After this interview, I observed the teacher conduct her lesson. The lesson began with the teacher at the front of the room using an overhead projector to fill in a worksheet taken from the textbook series. She spoke to the students briefly about singular and plural verbs and began the worksheet exercise by reading the first example, "A horse is stuck." The answer was already filled in on the transparency. She read the next sentence, saying the word *blank* where the answer should have been, then called on students to fill in the answer[2]:

1	TEACHER:	A horse is stuck.
2		The horses *blank* stuck.
3		[Calls on African American student.]
4	AF AM STUDENT:	The horses is stuck.
5	WHITE STUDENT:	Horses are stuck.
6	TEACHER:	We didn't say "horse are stuck."
7		[To African American students.]
8		Would you say "I is hungry?"
9		Do we say "We is hungry?"
10		No!
11	AF AM STUDENT:	I do, I do.
12	TEACHER:	But you're not supposed to!
13	AF AM STUDENT:	I say "I is going."
14	TEACHER:	But you're not supposed to say
15		[reaches for an example in the manual]
16		I is (going).
17		There are words that sound right,
18		and there are words that are right with
19		these subjects, and you just have to
20		learn them.
21		
22	AF AM STUDENT:	I was hungry.
23	AF AM STUDENT:	No. I say, I hungry [laughs].
24		[Laughter from his classmates.]

In this example, this teacher's beliefs about her students' inability to make verbs agree with their subjects in Standard English were enacted in a practice that excluded students' language resources as valid, however reductionist it was. Her use of pronouns ("we/you") positioned African American students as outside the Standard-English-speaking community that is normalized in U.S. schools. In this literacy event, reciprocal distancing was initiated when she asked questions that elicited what she considered "wrong" answers from African American students ("Would you say, 'I is hungry'?"). As a consequence, the teacher appeared to inhibit the construction of a shared context for literacy learning at the level of grammar by excluding students' linguistic resources from classroom literacy events.

Although the fill-in-the-blank exercise observed in this classroom is problematic as a tool for literacy learning, it may not be the most academically disadvantaging aspect of this lesson. The teacher's racialized language ideology, combined with an autonomous definition of literacy as a decontextualized set of skills (Street, 1995), denied the students access to meaning making through their own language and literacy practices. A pedagogy based on a definition of literacy as a social practice would value students' cultural and linguistic practices as legitimate resources in literacy instruction or would have used these practices in a way that assisted students in understanding the grammar of their own language. Students who learn to distinguish the grammatical differences between Standard English and AAVE are better prepared for the school-based literacy they will encounter throughout their education (Elsasser & Irvine, 1985; Perry & Delpit, 1998).

EXCLUDING STUDENTS' LITERACY KNOWLEDGE

The second study describes how one urban kindergarten teacher's language practices in both reading and writing events limits students' participation to watching the teacher, denying them the opportunity to bring their own language and literacy to the interaction.

The kindergarten classroom was colorful, well appointed, and child centered. The familiar design of the double-sized classroom (kitchen/home area, blocks, easels, puzzles, etc.) might be found in most early childhood classrooms in the United States. The scheduled activities were also typical of early childhood classrooms and included activities such as morning circle, center time, whole-class story time, and journal writing. On any given day, students could be seen going about their morning routine of singing, working in groups, and playing together. The teacher planned for journal writing to be a part of this daily schedule; however, time often grew short and writing did not occur.

Reading events in this classroom occurred when time allowed, and were limited to whole-class read-alouds orchestrated by the teacher. Occasionally, students had time to read independently; however, the teacher restricted access to books. Very few books were available on a daily basis because the majority of them were stored away from student access in a teacher-only cabinet. The only reading instruction I observed consisted of read-alouds, in which the teacher selected the books, read them to the class as a whole, and periodically asked prediction questions and what Heath (1983) has described as "what" questions. This form of questioning is a common discourse practice in White middle-class families and is normalized in schools.

The following example of this type of questioning comes from the reading of *Rosie's Walk*—a popular book in kindergarten throughout the United States—and is often used as a scaffold for students' understanding of prediction and directionality. The story follows a hen named Rosie through a number of adventures over, under, through, and around a series of obstacles while a fox tries to capture her.

131	TEACHER:	What do we see in the pictures.
132	STUDENTS:	A fox
133	TEACHER:	.hhhwhat's the fox doing
134	STUDENTS:	A chicken=
135	SHAMIR:	He's gonna eat her.
136		*((points to book))*
137	STUDENT:	=it's a chicken
138		it's a chick-
139	TEACHER:	Rosie is a chicken
140		*((looking at student))*
141		or a female chicken is called a he:n::
142		*((turns the page))*
143	STUDENT:	He*n*:
144		he*n*:

The teacher followed what she understood to be a whole-language technique or lesson structure in which the goal was to teach prediction. However, as the reading activity continued, the students did not have access to the text in the form of discussion about what was being read, despite their efforts (Larson, 2002). The classroom discourse structure was limited to a strict IRE (initiation, response, evaluation) pattern that required that the students recite the teacher's understanding of the text (Gutierrez, 1993; Mehan, 1979).

In the above example, the teacher corrected the students' words for something in the story into what she considered to be a more acceptable word. In lines 137–144, she corrects the students' word "chicken" to her "hen." One student responds by mimicking her pronunciation (lines 143–144). *Chicken* is an appropriate word to describe Rosie, so the correction seems unnecessary. Perhaps the teacher thought it was important for students to know similar words for chicken or more detail about the word ("a female chicken is called a he:n::", line 141). However, she continued to replace students' words with hers throughout the rest of the reading (e.g., "haystack" for "grass"). I am not suggesting that vocabulary building is not an important and valuable goal in early childhood; however, to do so in ways that replace the students' words with an arbitrarily determined word restricts students' participation and excludes their language resources in the construction of literacy knowledge.

Writing instruction occurred rarely in this classroom, and when it did, the students were restricted to watching the teacher write. There were few, if any, opportunities for students to write freely due to the focus in this classroom on doing writing exercises and learning what the teacher determined were proper writing behaviors (Edelsky, 1991). Writing activities centered on developing competent letter formation with little or no time for elaborated student-generated text, despite the teacher's goal of drawing on students' own literacy, which she articulated in interviews. I have discussed this activity at length elsewhere (Larson, 2002) and will only briefly describe one part of the writing period to demonstrate the dominance of White middle-class language practices and their consequences on students' access to meaningful participation.

In the following excerpt, the teacher was assisting Jerome in writing a story about his mother taking a bath:

256	TEACHER:	"M"
257		((writes the letter on paper))
258	JEROME:	((looks at her letter then writes "M" on his paper))
259	TEACHER:	"O::: ↑"
260		((writes the letter))
261		It's a circle,
262	JEROME:	((writes the letter))
263	TEACHER:	and then we put ano↑ther "M"
264		((writes the letter))
265	JEROME:	((writes the letter))
266	ALIA:	(here's an "M")
267	TEACHER:	((looks at Alia and smiles))
268		(5.0)
269		Alia↑
270		one more time
271		and I'll have to send you to another table
272		((nods toward another table))
273		you need to sit and quietly work.
274		"M-O"
275		((to Jerome))
276		and what did you just write,
277	JEROME:	Mom,

As this interaction began, the teacher wrote the letter "M" on her paper as Jerome watched, then copied on his own journal page (lines 256–

258). This pattern of watching the teacher write, then copying, continued for the remainder of his writing. Scribing students' stories is common practice in early childhood classrooms in the United States. However, this teacher did not scribe stories; rather, she wrote letters for students to copy. In this way, the teacher positioned students in the participation framework as observers or copiers of her text. The limited nature of available roles was reinforced in lines 266–273, when the teacher firmly denied Alia the opportunity to shift to an assistance role when she tried to show her letter to Jerome, then threatened a disciplinary consequence that would exclude her ("one more time and I'll have to send you to another table"—lines 270–271) if she continued her efforts to help Jerome.

In line 276, the teacher asked Jerome, "What did you just write?" With this utterance, she gave the credit for writing the word "mom" to Jerome when, in fact, she wrote the word and he copied it. This accommodating stance was reflective of the verbal strategies of White, middle-class American mothers documented by Ochs (1992). Furthermore, her implicit modeling of the writing process decontextualized the teacher's modeled writing from students' own processes. As a result, students had difficulty making connections between what the teacher was modeling and what they were doing as novice writers. The tightly controlled discourse structure restricted opportunities for interaction among the students and enabled the teacher to take all the responsibility for writing, contradicting her classroom rule that students write their own stories.

This teacher articulated many times in interviews similar beliefs about her students that I described earlier. At one point she told me she thought her students were "animals." I immediately reacted with astonishment and asked what she meant. She went on to invoke the longstanding deficit model argument of cultural deprivation, citing the same museum trips and home reading practices as the teachers in the textbook study. These beliefs were the foundation of her pedagogical decisions. I pushed further and talked about the concept of multiple literacies and the idea of using students' sociocultural knowledge in the construction of school-based literacy to no avail. Discouraged, I gave up. I tried on several occasions to meet with her to view the videotapes of her practice, hoping she would see what was happening for herself, but she canceled all our appointments, citing her busy schedule as the reason each time.

THE POWER OF DISCURSIVE PRACTICES TO MASK DIVERSITY

In the classrooms briefly described here, the instantiated school-based literacy served to persuade students as objectified "other" to internalize White middle-class language and literacy practices as normative. The teachers in these studies appeared to avoid race by focusing on students' ability. The enforcement of the teachers' practices masked the diversity of the students' language and literacy practices. As a result, these teachers continued to "underteach" (Delpit, 1995, p. 175) their students as they denied meaningful access to text construction.

The power of discursive practices lies in the construction of multiple positions (e.g., having more that the position of object of instruction available) within which participants are assumed to be capable of exercising choice in relation to those practices (Davies & Harré, 1990). In the classrooms I have described in this chapter, the choice of positions was limited to what roles the teachers made available through tightly controlled participation frameworks. I argue here that, by removing students' choice of positions, teachers' language practices excluded the students from a mode of participation that used their sociocultural knowledge in the active construction of literacy knowledge.

Patterns of participation in literacy activity determine how meaning is constructed in schools, by whom, and for what purpose (Luke, 1994). By understanding these patterns of participation, educators and policy makers may gain insight into how current Language Arts pedagogy restricts access to more meaningful and inclusive literacy practices. By paying attention to how this power struggle happens discursively, literacy researchers concerned about students' marginalization will be able to understand how to construct richer contexts for literacy learning—contexts in which both students' and teachers' cultural and linguistic practices make up the sociocultural knowledge of the classroom.

In sum, this research on the discursive practices of classrooms may help literacy researchers understand more fully how various racialized discourses are patterned within and across participation frameworks, which discourses are privileged, by whom, and how these patterns of interaction mediate learning. This research-based understanding of how access to participation is mediated by classroom language and literacy practices can provide an important base of knowledge for reforming the teaching and learning of literacy. Understanding how race is implicated in micro interactions in classrooms may help us move teachers toward more inclusive language practices.

THE DILEMMAS OF NEGOTIATING RACE

My own struggles with negotiating race in these projects have presented me with several unresolved dilemmas or tensions. On the textbook project, in agreeing to make my report confidential and to writing an executive summary that eliminated racial issues, I participated in the district's cover-up of my findings. I felt I had no choice, because the dean of my school of education had asked me to work with the district on this project in an effort to establish and maintain good relations between the district and my university. Furthermore, as a university representative, I felt that my professional standing in the community would be jeopardized in ways that I could not accept. For example, I may have been denied future access to research in NCSD. In my current position as chair of the Teaching and Curriculum program, I am responsible for placing student teachers in this district and my ability to do my job may have been compromised. Lastly, my three children attend school in NCSD and I was unwilling as a mother to make things any harder for them than it already is having a mother who teachers know is a professor of education at the university.

Another tension came with the choice to use an assumed shared indexical field (e.g., tolerating the air of collusion described earlier) with White teachers to expose larger societal beliefs about African American and Latino students as they are enacted in face-to-face interaction. To use a colluding stance and not challenge their negative assumptions to get the data was a choice I made because I felt it was more important to expose the insidious workings of the deficit model as it plays out in today's classrooms. To me, it is about the children. It was painful to watch children's faces as teachers excluded them or belittled their contributions. I found myself imagining my son Marcus and what these practices would do to his spirit. I think now, as I did then, that not to document these practices and expose them in my writing and presentations would mean I was *in* collusion and a part of the marginalization of African American and Latino students. By taking this work public, I hope to call attention to unspoken racialized assumptions in ways that will provoke change.

Feeling bad about what I observed in this research is not enough, however. What do I do about what I have found? As mentioned, I negotiated multiple and conflicting identities in this research: White, middle-class woman; university researcher; mother; activist; department chair; community member. Existing in these multiple contexts opened up spaces in which to take action. For example, a change in central office leadership enabled me to discuss my original findings with the new curriculum director, an African American woman, who took the original administrator's place. I described my work to her, the process of covering the results that had occurred, and shared a published article with her. Unlike her predecessor, she took action. She asked me to be the keynote speaker at a large professional development conference in my roles of university researcher and department chair. I discussed the research at this presentation and followed up with multiple smaller workshop-style talks in which we discussed my work and other research on AAVE with classroom teachers.

In my role of university researcher, I received a professional development grant from New York State to work with teachers in this district over a 5-year period. In this ongoing university-school collaboration we focus on changing traditional literacy practices and examining our underlying assumptions about students, teachers, each other, and literacy. The experiences I described in this chapter and the struggles I face as a mother of children in NCSD play a significant role in my participation in this group. I find that we move slowly and painstakingly, but we do move. For example, one teacher said after a conversation that was leaning toward negative comparisons between urban and suburban children that "urban kids are the same as suburban kids." This was a small change from her previous stance, but change nonetheless. This collaboration and the push to change ideologies continues.

As a teacher educator my courses on literacy learning are designed to get preservice teachers to think about their assumptions and to use a sociocultural theory of learning to understand ways to actively use their students' language and literacy practices in their curriculum (Ball, 1995; Ladson-Billings, 1994, 2001; Lee, 2001). This chapter itself is an articulation of my subjectivity and follows recent work by Majors (2001) in which she articulates her own assumptions as an African American woman that were revealed in her analysis of ethnographic research data. Finally, I am a staunch advocate for my son as he enters this same school system as a kindergartner.

I see the possibility of the research growing out of the tensions that arise in the public revelation of an embedded deficit ideology I found in this research. I have seen lately that there seems to be a consensus that the deficit model ideology in schools is something of the past. Colleagues speak about the issue as though it no longer exists. With the research I have described here, I hope to reveal that not only is a deficit model ideology not a thing of the past, but something that is active and dangerous. Some of the things teachers said during interviews in the studies described here dramatically represented this ideology. For example, when I asked questions such as, "What do you mean by culturally deprived?" one teacher responded with, "My students are animals." Or when I asked about practices she used to support student language learning, another teacher reported that she sent home tongue depressors with African American students so they could learn to use their mouths properly. These are indeed appalling and frightening practices. By bringing this ideology and resultant practices to a public sphere through research and through my professional development work with teachers and preservice teachers, I hope to effect meaningful change. Changing these embedded ideologies and resultant discriminatory practices is, after all, the point.

NOTES

1. Portions of this discussion appeared in Larson and Irvine (1999), "We call him Dr. King": Reciprocal distancing in urban classrooms. *Language Arts, 76*(5), 393–400.

2. The following transcription conventions, adapted from Atkinson and Heritage (1984), are used in the examples given:

Colons denote sound stretch (he:n::); brackets indicate overlapping speech; outward-facing brackets (<>) indicate slowed speech; inward-facing brackets (><) indicate faster speech; equal signs (=) indicate closely latched speech or ideas. For example:

> STUDENTS: A chicken=
> SHAMIR: He's gonna eat her.
>   *((points to book))*
> STUDENTS: =it's a chicken

Intervals of silence are timed in tenths of seconds and inserted within parentheses; short, untimed silences are marked by a dash when sound is quickly cut off (chick-) or with a period within parentheses (.). Rising intonation within a utterance is marked with an arrow (i↑s); rising intonation at the end of an utterance is marked with a comma (so,); falling intonation at the end of an utterance is indicated with a period (pictures.); descriptions of speech or gestures are italicized within double parentheses [*((puts finger to mouth))*]; single parentheses surround items of doubtful transcription.

REFERENCES

Atkinson, G. M., & Heritage, J. (1984). *Structures of social action: Studies of conversational analysis.* Cambridge, UK: Cambridge University Press.

Bakhtin, M. M. (1986). *Speech genres and other late essays* (C. Emerson & M. Holquist, Eds.; V. W. McGee, Trans.). Austin: University of Texas Press.

Ball, A. (1995). Text design patterns in the writing of urban African American students: Teaching to the cultural strengths of students in multicultural settings. *Urban Education, 30*(3), 253–289.

Davies, B., & Harré, R. (1990). Positioning: The discursive production of selves. *Journal for the Theory of Social Behaviour, 20*(1), 43–63.

Delpit, L. (1995). *Other people's children: Cultural conflict in the classroom.* New York: The New Press.

Du Bois, W.E.B. (1989). *The souls of black folks*. New York: Bantam. (Original work published 1903)

Duranti, A. (1997). *Linguistic anthropology*. Cambridge, UK: Cambridge University Press.

Dyson, A. (1993). *Social worlds of children learning to write*. New York: Teachers College Press.

Edelsky, C. (1991). *With literacy and justice for all: Rethinking the social in language and education*. New York: Falmer Press.

Edelsky, C. (1996). *With literacy and justice for all: Rethinking the social in language and education*. London: Taylor and Francis.

Elsasser, N., & Irvine, P. D. (1985). English and Creole: The dialectics of choice in a college writing program. *Harvard Educational Review, 55*(4), 399–415.

Foucault, M. (1979). *Discipline and punish*. New York: Vintage.

Freebody, P., Luke, A., & Gilbert, P. (1991). Reading positions and practices in the classroom. *Curriculum Inquiry, 21*(4), 435–457.

Gee, J. P. (1996). *Social linguistics and literacies: Ideology in discourse* (2nd ed.). London: Taylor & Francis.

Gee, J. P. (1999). *Introduction to discourse analysis: Theory and method*. London: Routledge.

Gee, J. P. (2001). Reading, language abilities, and semiotic resources: Beyond limited perspectives in reading. In J. Larson (Ed.), *Literacy as snake oil: Beyond the quick fix* (pp. 7–26). New York: Peter Lang.

Goffman, E. (1974). *Frame analysis*. New York: Harper & Row.

Goffman, E. (1981). *Forms of talk*. Philadelphia: University of Pennsylvania Press.

Goodwin, C. (1981). *Conversational organization: Interaction between speakers and hearers*. New York: Academic Press.

Goodwin, C. (1996). Transparent vision. In E. Ochs, E. Schegloff, & S. Thompson (Eds.), *Interaction and grammar* (pp. 370–404). Cambridge, UK: Cambridge University Press.

Goodwin, M. (1990). *He-said-she-said: Talk as social organization among black children*. Indianapolis: Indiana University Press.

Goldberg, D. (1993). *Racist culture*. Oxford, UK: Blackwell.

Gutierrez, K. (1993). How talk, context, and script shape contexts for learning: A cross-case comparison of journal sharing. *Linguistics and Education, 5*, 335–365.

Gutierrez, K. (2001). Smoke and mirrors: Language policy and educational reform. In J. Larson (Ed.), *Literacy as snake oil: Beyond the quick fix* (pp. 111–122). New York: Peter Lang.

Hanks, W. (1990). *Referential practice: Language and lived space among the Maya*. Chicago: University of Chicago Press.

Heath, S. B. (1983/1996). *Ways with words: Language, life, and work in communities and classrooms*. Cambridge, UK: Cambridge University Press.

Irvine, P. D. (1995). *Pueblo perspectives on schooling*. Unpublished doctoral dissertation, University of New Mexico, Albuquerque.

Ladson-Billings, G. (1994). *The dreamkeepers: Successful teachers of African American children*. San Francisco: Jossey-Bass.

Ladson-Billings, G. (2001). *Crossing over to Canaan: The journey of new teachers in diverse classrooms.* San Francisco: Jossey-Bass.

Lankshear, C., & Knobel, M. (2002, February). *Steps toward a pedagogy of tactics.* Keynote address at the annual conference of the National Council of Teachers of English Assembly for Research. New York, NY.

Larson, J. (1999). Analyzing participation frameworks in kindergarten writing activity: The role of overhearer in learning to write. *Written Communication, 16*(2), 225–257.

Larson, J. (Ed.) (2001). *Literacy as snake oil: beyond the quick fix.* New York: Lang.

Larson, J. (2002). Packaging process: Consequences of commodified pedagogy on students' participation in literacy events. *Journal of Early Childhood Literacy, 2*(1), 65–95.

Larson, J., & Irvine, P. D. (1999). "We call him Dr. King": Reciprocal distancing in urban classrooms. *Language Arts, 76*(5), 393–400.

Larson, J., & Maier, M. (2000). Co-authoring classroom texts: Shifting participant roles in writing activity. *Research in the Teaching of English, 34*, 468–498.

Lee, C. (2001). Is October Brown Chinese? A cultural modeling activity system for underachieving students. *American Educational Research Journal, 38*(1), 97–141.

Luke, A. (1992). The body literate: Discourse and inscription in early literacy training. *Linguistics and Education, 4*, 107–129.

Luke, A. (1994). *The social construction of literacy in the primary school.* Melbourne, Australia: Macmillan.

Majors, Y. (2001). Passing mirrors: Subjectivity in a midwestern hair salon. *Anthropology and Education Quarterly, 32*, 1.

Mehan, H. (1979). *Learning lessons.* Cambridge, MA: Harvard University Press.

New London Group. (1996). A pedagogy of multiliteracies: Designing social futures. *Harvard Educational Review, 66*(1), 60–92.

Ochs, E. (1992). Indexing gender. In A. Duranti & C. Goodwin (Eds.), *Rethinking context: Language as an interactive phenomenon* (pp. 335–358). Cambridge, UK: Cambridge University Press.

Perry, T., & Delpit, L. (Eds.). (1998). *The real Ebonics debate: Power, language, and the education of African-American children.* Milwaukee, WI: Rethinking Schools.

Smitherman, G. (1986). *Talkin and testifyn: The language of Black America.* Boston: Houghton Mifflin. Reissued with revisions, Detroit: Wayne State University Press. (Original work published 1977)

Smitherman, G. (2000). *Talkin that talk: Language, culture, and education in African America.* London & New York: Routledge.

Street, B. (1995). *Social literacies: Critical approaches to literacy in development, ethnography, and education.* London: Longman.

CHAPTER 5

Successful Strategies of Latino Students: Bringing Their Worldviews to Their Studies

Marilyn S. Sternglass

When I decided that I wanted to leave my position at a midwestern university, it was because I wanted to find a college where my background in linguistics and composition would be more usefully employed to work with an urban population of students and teachers. No institution could have been more urban and inner-city than City College of New York, so I was delighted to be offered an appointment there in the fall of 1985. Having had experience teaching in and directing basic writing programs, I knew that City College would provide me with opportunities to use my background for both teaching and research.

After arriving there, I read an article by Patricia Bizzell (1986) in *College Composition and Communication* urging study and reflection on how basic writers incorporated their worldviews into their academic experience. The idea for doing a longitudinal study was thus born, and I set about trying to find funding for an extensive study. Unable to acquire such support, I decided to undertake the study in the fall of 1989 by teaching one section of each of the three levels of composition then offered, English 1 (the first basic level), English 2 (the second basic level), and English 110 (the one-semester freshman composition course). The population of the classes (53 students randomly assigned) met the diversity of the college: 21 African American, 26 Latino, 4 Asian, and 2 White. Thirty were males and 23 were females. Twenty-five were born outside the continental United States, including three born in Puerto Rico. Students in English 1 and English 2 were placed in the courses on the basis of their performance on the inappropriate, timed, impromptu Writing Assessment Test (WAT). Students in English 110 had multiple routes into the course: initial placement on the basis of the WAT; completion of one or two semesters of basic writing; completion of one, two, or three semesters of English as a Second

Language (ESL); or as transfer students who had not yet successfully completed the English composition requirement. I ended the study after 6 years with complete data for nine students and partial data for the others.

I hoped that in examining how the worldviews of the students impinged on their academic experiences and their life experiences, I would have an opportunity to discover how their backgrounds affected their learning. The student population at City College was comprised of students from diverse racial and ethnic groups and I knew that the writing experiences of such groups had not previously been followed over time in research studies. I also realized that the socioeconomic backgrounds of these students would entail demands for work and family responsibilities that would greatly affect their academic progress. Bringing these factors together in a longitudinal study could thus contribute knowledge not then available about how such students adapted to the college environment. The significance of their racial and ethnic identities was introduced by the students themselves in the interviews and in their responses to the academic tasks.

I decided that in reporting my research I would make myself as unobtrusive as possible and let the students' interview comments and writing make up the bulk of the presentation. At the beginning of the study, I was a White, 57-year-old Jewish woman, whom I believe was perceived to be a sympathetic and politically liberal person who had chosen to teach at this college in Harlem. Over the years, the students who decided to remain in the study became increasingly comfortable with sharing experiences of their personal lives and how these experiences affected their work at the college.

The need for longitudinal research was great at the time of my study, and it is even greater now. The expectation back in the late 1980s was that a semester or two of remedial instruction would provide the "quick fix" needed so that underprepared students could almost instantly acquire the "skills" required to advance in their academic work. The belief today by administrators and boards of trustees of many 4-year colleges is that such students should not even be given this opportunity, but they should be assigned to overworked community college faculty in oversubscribed writing classes where the even "quicker fix" is demanded—one semester or you're out. It was my conviction that students who began at basic writing levels had the ability to succeed at their studies, but proof would have to be provided to decision makers.

Longitudinal research could uncover the pathways that would be followed by individual students and identify the conditions that would gradually lead to increased competence in meeting academic demands. I quickly began to recognize that their progress would not be linear and would be greatly affected by the particular instructional settings they were in. I knew that poor prior preparation and socioeconomic factors would combine to place many students in extraordinarily difficult circumstances. And that indeed proved to be the case.

Another reason that I felt so strongly about doing longitudinal research was that I believed that the remedial approach of working on basic skills was the wrong approach. Linguistic features that were so harshly criticized could be ameliorated over time; what the students really needed was to become more adept at handling reading and writing processes, particularly those that enhanced learning. Learning has been identified as having three stages: recall, particularly of facts; analysis and synthesis; and the creation of new knowledge. I believed that if students were challenged gradually over time they would be able to handle the analyses of increasingly complex reading materials and that writing would be the means by which this could be accomplished. Further, it was likely that the specific worldviews the students brought to their academic courses would enable them to critique certain assumptions and offer their own insights to their disciplines. This, in fact, happened. But it had not yet been demonstrated in any long-term study that underprepared students would gain such abilities, and the purpose of my study was to show that this would happen over time and with the appropriate instructional support.

I was fortunate to find support at City College where the deans of humanities over the years of the study gave me one course off for each semester to enable me to do the research. In addition, I received support from the Professional Staff Congress-City University of New York Research Foundation and the Research Foundation of the National Council of Teachers of English so that I could hire graduate student assistants to Xerox student papers and exams, draw up transcripts, and observe classes. This left me time to do all the interviewing of the students and start with the analysis of the materials.

When I spoke at the NCTE Assembly on Research in 1999, I talked about the experiences of some of my African American students, but when the editors of this volume approached me about writing a chapter, I told them that I would prefer to write about my Latino students. I made this decision because I felt that these students needed to be represented since their language and cultural experiences differ from those of the African American students whom I felt would be well represented in this book.

BACKGROUNDS OF TWO CASE STUDY EXAMPLES: DELORES AND CARL

The experiences of two Latino students who participated in a 6-year longitudinal study of writing and learning at the City College of City University of New York (CUNY), from 1989 to 1995, provide evidence that recognition of stereotyping served as a strong impetus to disabuse others of characterizing them as members of a group with only negative traits (Sternglass, 1997). It is essential not to overgeneralize either about the students' backgrounds or their attitudes toward their lifetime experiences. Delores (a pseudonym), from the Dominican Republic, came from a strong family background in the sense that her mother, who worked very hard to support the family after her husband left her, became an effective role model for her daughter, who found that all the men in her family had failed her: father, stepfather, brother, boyfriend. Delores became very sensitive to the issue that skin color affected the way that individuals were perceived, and in her combined BA/MA in Psychology, which she earned in 6 years, she studied how the self-esteems of Latinos of different backgrounds were influenced by their shade of skin color.

Carl (a pseudonym), with Ecuadorian roots but born in the United States, never identified himself with negative stereotypes of Latinos and thus never fought actively against such stereotyping. Gradually acknowledging his homosexual identity to himself and others, he vigorously fought against the stereotyping of homosexuals. He eventually went out of his way to inform his mother and sisters of his orientation, but he was warned by all of them never to let his father know about his homosexuality because they believed his father would disown him. With a strong academic record and skills in writing, Carl began with part-time and then moved to full-time work at a major New York newspaper, delaying his graduation until he could fulfill the necessary requirements for his degree in communications with evening school classes.

So each of these students identified social issues that were very important to them and they were thus able to incorporate their worldviews into their academic and personal lives. Writing became a crucial tool for each of them to convey the messages they felt were important to communicate to others.

USING WRITING AS A MEANS FOR COPING WITH STEREOTYPING

Two of the students in my larger study (Sternglass, 1997) had direct experiences with stereotyping, but they reacted in completely opposite ways. I provide here an example of what happened to one of the students in this larger study, Ricardo (a pseudonym) (note that his work will be mentioned only in passing here), to contrast his reaction with that of Carl, one of the case study students presented in depth here. In an autobiographical paper he wrote for the English 2 section that I taught in the fall of 1989, Ricardo wrote about an experience he had while working in a photography shop shortly after his arrival in New York City. All excerpts from student writing in this paper are presented without any changes in spelling, punctuation, or grammatical constructions. Occasionally a parenthetical word is inserted to clarify the meaning.

> While in my job as a camera [in a camera shop] I became one of the best salesman for the company. I was making over $25,000.00 a year at the age of twenty two. But I was uneasy at this job. The racism and prejudice that was evident was making me look for ways to get out of it. And finally one day a manager saw me in the stock room pulling merchandise for a sale that I was working on. He came to me an shouted "that I was the same as all the others Puerto Ricans, that I was a thief." I have never killed anyone but he got very close to be the first one. I had never been insulted like that in my life. I told another the manager what had happened and he laughed in my face. That made me mad. I presented a complaint to the store manager and he said to forget about it and that he apologized on behalf of the other. I left that job a couple of months later when I found a job at another camera store. Several jobs followed until I decided to change my career.
>
> It hasn't been easy to start all over again. I'm giving it the best I got. The financial responsibilities and the cost of living in New York are obstacles that are making it very difficult. I plan to get my degree in Film & Video. I want to be able to use my art to educate people; an prepare them to fight against the injustices and the prejudices that bear all over us. You don't need weapons to create awareness. You need books to eliminate ignorance. We can only do it, if we have the education.

Although he was clearly incensed by this experience, from the very beginning of his college studies, Ricardo recognized that he needed to channel his energies and resources into productive ways to combat racism. He came to realize that his language in his college writing was not always tempered; he learned to adjust it so that he could be more effective in having his arguments legitimized.

Stereotypes of Latinos had little effect on Carl because he believed himself so Americanized that he bore little relation to those who were characterized as having negative traits. Part of this attitude resulted from the separation he felt between his parents and himself. Since Carl's parents had strong Ecuadorian traditions and mores, their son's distancing himself from the family was particularly difficult for them to accept. Carl described his feelings in a paper he wrote for the freshman composition course I taught in the fall of 1989, his first semester at the college. The students had been asked to compare their experiences with those of Richard Rodriguez. Carl wrote:

> Coming from a Spanish background myself, I understand and have gone through what Richard Rodriguez wrote about. The drifting apart from his family and uncomfortableness are things quite familiar to me but there are also some factors that make us different.
>
> Speaking to Spanish relatives has been as difficult a task for me to do as it is for Richard Rodriguez. I feel uncomfortable when I'm forced to visit with friends or family from Ecuador because I am unable to answer their questions so my parents must act as a go between to bridge the gap in our communication problem. . . .
>
> What separates Richard from myself is that he seems to feel guilty for the drifting. I feel uncomfortable and at times wish Spanish friends or relatives would never come over but I never feel guilty. My attitude has always been—this is the U.S., you have to speak the language and go with the flow of things. This has been a constant source of argument with my parents and three of my sisters, all of which were born in Ecuador. . . .
>
> Part of the blame of my lack of ability in being able to communicate could be placed on my parents. They never forced or even asked us to speak Spanish around the house so with each year my ability to speak the language got worse, though I can understand most of it. I don't blame them for the way I am but then they can't blame me for answering their Spanish spoken questions with my English spoken answers.

In light of Carl's feelings about the attempts to confine him within his parents' traditions, it becomes easier to understand his response to his experiences while he was a high school student. In a writing assignment that he wrote for the freshman composition course in preparation for a paper on the topic of stereotyping, Carl presented his perspective on his relationships with his classmates, emphasizing his separation from the usual stereotypes:

> I've never been stereotyped as a "typical hispanic" in a mean spirited way. In high school, the lunchroom was filled with racial jokes. There I was typecast as a "typical hispanic" which meant I was on welfare, that I came from a big family, that there was numerous possibilities on who my natural father was, that I carried a switch blade, that I wore lots of multicolored outfits and that I stole car radios in

my spare time when I wasn't eating rice and beans or dealing drugs on the corner. The guys saying these things meant it as a joke and I took it as one. These things don't bother me as anyone who does feel that way is not going to change.

Issues of group versus individual identity are described by Tatum (1999). In her research, she found that Whites frequently experienced discomfort and anger from the frustration of being seen as a group member rather than as individuals. "People of color learn early in life that they are seen by others as a member of a group" (p. 102). Tatum pointed out that "[i]f viewing oneself as a group member threatens one's self-definition, making the paradigm shift from individual to group member will be painful" (p. 103). This seems to be the case for Carl, who strongly asserted his separation from the characteristics assigned to a "typical Hispanic" by his classmates. In the excerpt just cited, Carl revealed an astonishing lack of sensitivity to the damage that negative stereotypes—with which he denies being associated—can cause to others. In the final paper, he again asserted his separation from these stereotypes, but he was more responsive to the harm that they could cause others:

> People, in my opinion, have never put me in the category of being a typical "dumb spic," who does poorly in school and can barely speak English . . . There will always be blacks and hispanics who do poorly in school, drop out and deal drugs on the corner. Even a small number is enough to give a tainted view of a whole race or groups.
>   . . . Stereotyping and discrimination go hand in hand. It is easy to give the characteristics of one person to a whole group or race but each person should be judged only on himself not his people. . . .

Here, Carl showed more sensitivity to the damage that stereotyping can cause, but there was also a self-protective aspect to his discussion, ensuring his right not to be identified with the negative characteristics applied to others. He did emphasize that each individual had the right to be judged solely on his own characteristics, but he did not castigate strongly those who employed stereotypical labels, nor did he propose any positive characteristics for Hispanics and Latinos.

Delores never indicated in any of her writing through the college years that she had had experiences in which she was stereotyped. But, in an interview in the spring of 1993, the end of her fourth year at the college (after she had been admitted to the combined BA/MA in psychology), she described to me her growing sense of a personal identity:

The first semester I went through a period of extreme anxiety and depression. The first semester in school was a big thing, my first actual year in college, a big thing. Looking back, every year I try to analyze what happened, have come to understand that I'm here, I'm a woman. Back then my English wasn't so well. I was taking remedial courses; things didn't feel so good.

The project at Lehman [a project at Lehman College of the City University of New York that accepted a small number of students to conduct individual research with special mentoring and which culminated with a Symposium on April 30, 1993 at which time the nine students who completed their research presented their work] really made me know—I tested myself. I could do it or I couldn't—fifteen started, nine finished. I had no doubt I could do it—got up three a.m. to do that paper and other work plus two jobs.

I know myself a little better. I know I have the perseverance to do what I want. I feel different. I'm a woman, a Latino woman, a Black woman.

Tatum (1999) points out that the parts of an individual's identity that do capture the person's attention are those that other people notice and that reflect back to the individual. "The aspect of identity that is the target of others' attention, and subsequently of our own, often is that which sets us apart as exceptional or 'other' in their eyes" (p. 21). Tatum also notes that

> ethnic identity and racial identity sometimes intersect. For example, dark-skinned Puerto Ricans may identify culturally as Puerto Rican and yet be categorized racially by others as Black on the basis of physical appearance. In the case of either racial or ethnic identity, these identities remain most salient to individuals of racial or ethnic groups that have been historically disadvantaged or marginalized. (p. 17)

Here, Delores proudly affiliated herself with three groups frequently characterized as minority ones: women, Latinos, and Blacks. By combining these group memberships—gender, ethnicity, and race—she declared pride in the person that the combination had produced, herself.

In the same way that there is a danger in characterizing others through stereotyped labels, so is there a danger for instructors to pigeonhole students of a particular racial or ethnic background as having similar traits, experiences, or attitudes. Although Ricardo and Carl were not in the same class, their different backgrounds and attitudes make it very clear that instructors must be sensitive to the differences between them as between any

individuals having a similar ethnic or racial background. Delores had growing confidence in herself and her proud identity as a Black Latino woman.
With research that comes to know students as individuals over long periods
of time, it is possible to respect differences between individuals within a
group as well as differences between groups.

SECOND-LANGUAGE INTERFERENCE IN WRITING

Just as with the variety in the students' backgrounds, so their experiences
with writing differed during their college experience. One of the students,
Delores, had second-language features in her writing in English. At an urban college like the City College, where roughly half the students were
born outside the continental United States, as were 25 of the 53 students
in the original cohort of my study, it would be reasonable to expect that
instructors of basic writing and freshman composition courses would be
knowledgeable and sensitive to issues of second-language development.
Some instructors were, but many had no formal or informal preparation
for working with students who had either second-language or second-dialect features in their writing.

More difficulty for second-language and second-dialect speakers came
from the institutional writing tests demanded of all students. Students placed
into the basic writing sections or the English as a Second Language (ESL)
sections had all failed the Writing Assessment Test (WAT), a placement
test required of all students entering any campus of the City University of
New York (CUNY) at the time of my study. The criteria of the test, although paying lip service to content and organization, heavily stressed sentence-level features and grammatical competency. Unfortunately, at the
time of my study, the readers of these essay examinations were almost
always literature faculty or part-time instructors who had no background
in issues of language development and who expected a level of competency
inappropriate to the students' patterns of language use. In fact, knowledge
that features of writing should be looked upon as patterns rather than
discrete items was virtually unknown to these readers. Thus, for example,
the absence of the -ed marker on 3 regular past-tense verbs out of a total
of 10 past-tense verb forms was frequently viewed as "three errors" by
these readers. They never saw these correct and incorrect verb endings as
part of a pattern, one that students knew but did not yet control automati-
cally.

Although the issue of patterns in second-dialect interference features
are the same as for second-language interference features, the origin of
these features differs markedly. In the case of second-dialect patterns, the

genesis is frequently the rendering of word pronunciations into written forms (Sternglass, 1974) and creolization from a simplified pidgin English necessitated by turning disparate African languages into a simplified English dialect.

Selinker (1984) has proposed a hypothesis, which he termed *interlanguage*, that purports that second-language learners pass through a stage of language ability in which systematic errors of various kinds appear. According to this theory, second-language users attempt to simplify the system by, for example, placing an -*s* ending on all present-tense verbs or on none. They may also overgeneralize rules (Horning, 1987). An example would be placing a past-tense marker on all past-tense verbs, including irregular verbs as in the forms *singed* or *runned*, just as young children do when they are first learning English. In fact, many of the practices of second-language learners resemble those of native speakers who are trying out the rules they have internalized, awaiting feedback from more proficient users of the language who can accept or reject their formulations. In the process of acquiring the proper rules, through formal instruction or through informal feedback, second-language learners frequently produce inconsistent results, achieving more control when they have time to monitor consciously the forms they are producing, particularly in writing, but being more inconsistent when under stress or time pressure, as in exams or in-class writing.

Evidence of lack of automatic control over language features should not be regarded as a negative; rather, it is an indication that the individual knows the appropriate form but requires additional time and attention for careful editing. Thus, in impromptu writing test conditions, as with the WAT at CUNY, evidence of inconsistency in certain standard features should not be regarded as lack of knowledge or mastery, but rather as an artifact of constrained conditions of stress and lack of adequate time for appropriate editing. Errors can then be seen to "represent an interlanguage stage in the development of writing skill and are indicative of progress rather than failure" (Horning, 1987, p. 32).

A CASE STUDY OF A DEVELOPING WRITER

Delores took the WAT twice before her enrollment as a freshman in the fall of 1989. In each of her writings, she manifested some of the problems common to second-language learners. She had only been in the United States for 4 years and 2 months the first time she attempted the WAT in February 1989. She took the writing test again in August of 1989, but once again she failed and she was placed into the English 2 section I taught. The second test paper revealed the problems she was having in addition to the grammatical features inappropriate for formal writing: she had a tendency to write run-on sentences and to repeat ideas rather than develop them. In response to a question on the WAT asking whether young people should postpone marriage until after completing their education, Delores wrote:

> My reasons are the following: Firstly, they will not be able to concentrate on their education. Secondly, they are just too young and might not be able to manage the task that involves being married.
>   School, takes almost all your time. Can you imagin yourself in school and at the same time being married, and with children to take care of? It is difficult to do both at the same time. As I said before, when young people are in school and get married; it will not be the same because all the concentration that she or he had before get married has gone. Now that student, won't be able to concentrate in his or her studies because [he or she] is attending to different things, which both need attention.

In addition to the obvious sentence-level features that Delores needed to work on further, this section revealed her frequent repetition of ideas without further development.

By one of the quirks of such testing, Delores had the same question on her exit test from the English 2 course. In this paper, although she raised the same point, she was able to deepen her response:

> The education process is a long process and requires the person a great amount of time and dedication. When a person is getting an education that person should only be concentrated on his or her career. Since the education process takes most of the person's time, it will be difficult for the person to concentrate on what he or she is doing at school and at the same time take care of the family. For instance, it will be difficult for a full time student to go to school for eight or nine hours a day and then go to work because he/she has a family to support. When a person is not married or has a family to take care of, this person will have more time to dedicate to school. Furthermore, this person will be more successful in he or her career because he/she has had more time to study.

Although this section of her paper continued to have some second-language interference features and some repetition, nevertheless, it introduced several ideas and discussed them rather than repeating a single point. Delores passed the WAT on this retaking and was admitted into the freshman composition course.

The excerpts from these two exam-takings reveal some of the features common to second-language learners: There are comma faults in both sets of papers, common for students who have likely overlearned some rules and attempt to insert commas wherever they believe it is possible they may be required. In the first paper Delores had difficulty with the phrase "getting married" although not with the phrase "being married," so learning this construction should not present any difficulty. She used "get married" twice correctly, and that may have led to her repetition of the inappropriate form. She omitted pronoun subjects twice, but that may be due to the hurried and stressful conditions of timed writing.

The second paper, written after Delores completed the English 2 course, contained inappropriate word order for English in the first sentence, a feature perhaps carried over from a translation from the first language. Except for two minor pronoun forms ("he" for "his" and the omission of "her"), again likely time-constrained mistakes and one incomplete word, Delores's sentence-level structures had improved considerably.

Repetition in writing continued to be a problem for Delores, but when she had had an opportunity to revise her writing in her writing class, Delores was better able to organize and present her ideas:

> The family is the most important institution in our society. The traditional family, as it is usually called, is composed of a father, a mother, and their children. Even though some measure taken to prevent the family from breaking up, the traditional family has been deteriorating over the last two decades. The most important reasons for this are the high divorce rate and the women's liberation movement.

With this introduction to her revised paper, Delores demonstrated that she had been able to formulate a plan for the organization of her paper and to eliminate most of the sentence-level features she had produced in her earlier papers, particularly those written in class or under testing conditions. This is not to suggest that sentence-level problems did not recur in her writing over the college years, nor that she had eliminated the repetition of ideas in her writing.

In fact, Delores's problems with repetition continued, as is demonstrated in the following excerpt from a paper she wrote in the fall semester of her second year for a psychology class on the effect of cognitive processes on aging:

> Memory is the aspect of the intellective functions which appears most vulnerable to change according to studies conducted by Berger.

These studies have agree that memory as a rule is the most suscepti-
ble part of cognition to the effects of physiological changes as people
age.

As researchers have found, the earliest and greatest losses is
those that occur in memory as people get older. There is strong support to the view that the memory process deficies increase in advancing age. Studies conducted by Jones and Kaplan indicate that memory defeats are one of the most visible physiological symptoms of
aging. Hughes (1959) also supports the datas of Jones and Kaplan
that some degree of memory lost is a fairly common charactiristic of
the aging process.

But, unlike her freshman composition instructor, who did not addresss the
quality of her ideas, her psychology professor wrote an extensive comment
on Delores's paper:

> My reactions are mixed. The topic is a very important one and you
> cover a number of the important aspects. It tends to be disjointed
> and many times you repeat basic points that you have already made
> rather than deepening or clarifying the discussion. And there are
> many places where the writing is awkward and unclear. Also there
> are many spelling and/or typing errors. So what would have been
> quite a good paper is hampered by poor writing. (Grade: C–)

Delores took this criticism to heart and told me that she planned to rewrite
the paper. (I do not have a copy of the rewritten version.) This kind of
specific comment was very useful to her because she was vitally interested
in improving her performance in her psychology courses. The professor,
who doubtlessly had little knowledge of second-language interference patterns, subsumed the sentence-level writing problems into a category of
"spelling and/or typing errors."

By the second semester of her third year, Delores was deeply immersed
in her major, psychology. She had gradually improved her work in her
Experimental Psychology course, the most difficult course of the major,
involving a great deal of statistical analysis. In one of 10 reports required
that semester, she had mastered both the style and content of the assignment, receiving a 94, and the comment by her instructor, "good report."

By the fall of the following semester, having been accepted into the
Project in Bronx Studies at Lehman College of CUNY, Delores prepared a
proposal for her final paper, which she tentatively titled, "Skin color as a
factor in self-concept and as an element of perception of Bronx's Puerto

Ricans and Dominicans by other groups." Her proposal introduced her topic in the following way:

> The 1990 Census found the Bronx to be the borough with the highest population of Latinos in New York City, specially those from Puerto Rico and the Dominican Republic and their descendants. Puerto Ricans and Dominicans share a similar Hispanic culture: Spanish as their mother language, similar hispanic heritage, same Catholic faith, a similar music rhythm, and taste for food. The fact that Puerto Ricans and Dominicans share several things in common makes them an interesting population to study in relation to the color of their skin and how does it affect their self-concept. Also, this population could be studied in relation how other groups perceive them in terms of their skin color.
>
> There are Puerto Ricans and Dominicans who, by virtue of their European-looking features (e.g., white skin, straight nose), can pass as White and be regarded as such. On the other hand, there are Puerto Ricans and Dominicans who because of their African-looking features and black color are perceived and regarded as Black.

This introduction revealed that Delores was beginning to understand the complexity of the issue she was about to research. This self-initiated project also reveals that she had identified a topic related to her ethnic and racial background that had not been previously researched and that was unlikely to have been initiated by someone not sensitive to the nuances in her life that she wanted to investigate.

A year and a half later, when Delores completed her paper, she had narrowed her topic somewhat, as the title of her final report reveals: "Skin Color and its Impact on Self-esteem of Latino College Students—Dominicans and Puerto Ricans." By the time she finished her study, Delores realized that she had been researching a difficult and sensitive topic. Part of her conclusion pointed out the range of factors she now understood that needed to be considered in assessing self-esteem:

> Although weak, there is a significant relationship between self-esteem and skin color of the sixty-four students. This finding gives some rationale to my hypothesis that in the populations of Dominicans and Puerto Ricans, the relationship is probably not zero. This means that these two variables (self-esteem and skin color) are some what related.
>
> One explanation for this significant relationship between self-esteem and skin color could lied in the fact that when I compared the

two groups (Dominicans and Puerto Ricans) in how worthy they valued the perceived self, Puerto Ricans seems to value themselves significantly higher than Dominicans.

The result could be explained in the sense that Puerto Ricans are, in the average, lighter-skinned than Dominicans and as such, when asked to rate themselves in a continuum of color from 1 to 10, they rated themselves significantly lighter than Dominicans. It gives rationale to the hypothesis that the lighter one is the better one feels about one self, the higher the self-esteem.

Another explanation for the finding that Puerto Ricans valued themselves higher than Dominicans, could be the fact the Puerto Ricans are lighter therefore, they feel more attached to the Anglo Americans for the virtue that they share a similar physical traits with the dominant group. It is important to notice that although the correlation between skin color and self-esteem was significant, I must say it only accounts for 9% of the total variance. This is that the variable of skin color is only related to self-esteem, for this population, 9% of the time.

If we really want to make an assessment of the other 91% of the variable that it is not accounting for one can say that time in the United States could also be a factor. Puerto Ricans have lived longer in the United States with a length of stay of 18.76 in the average, while respondents from the Dominican Republic had an average length of stay of 8.89. Perhaps the longer the stay the more one is acculturated to the customs and norms of the United States, the better English one knows, the better an economic position one has secured for oneself. The stronger an ethnic identity one has, and the better relation one has sustain with the dominant group (Phinney, 1991).

As this last part of the analysis is revealed, Delores had been able to confirm her hypothesis, but she had also become sensitive to the difficulties involved in trying to tease out the significance of a single factor within the complex lives of individuals and groups.

Delores's own sense of self-confidence and self-esteem had grown gradually over the years she had been in the United States. She went through a period of "extreme anxiety and depression" during her first semester at the college, perhaps due to her lack of confidence in her ability to perform successfully as a college student. But by the end of her fourth year at the college, she had proven to herself (as well as to others) that she had the ability to succeed in her studies and in her life, having been accepted to both the Bronx Project and the combined BA/MA in psychology.

The persistence of second-language interference patterns continued in

Delores's writing; even in her final paper for the Bronx Project, there were a few examples of second-language interference features that lingered. But what is more important in the evolution of the writing demonstrated by the excerpts from her work is the growth in the complexity of her thinking. Writing had given her the opportunity to reflect on serious problems and develop cogent reasons to support the positions she wished to espouse. She also used writing to promote sensitivity in her readers to the particular issues of concern of minorities with specific emphasis on Latinos.

WORLDVIEWS: USING WRITING TO NEGOTIATE AN IDENTITY

The major social question that Carl confronted in his writing was the public attitude toward homosexuality. Carl saw two aspects of his identity—being a Latino and being gay—as completely separate orientations in his life, except for his conflict about his father's attitude toward homosexuality, which Carl attempted to submerge. Being a Latino, he felt, was essentially irrelevant to his life; being gay was a predisposition that was a badge of honor to be strongly defended. In a paper he wrote for a psychology course in the spring of his fourth year at the college on the topic of homophobia, Carl wrote about the evolution of his own private and public perspectives:

> As for me, my first encounter with a gay person, or least someone I perceived as gay, came in high school. There was a guy in my class, his name was D_____ N_____ who had some of the stereotypical mannerisms of a gay person. I feel ashamed of my actions now but I felt I had to make fun of him in order for people not to think that I was gay too. I joked about him constantly and everyone thought I really had it in for the guy. These days, I wish I had been strong enough, more sure of myself, to have reached out and extended my hand in friendship because he and I could have benefited from knowing that we were not alone in the school of 4,000 students.

Here, Carl acknowledged that his intense overt hostility was a protective device, since he was still insecure and unsure about his own sexual orientation and acceptance by the in-group was paramount to him. This behavior during his high school days was entirely compatible with the protective armor he wore about not being stereotyped through the negative characteristics his friends assigned to Latinos.

In a later section of this same paper, Carl described his mixed feelings on observing a Gay Pride Parade the year that he was entering college:

> I have been guilty of being homophobic. Back in 1989, I was on my way to work and I happened by Central Park where the Gay Pride Parade participants were gathering. At that point in time, I was still struggling with my sexual orientation. I was put off, almost scared by the men in drag, the very masculine women, the leather crowd, the pierced bodies of some of the participants and all the "oddities" of the parade. My mind wasn't able to deal with the shock of it all, I was scared that I would turn into one of them, never realizing that there were people within the gay community who weren't like that, that if nothing else, our community was about diversity and that everyone had to be accepted. Just as I wanted to be accepted by my straight friends, I would have to be willing to accept gay people who were different from me.

Through his recognition of the need for him to go through a period of acceptance, Carl acknowledged that others would also have to learn tolerance, even though they might not be having the same experiences he was having.

By the time Carl joined a public parade himself, he had come to the realization that only his overt declaration of his sexual orientation would allow him to become a true advocate for changing others' perceptions of homosexuality. In the concluding section of this paper, Carl described his feelings as he participated in the march on Washington in 1993:

> The March on Washington on April 25 showed America the diversity of the Gay, Lesbian, and Bisexual community. The participants, in all shapes, sizes and colors, were individuals who represent all walks of life. And no matter what the count of the marchers was, 300,000 or 1.1 million, the impact remained the same: America saw *us* as human beings, real people, individuals, rather than strange, unusual or dangerous people who ought to be shunned. Despite the differences among *us*, all of the speeches that afternoon echoed the same theme: unity, perseverance, and the need to combat ignorance about homosexuality relentlessly. *We* want people to know who *we* are; indeed, this goal is imperative. *We* will not step back into the closets that confined *us* [emphasis added].

His mentioning that participants came "in all shapes, sizes, and colors" is the closest he came to acknowledging these dual aspects of his own identity. Two other points can be made about this section of Carl's paper: the first is his obvious willingness to identify himself publicly as a member of this group and the second is his pride in the diversity that he had feared a few short years before. Through his acceptance of this diversity, he can express his self-esteem in his public identity as a homosexual person.

Interestingly, his mention of coming out of the closet became the basis for a paper he initially prepared for a college course that was eventually published in the *New York Times*. In the spring of his third year at the college, Carl wrote a proposal for a journalism course in which he stated his intention to write about the first thrift store in New York City that gave its proceeds to AIDS research. He indicated his intended emphasis in the last part of his proposal:

> If I focus on the first store, I can pursue the story in terms of the people who shop there: Are they victims of AIDS? Their friends? Do they know that the proceeds go to AIDS research? I can also look at the owners of the store: Have they had problems in running the store? How much business does the store do? Are they supported by any outside sources?

Carl's instructor was less than enthusiastic about the direction of this paper, commenting on the proposal: "What will be the 'news' focus, as opposed to a profile of the store?" Because of work conflicts, Carl dropped the journalism course, but he decided to pursue this story, eventually writing it in the feature style he believed it deserved. The article later appeared in the Metropolitan Section of the *New York Times*, where Carl was then employed on a full-time basis, taking the still required communication courses at night. The opening section of the article gives a sense of the tone Carl felt appropriate for the story:

> From an 18th-century Samurai longbow to the antique elephant headdress to the hats of Gypsy Rose Lee, The Out of The Closet Thrift Shop offers more than just exotic items. The store, founded by gay men, offers its customers a chance to participate in the fight against AIDS.
>
> Located on 81st Street between Second and Third Avenues, the store was opened last June by four friends who saw it as a way to raise money for dozens of AIDS organizations desperate for funding. The store donates all of its profits to AIDS groups.

Channeling his interests, abilities, and contacts to reach a large audience, Carl demonstrated the effectiveness of using the mass media to further a deeply felt cause. Moreover, Carl demonstrated that he had incorporated the personal social issues so important and relevant to his life into his public persona. Writing was the outlet that gave him an opportunity to persuade others of the validity of his views.

Although Delores would never have given herself the label "feminist," over her college years she grew more sensitive to the complex identities women assumed, examining the complicated choices women have to make in regard to family and professional opportunities. She considered these complexities in many papers she wrote in different courses. In an early paper in her freshman composition course, her second semester at the college, she wrote about the changes that were occurring in the traditional family:

> In summary, I would like to say that even though the women's liberation movement has brought many changes in the role of the American women, the real woman can take care of the family, and at the same time be able to help her husband and the family financially. The liberation of women has not only shown the American woman that she can go out and take care of businesses, is also the American woman that she can be a good wife, a good worker, and the most important, a real mother, if she wants to be so. I think if women try to be efficient in their public and personal lives, there is still hope for the traditional family.

It seems likely that Delores's views had been strongly influenced by her experience with her own family situation. In an interview the spring of her fourth year at the college, Delores described her relationship with her mother and other family members:

> I know myself a little better. I know I have the perseverance to do whatever I want. I feel different, I'm a woman, a Latino woman, a Black woman. I don't have doubt I can do these things. My family always supports me. I have a lot of good friends.
>
> Without being the way I am, I couldn't do it. The main part is coming from me, the motivation. My financial situation is not so good. I always see my mother struggling. My parents divorced when I was five. My only identification was with my mother struggling— like her I am trying to struggle. All men who passed through my life have disappointed me. Father, boyfriend, stepfather, I'm not proud of him, my brother is not a strong male figure. Only my mom doesn't disappoint me. My mother went through a lot, so can I. My mother's hard work tells me a lot.

In the fall of the next year, Delores wrote a paper for her Social Psychology course about how her sense of being a woman had been strengthened:

> Finally, living in the United States not only has strengthen my sense of a woman, but also my sense of ethnicity and the color of my skin, so that I do not only see myself as a woman, I also see myself as a Latino black woman. Woman in the sense that it is my gender and I will do my best to enhance it and work for the advancement of other woman. A Latino woman in the sense that I am a Hispanic person in this country and I would work for the advancement of the Latino woman, which up to the present lacks recognition. A black woman because as the Latino, the black woman is lacking the recognition deserved.

In this fleshing out of her previous statements of her strong sense of identity, Delores reflected on the lack of status accorded to women of her background, especially Black Latino women. It can be seen again how her study for the Bronx Project encompassed vital issues for her to probe.

Through these excerpts from Delores's writing, it became clear that she had evolved a strong and dignified sense of self. Personal and professional experiences had come together to provide her with the self-esteem that would lead her to a satisfying and productive life. She had both the desire and the ability to scrutinize areas that were meaningful to her and to design research projects that would contribute knowledge to the larger society that it might not have recognized as worthwhile to pursue.

Incorporating their worldviews into their writing added an important dimension to these students' academic experiences. They discovered that the events and the encounters they had in their lives could be used to inform and educate others whose background experiences differed from theirs. Their knowledge had the potential to add new understanding to the perspectives of others in the society.

THE VALUE OF RESEARCH OVER TIME

Research over time has been the basis for following the development of these Latino students. All students, those initially disadvantaged by having to study in a second language and those fortunate enough to study in their native language, need time to develop and demonstrate their intellectual capabilities. One of the students, Delores, might easily be passed over today for admission to a 4-year college because of the second-language features she manifested in her writing at the time she applied to college. Little if any consideration would have been given to her intelligence and drive to succeed and to contribute in meaningful ways to the larger society. But she was fortunate enough to have been in a situation where students with second-language and second-dialect features in their writing were given the opportunity to add academic English language skills to their language repertoire while at the same time they could foster their cultural and racial identities in ways that would allow them to make serious contributions to their own and the larger community. The other student discussed here, Carl, who had no features in his writing that identified him as anything but a user of conventional, standard English, eschewed his family background and identity but pursued the credibility of his gender orientation while reflecting some small sensitivity to the plight of members of minority races and cultures who had not had the benefits he had experienced academically in his upbringing.

Writing is the essential tool that fosters such development. No excuse should be offered to deny students the opportunity to practice formal writing throughout their academic studies. Too often, teachers despair about the initial abilities of their students and do not provide the writing activities that are so essential. In a letter to the *New York Times* on July 16, 1999, Professor Dexter D. Jeffries expressed his dismay at the attitude of many professors at the community college where he teaches:

> [A] Colombian immigrant has been robbed of a chance to achieve what she deserves in the United States by professors who routinely do not give writing assignments or do not check them. The excuse that "I never assign writing" echoes through the hallways of the community college where I teach.

Such an attitude is frequently fostered by legitimate difficulties second-language and second-dialect speakers have in composing academic texts. Forced to wrestle simultaneously with difficult concepts and the language to express these concepts, students with second-language backgrounds struggle to produce work that will be comprehensible to themselves and their instructors. But, as my study reveals, over time the students do master both the concepts and the conventions, bringing to their fields the perspectives and insights that their particular worldviews contribute.

Faculty both in composition programs and discipline areas could do more to alleviate the stresses that second-language students encounter as they respond to the demands for academic writing. It should be a given that those entrusted with the teaching of writing have fundamental knowledge about language-development issues. Coordinators of writing programs thus have a clear responsibility to provide materials and workshops for their instructors that will sensitize them to the bases for the features that second-language students will present in their writing. If such instructors have knowledge about the developmental sequences and patterns of the linguistic features produced by second-language learners, they will be able to provide the assistance and encouragement that their students deserve. Discipline area faculty also should be made aware of such language-development issues and given advice on the best ways to respond to their students' papers. While it is true that urban colleges and universities may enroll greater numbers of second-language learners than rural or small-town institutions, the demographics of the United States are changing rapidly, so that all sites of higher education are likely to find students with second-language backgrounds as part of their population. These students deserve informed instruction.

As the students are given opportunities to confront stereotypical images of race, class, gender, and sexual orientation, they bring valued perspectives to issues that the society sorely needs to reconsider and reconceptualize. It is a matter of the highest priority that institutions of higher education acknowledge and respect the importance of developmental learning and offer adequate time and opportunity to students of all backgrounds to demonstrate that they not only have the capability to succeed, but they have the ability to bring important fresh perspectives to significant questions and issues that must be faced in the coming years.

REFERENCES

Bizzell, P. (1986). What happens when basic writers come to college? *College Composition and Communication, 37,* 294–301.

Horning, A. (1987). *Teaching writing as a second language.* Carbondale, IL: Southern Illinois University Press.

Selinker, L. (1972). Interlanguage. *International Review of Applied Linguistics 10,* 209–231. Rpt. in J. Schumann & N. Stepson (Eds.), *New Frontiers in Second Language Learning.* Rowley, MA: Newbury, 1974.

Selinker, L. (1984). The current state of IL studies: An attempted critical summary. In A. Davies, C. Criper, & A.P.R. Howatt (Eds.), *Interlanguage* (pp. 332–343). Edinburgh, UK: Edinburgh University Press.

Sternglass, M. S. (1974). Close similarities in dialect features of black and white college students in remedial composition classes. *TESOL Quarterly, 8*(3), 271–283.

Sternglass, M. S. (1997). *Time to know them: A longitudinal study of writing and learning at the college level.* Mahwah, NJ: Erlbaum.

Tatum, B. D. (1999). *"Why are all the black kids sitting together in the cafeteria?": And other conversations about race.* New York: Basic Books.

PART III

Making Visible Power and Discrimination

Tenth-Grade Literacy and the Mediation of Culture, Race, and Class

Melanie Sperling

I am walking through the parking lot of McDonough High School in San Francisco toward my car.[1] I am coming to the end of my data collection in Kristin Jencks's 10th-grade English classroom, where nearly every day for 6 weeks I have observed her students studying literature and working on their writing. Such activities are the "givens" of a high school English class, yet this classroom causes me to problematize such givens, to see them with new eyes. The kids reflect the school demography to perfection: they are primarily working-class Latino, Southeast Asian, African American, a few recent immigrants from Eastern Europe, and some Whites. Their teacher, like many other teachers in the school, is White. She has taught kids such as these—underserved minorities and newcomers to this country—for over 20 years, and cannot see herself teaching any others.

The students in this class populate a school that sits at the edge of a little-discussed and not-so-obvious boundary dividing two San Francisco neighborhoods. On one side of the boundary, the school's side, lies the beginning of a tough inner-city neighborhood, infused with the fearfulness that accompanies its relative poverty. In contrast, the neighborhood on the other side of the boundary couples a deeply entrenched middle class with a culturally and socially diverse, sometimes politically active, and artistic population. The exterior of McDonough seems to fit in with this side of the boundary: It is a large, imposing, relatively modern structure on a huge boulevard. But the building is surrounded by a chain-link fence that closes it off from its surroundings.

Like Ms. Jencks, I like this 10th-grade class. I have come to look forward to seeing the kids each day and am disappointed when, as invariably happens, one or more of them does not show up. I like their humor, and I am sometimes blown away by their conversational facility and inventiveness. I am curious about their writing; I am curious about their thoughts as they sit at their desks. Moreover, I am curious about what is really happening whenever one of them is called out of class to the main office, to a phone call, for instance, and to whatever in their lives outside this classroom takes them away from 10th-grade English.

I have come to know the class's routines. Dean gets to class late—when he gets there at all—because, he says, he oversleeps, so Ms. Jencks convinces other students in the class to phone him before they leave for school themselves, to be his alarm clock, to keep him out of trouble. But her plan only partially works, because the kids often forget to call. Matthew has announced to the class that he is being "kicked out of the house"—the reasons for this I never learn—but may be able to live with his sister, although several kids in the class offer to put him up with them. There is much talk about Matthew's losing his home, and Ms. Jencks, the kids, and I wonder independently where he is each day before he comes to school in the morning and after he leaves in the afternoon. Katherine calls herself a poet—she writes when she is at home as well as when she's at school, and her father, with whom she lives in a single-parent family, encourages her talents as he shares them himself. Michael, who has a brother in the county jail and whose family sorely needs money, is promised a job helping a carpenter do summer work at Ms. Jencks's house if he can bring his course grade up to C before June. At this point in the school year, it is a horserace between the carpenter and the report card.

I am also aware of the institutional pressures on these kids and on Ms. Jencks. The school can't seem ever to provide Ms. Jencks's students with enough writing paper, so Ms. Jencks brings her own supply to the classroom and frequently replenishes it. With a library that has many more shelves than books to stack on them, she also brings books for her students to read and videos for them to watch. She brings stories about her own life to share with them when they tell their life stories to her (she and the student Algeria, I learn with Algeria's classroom peers, are both afraid of airplanes). In the middle of the school year, at the time that I am collecting classroom data, Ms. Jencks contracts pneumonia and must stay home for 2 weeks. The class gets a stream of substitute teachers who cannot possibly know these students and their classroom routines as Ms. Jencks does, or as I do for that matter, and the classroom "flow" is dramatically disrupted.

In spite of this disruption, the class appears to have developed together around the spirit of personal experience—the students' own, and the lived experiences of others in the world outside of school. Ford's memory, written in a compelling narrative, about once being locked in a closet as a child, Sean's about a childhood hospital stay, Matthew's about riding the city bus from school and physically striking a female companion, sit side by side with those of former student Lawrence, a lawyer and activist who visits the class and shares with them his journey from turbulent adolescence at McDonough High to calm adulthood. And these experiences together form a kind of backdrop when the class encounters Maxine Hong Kingston's written memories of Japanese internment, Malcolm X's of his life journey as Black civil rights activist, and Sandra Cisneros's fictional portraits of Latina childhood. It strikes me, as I first take it all in, take notes, and tape record the goings-on, as a multivoiced classroom in a fine Bakhtinian sense, with voices past and present giving meaning to one another. And that is Ms. Jencks's intention for it, I realize as she explains her teaching philosophy to me.

While the intention may be more purely conceived than classroom reality can be, it is with thoughts of this classroom as a social community that I walk through the parking lot toward my car. I become conscious of another person near me, also apparently walking to a car, and also, like me, a White woman. Unlike me, I learn, she is the mother of a ninth-grade girl at McDonough. "Are you a teacher?" she asks. Even when I tell her that I do not teach at this school, she asks if I can help her, and her eyes well up. Her daughter, she tells me, has come to dread going to this school each day and up until today, when the mother has come to McDonough and spent time here herself, this turn in her daughter's character has had her baffled. "But now," the woman says, "I know what she means. This place . . . " and she sweeps the length of McDonough's fences with teary eyes. She both jars and touches me, for I think I recognize the social reality that she brings into this picture. I surmise that she cannot bear to have her daughter in a school without enough materials, even writing paper, to help her be a student; with a library sparsely filled with people, let alone books; with teachers' time occupied by students from a range of backgrounds that she cannot even begin to guess about and who are less likely than not to go on to college after high school—in short, in a school unable to give her daughter a White, middle-class education. At that moment in the parking lot, we are, together, Everymother, and at the same time, we are outsiders of sorts, and I cannot help her. I can only try to say comforting things.

This experience, which haunted me at the time, raises many issues for me now about why I conducted research on the teaching and learning of writing in this urban school. I know that the primary reason was, and still is, the urgency of urban problems coupled with a society often so at odds with itself as to confuse language and literacy politics—for example, the gate-keeping uses of large-scale assessments—with sound pedagogical goals for reading and writing. The politics surrounding literacy learning and instruction come up in virtually every English classroom—they come up in the suburbs, too, and I have studied suburban classrooms as well, one of which I discuss later as it figured into this study of Ms. Jencks's class, providing a foil for this urban setting. But the sense of urgency can be particularly pronounced and visible in schools where students in large numbers often need great academic help and where school can easily come to be a lower priority for them than the everyday challenges that come from living in a low-income urban environment and that can easily infringe on class time. The social and political tensions around schooling that suburbia may be able often to overlook have had profound implications for students in urban settings.

Another reason that I studied this urban classroom is closely related to the first. It is nearly impossible to escape the alarming statistics on school achievement that get paraded in the newspapers with increasing frequency, in which students and schools in low-income urban settings invariably show the poorest achievement levels across the country (see also Cazden and Greene & Abt-Perkins, this volume). National concern about student reading and writing achievement, reflected in the daily press as well as in academic conversation, is nothing new. Yet the growing recognition both inside and outside the academy that literacy achievement levels, as well as instructional practices, pattern disturbingly along social, cultural, and racial lines fuels much of the present-day political and social uneasiness over how and whether students across these lines are learning to read and write. It has become almost a commonplace that top-performing schools in reading and writing tend to be located in White, middle-class, often suburban areas, that low-income urban areas are associated with bottom-performing schools, and that literacy instruction for students who get labeled as *cultural* or *racial minorities* can lag seriously behind theoretically informed and cutting-edge pedagogy (see, for example, the NAEP, 1994, reports on demographic trends in reading and writing practices and student achievement [Applebee, Langer, Mullis, Latham, & Gentile, 1994; Valdes, 1992]). This situation must be understood for its complexity in order to be well remedied.

I indicated at the beginning of this chapter that I observed Ms. Jencks's students studying literature and working on their writing. As easy as it is to observe these activities, and to recognize them when you see them, it is not at bottom so easy to define them. During this study of reading and writing in high school English classes, I discovered for myself how ever-shifting reading and writing can be, as they play out remarkably differently in different communities. They are shaped by the particulars of the communities, schools, teachers, and classrooms. And while tests measure some instantiations of reading and writing, they surely ignore others.

So I study urban classrooms because I need to know what goes on inside them, to see how literacy there—reading and writing—is construed, taught, and learned, so that my work might be a productive part of the effort to improve education for the students who, when they reach adulthood, can be like Ms. Jencks's former student Lawrence and one day help society make civic and cultural life the fairest it can be for all its citizens. I do not study urban classrooms to learn about "bad" teaching, of which, unfortunately, we hear much, but rather to see how purportedly good teaching plays out in settings where teaching and learning can be readily compromised by forces that are too often invisible both to the participants as well as to the researchers who study them. What, under such conditions, are students in case-study urban classrooms learning about writing, and how are they learning it? Moreover, what, ultimately, is good teaching?

THE SOCIAL AND CULTURAL EXPERIENCES
THAT SHAPE MEANING

Three related assumptions about writing and learning guide this research (see Sperling & Woodlief, 1997). The first is that writing is a socially constructed meaning-making activity. As such, writing is part of the broader social-cultural-political contexts in which it is situated. This assumption is informed theoretically by Vygotsky's (1962, 1978) sociocognitive theories of language and learning, which assert that individuals construct knowledge, skills, and values through social interaction with others. It is also informed by the related sociocultural theories of Bakhtin (1986) which suggest that an individual's thoughts and actions do not exist apart from those of other people.

Following these theoretical perspectives, I search for classroom meaning in classroom social interaction. Such meaning, I believe, can help inform teachers in focusing attention on what are, in the everyday rush of classroom talk, often fleeting but critical moments of literacy-in-the-making.[2] The following moment, when Zakia, an African American student, entered a class discussion on Malcolm X, exemplifies my focus:

ZAKIA: I was gonna say like, um. A lot of people, like he could be just like everybody else in the sense that, you know, people get stuck in a way, and everything like that, but when something tragic or something really goes wrong, oh, so maybe he thought, oh being a hustler was gonna be OK and everything, and did the things he did, but when he got sent to jail you have to change your life "cause you don't" wanna be there.

JENCKS: OK, OK, so you could write an essay on the, what would you call them, the changing experiences in his life . . . that would be a good idea, that he's a human being, like the rest of us, and he had life experiences which changed him.

When I have discussed this particular interaction in reports on the study of this classroom (e.g., Sperling, 1995; Sperling & Woodlief, 1997), I discussed it as one in which the student, through the opportunity afforded by discussion, could think and be helped in her thinking on a number of levels. She could hypothesize about Malcolm's life ("so maybe he thought, oh being a hustler was gonna be OK and everything, and he did the things . . . "), engage with her peers ("he's a human being like the rest of us"), and raise specifics to the level of abstraction or generality ("whenever something tragic happens, people change"). I also noted how Ms. Jencks supported Zakia as a thinker by taking up her ideas, and how she fostered her as a writer by framing these ideas as material for writing.

The second assumption behind my work is that students' writing processes are undergirded by an interrelated web of social and cultural experiences that get expressed through language, a linguistic intertwining of connections between students and their multiple social worlds—including the worlds inside and outside the classroom setting (also a Bakhtinian notion).

For example, I could not help but be interested in particular in Matthew, who is African American, because he spoke so much, much more than any of the other students in the class; in fact, more than all of them put together. The topic that took up the whole class period was the acquittal of the four police officers who had been accused of beating Rodney King. In the example below, Matthew speaks directly to Ms. Jencks and his peers as he questions the reason for Rodney King's beating:

> How he [Rodney King] gonna provoke that [the beating]? He was down on the ground, he was practically dead. He was almost beat unconscious. And they [the court] said and they said they dropped the charges [against the police] due to lack of evidence. C'mon man. Well he [King] was telling [the police] beat me beat me please beat me. C'mon man.

When I encountered Matthew's spoken discourse, as in this example, reading Mitchell-Kernan (1973) helped me to speak about his African American style and its artistic merit (p. 324). Reading Smitherman (1977) helped me to speak about the likely value to Matthew as an African American of "entertaining" (p. 3) his peers through talk. Together with Labov (1972), who is White, these African American researchers also pointed me toward such language features in Matthew's discourse as pitch, rhythm, repetition, multiple negatives; and such rhetorical strategies as irony, boastfulness, narrative structuring, mimicking others' speech mannerisms, and making complex arguments in few words. Some of these features and strategies appear in Matthew's speech above. His discourse expressed his identity along with his ideas, and, to the benefit of the class, it did so in a manner that also captured students' attention. It tended to be at once expository and rhapsodic, argument penetrated by irony, and in being so helped shape his connection both to his fellow students and to the world outside the classroom.

The third major assumption of my research follows from the first two: Students' learning is fostered by teaching that is, in Ladson-Billings's (1994) words, "culturally relevant," that "capitaliz[es] on student's own social and cultural backgrounds" (p. 10). It was on this assumption, not incidentally, that the school district where McDonough is located decided that the 10th-grade English curriculum across schools be focused on what they call "the ethnic experience in literature." And it is this focus that in large part drew Ms. Jencks to teach this class. My own interpretation of what went on in this classroom, its expression of community and its literacy practices, grew largely from the idea that the classroom fostered literacy by drawing on the cultural capital or "funds of knowledge" (Moll, 1992) that the students brought to it.

As with the other assumptions guiding my work, this last assumption, too, was not without its issues. For the infusion of students' social and cultural experiences into conventional notions of "doing school" surfaces in all classrooms and did in this one. How such notions play out in specific contexts can be key to understanding students' differential classroom experiences, in particular, when classrooms reflecting students' varying cultural, social, or racial experiences also reflect differential academic success.

When I studied Ms. Jencks's classroom, then, one of the questions that I wanted to probe was whether the events and interactions that took place there could only have happened in that particular classroom context or whether they might transcend this context. For that reason, at the time I studied Ms. Jencks's 10th graders, I also studied Ms. Smith's 10th-grade English class at Cedar High, located 20 miles from San Francisco in a relatively affluent suburb. Like Ms. Jencks, Ms. Smith enjoyed a fine reputation as an excellent teacher. But her students were for the most part middle to upper middle class and White, and, like virtually all students at Cedar, they all planned to go on to college when they finished high school. I note here that in this school, race seemed invisible. And in this classroom, there was no talk of race and no talk of Rodney King or of the then-current verdict that had caused riots in Los Angeles and that predicted chaos in other large cities, including San Francisco.

BACK TO THE PARKING LOT: THE CONTRADICTORY
ASSUMPTIONS OF LEARNING INSIDE AND OUTSIDE SCHOOL

Wrapped up in my theoretical assumptions about learning are three related components: knowledge, skills, and values, which are inseparable as the meat of teaching and learning (Vygotsky, 1978). For a researcher, this inseparability is double sided, for I forge my own knowledge, skills, and values in the process of studying those of other people.

The experience in the parking lot highlighted for me how conflicting and contradictory these related components can be. For example, as I was beginning to think of Ms. Jencks's classroom as a community in which shared personal experiences and text-based narrativized experience could become, to good effect, the focus and thrust of literacy, I was brought face to face with a distraught mother and the unavoidable, some might say cruel, reality of this school. This is a school in which hundreds of children representing a broad spectrum of racial, social, and cultural backgrounds are supposed to acquire a decent secondary education. Yet the school lacks material resources. It is a large and sometimes dangerous place (two uniformed guards patrol the automobiles entering and leaving the parking lot, not a feature at Cedar High). Many of the students, for a variety of reasons, find little to come to school for, including Dean in Ms. Jencks's 10th-grade English class. And, also for a variety of reasons, its teachers' goals and ways, even those of Ms. Jencks, may sometimes conflict dramatically with the goals and ways of others outside the classroom, such as this mother's, as they attempt to make the classroom responsive to the range of students they see each day and thereby introduce competing conceptions of learning literacy, of doing school.

What I know and value about literacy—in particular, that it is a complex functional process that is exquisitely context-bound—plays out before me in Ms. Jencks's classroom. Here, literacy learning gets shaped by authorship and readership that are tied to cultural and racial experiences; here, literacy invites students to join the mix of authors they are reading as writers among these writers. How am I to reconcile this literacy with what I am tempted to guess is the wish of the mother in the parking lot to get her daughter away from this school, including its English classrooms, as quickly as she can?

LITERACY AS A FUNCTION OF RACE, CULTURE,
AND CLASS IN TWO CLASSROOMS

This question forces me to reflect on my own stance toward "difference," which is to say, my own stance toward race, class, and culture and their relationship to the goals of school, to literacy learning, to definitions of literacy. And it was from this "self-consciously unencumbered" stance that I wrote about Ms. Jencks's and Ms. Smith's classrooms.

Ms. Jencks's Classroom

Ms. Jencks's classroom focused attention on already lived experiences—both the students', which were often the topics of their discussions, and those of individuals outside the classroom, ranging from the authors they read to politicians, from persons in the current news to fictional characters. Writing became a process in which students melded their own lives into the mix of this broader population and its literacy events—authors' particular struggles against racial bias, for example, which resulted in their choices to become not just writers, but writers of cultural, social, and racial experience; or media perspectives and coverage of current racial strife. Matthew's comments, for example, in the class discussion of the Rodney King police case, became key information that many other students in the class incorporated into their essays on this event (Sperling, 1995).

Talk such as Matthew's, on the one hand, and Zakia's on the other, tended to minimize the social distance not only among the students or between the students and teacher, but also between the students and the topics of discussion. The students tended to discuss topics in ways that suggested that they were taking the perspective or point of view of the subject or person that they were talking about (for example, Rodney King or Malcolm X) or of the subject or person that other students in the class were writing about—Katherine's getting lost in the woods, for example, or Malcolm X's conversion away from Islam.

In short, in Ms. Jencks's class, literacy tended to be tied to life recounted; whether the reading or writing was expository or narrative, literacy both invoked and added to life experiences that became the "center of gravity" of the work of the classroom.

Ms. Smith's Classroom

In contrast, Ms. Smith focused attention not so much on students' already lived experiences as on experiences that this teacher created for her students in order for them to do the work of school, such as the experience of gathering information for a research paper. In this classroom, these teacher-orchestrated experiences focused discussion and became the topics of students' writing. Writing became a process of students' getting themselves, through their discussion and writing, into the mix of school-like literacy events such as finding research topics to write about or discovering interviewees to talk to for information on a research topic. Helping to construct the school-based community of writers that was developing in this classroom, Ms. Smith often related the students' processes of writing their papers to those of her former students (as Ms. Smith said one day of a paper written by a former student that she was about to read to the class, "This is by a young woman named Helen Lender, who is now a sophomore at U.C. Davis, and she wrote it when she was just your age").

It was not surprising for me to discover, in looking closely at their classroom discourse, that these students frequently displayed their common "studenthood" through their class discussions. This display occurred in part through what they talked about, their common writing assignment. But it also occurred through the parallel ways in which they talked about their common work, as I illustrate in the following examples of students' various opening remarks excerpted from a discussion about obtaining interviews for their papers (parallels noted in emphases supplied below):

> ARNOLD: *Well, I met* this doctor that works out in the gym . . .
> INGRID: *Well, I just think* that it's real hard to get interviews . . .
> JOHN L.: *Well*, uhm, Jasmine and *I have done* two interviews . . .
> ALEXANDRIA: *Well*, Michelle and *I interviewed* Mrs. [tape unclear] yesterday . . .

In short, in Ms. Smith's class, literacy tended to bend to and extend the doing of school. Through their reading and writing, students' commonly shared school experiences, and their identities *qua* students, came to the fore.

The Two Classrooms

Each classroom showed students interacting and constructing knowledge, skills, and values in ways particular to that classroom—to its students, its teacher, its texts, and its topics.

Of particular interest is the way that literacy in these classrooms—its processes and its teaching and learning—was mediated through the particularities of each classroom, including who the students were and what each teacher was able to draw out from, as well as add to, students' prior school as well as personal lives. In this sense, literacy in these classrooms was ultimately a function of culture, race, and class, as it came to be shaped and lived out differently in each setting. In this sense, too, culture, race, and class were mediated by the literacy taking shape in these classrooms. While rich constructions of literacy unfolded in these two contexts, they were different constructions and only one, Ms. Smith's, mapped most readily onto the "essayist" construction tapped in conventional assessments.

Despite the differences in the two classrooms, certain commonalties transcended the two. Specifically, in both classrooms, discussion guided students' writing. Discussion shaped knowledge, skills, and values as, along with the teacher, students connected socially and intellectually both to one another and to the world outside the classroom.

In making such social and intellectual connections, the students and teachers in both classrooms created a wide range of roles for themselves in which to speak and act. Discussion both shaped and reflected roles such as learner, writer, reader, buddy, as well as that of representative (of many stripes) of the cultures and communities existing for the students and teachers outside of school.

THE EXPECTATIONS OF SCHOOLING

Sizer (1985) writes: "A successful classroom is one in which students and teacher agree on what they are about and on the rules of their academic game" (p. 154). In order to be successful classrooms from others' perspectives, I would argue, such agreement between teacher and student must also meet some notions or expectations in general for what school should be about. As a researcher in this study, I addressed such issues, asking the question of how and what students in each classroom were learning about literacy and about themselves, and speculating on what others might say about such learning. From such perspectives, were these both successful classrooms?

With these questions in mind, I bring up a key point about classroom interactions in the two settings that I studied. Such interactions, in constructing knowledge or learning, were not always smooth. Yet, in such moments, the way teachers and students each construed the work of the classroom were underscored and, perhaps not surprisingly, so were each classroom's centers of gravity—Ms. Jencks's, to highlight life experience as central to the literacy learning process, and Ms. Smith's, to highlight the doing of school. I illustrate this observation below, as I discuss some contentious moments.

RACE AND CULTURE AS SOURCES OF CONTENTION IN WRITING ABOUT LIFE EXPERIENCE

The main writing assignment in Ms. Jencks's class was to explain and analyze an event that changed students' lives, an assignment called "Hero's Journey." In the first excerpt below, Ms. Jencks suggests how Huong might write about her experience coming to America from Vietnam:

> JENCKS: Huong, who might you describe at the beginning of your story of coming to America, what's a person you might describe? . . . Somebody from Vietnam that maybe didn't come with, that's still, that stayed there, like a grandma?
> HUONG: Nobody stayed.
> JENCKS: Not in your family? Uh, how about a place, like a house or a village? A classroom? OK?
> HUONG: [silence]

In the next excerpt, Ms. Jencks tries to help Michael, an African American student, find a topic to write about:

> JENCKS: Were you ever really really sick? And you thought you weren't gonna get better? Was there uh experience in your neighborhood, that was kinda scary? A fight?
> MICHAEL: There was a fight but they weren't scared.
> [Ms. Jencks makes other suggestions; Michael's responses are unclear; Ms. Jencks continues:]
> JENCKS: Have you ever had to deal with racism?
> MICHAEL: Not really, I never been confronted.
> [Ms. Jencks makes more suggestions. Michael is silent.]

In these two excerpts, the class's center of gravity seemed to cave in as students appeared oppositional either through silence or through contradiction. These particular kinds of contentions occurred most often when the topic touched on students' cultural or racial experiences, as in the examples above. And at these times they appeared to bring conversation to a halt. As it turned out, Huong did write her essay on her experience coming to America from Vietnam, but Michael wrote his on running track and made no mention of racial experience.

Contention over Doing School

The main writing assignment in Ms. Smith's class was to write about a topic of interest while also incorporating into the essay the writer's experience getting information on and writing about the topic, a kind of assignment known as an "I Search" paper. This task within a task pressed on students to negotiate unfamiliar strategies for writing, as the "Hero's Journey" had done in Ms. Jencks's class. It was a challenge, for example, for some students to write about doing the search for information, as in the following exchange between Ms. Smith and Emily in a class discussion on this topic:

> SMITH: Just spit it out [the story of doing the information search], OK. Just spill it out of your head. [mimicking writing:] "I [rhythmically spoken] duh-duh-duh." Just tell me the story. If you don't know a lot, say=
>
> EMILY: =Can we [the students, in doing the task] just list it [steps taken] instead of=
>
> SMITH: =Say again?
>
> EMILY: Can we list them?
>
> SMITH: No. I'd like some sentences please. So tell what you already know.
>
> EMILY: On the back [of the assignment sheet]?
>
> SMITH: On the pink sheet. Just write right on the sheet.

Emily seemed to know that a person can't "just tell" about something that happened, a person can't really just "spill it out," as Ms. Smith suggested, when writing in a particularized, relatively formal, and consequential context such as the classroom. Rather than do the complex task of writing a story, Emily asked to just make a list. Ms. Smith didn't accept this alternative, however. Emily, along with all the other students in the class, ended up following Ms. Smith's guidelines for doing this writing task in the specified way. In one sense, the contention between Ms. Smith and Emily was productive. It helped shape Emily as a writer in parallel with the other student writers in the class (note Emily's emphatic use of the collective "we" in asking her question), and it helped shape all of them as doers of school. In another sense, as Emily clarified for herself what it was that Ms. Smith found acceptable, this kind of conversation was more stereotypical than Ms. Jencks's of what school learning is about.

Classroom Differences: The Role of Cultural and Racial Identity in Doing School

In both classrooms, as illustrated in the sections above, the teachers' job was to help and guide their students toward their expectations, which the students sometimes agreed with, sometimes resisted. Yet in each classroom, the nature of the assignments, the nature of the curriculum, the teacher herself, and the particular students, worked toward particular ways of both defining and enacting any teacher-student congruence or conflict.

In Ms. Smith's classroom, goals for literacy were future oriented in the sense that the students were college-bound, and a large part of Ms. Smith's job as she saw it was to point students to college expectation. Her approach to them and to the topics they were studying could be somewhat distanced, and characteristics of personal life in the general sense, in particular, "race," "class," and "culture" as generalized constructs, as well as students' own life characteristics, that is, their own race, class, and culture, could remain implicit, even invisible.

In contrast, Ms. Jencks's classroom, while pointing students toward the possibility of future success (for example, of the type that is reflected by successful African American, Latino, and Asian authors), was still of necessity "present oriented." That is, Ms. Jencks saw her job as helping students to define themselves for a safe and productive present, "selling academics" as she fostered students' moment-to-moment choices to be academically involved. She inspired, provided role models, and presented class work that she hoped would be personally involving. She also asked students through their literacy practices, their reading and writing, to negotiate not only challenging personal experiences but essential characteristics of their individual lives, including cultural and racial identity. In this classroom, then, writing, and the writing process, had much to do with students' inner spirit, or, in one of her student's words, "soul."

MAKING SENSE: WHAT SHOULD SCHOOL LITERACY ULTIMATELY BE?

At the beginning of this chapter I discussed my reasons for studying a classroom such as Ms. Jencks's. Yet I cannot write of these reasons without also mentioning that, in breaking with the stereotype of the conventional 10th-grade English class, Ms. Jencks's classroom has been, for me, the object of both concern and criticism, expressed in different ways by different kinds of people.

One of these people was Zakia's mother, who spoke to me before I undertook the research. She had a different kind of connection to this classroom than I, including both a personal and professional stake, and she was not certain that she wanted Zakia to participate in the study. At the time I began to observe Ms. Jencks's classroom, Zakia's mother was a student at a nearby university in the field of anthropology. She had read too much anthropological research, she told me during a phone conversation, that patronized African American subjects or that in other ways showed African Americans in a poor light. How could I assure her that I wasn't going to produce just one more study that got it wrong? Our conversation helped take me out of the research trees and into the forest, to a far-reaching research world that, by its very existence and largely unbeknownst to me, filters my work and, doing so, takes it out of my hands. It also impressed on me the authority of this woman's life, and Zakia's life, over my own, which I could try to learn from but, ultimately, could never fully know.

Others have expressed criticism about Ms. Jencks, in particular a student in my seminar, as well as a colleague, who wondered whether Ms. Jencks's interactions with her students, for example, the interactions with Huong and Michael shown earlier, were sometimes actually racist, as they presumed that these students' experiences with culture and race could and should be topics to write about. In the case of the graduate student, the question was also whether I myself wasn't racist in speaking of student talk through a sometimes racial lens. This is a legitimate question. Yet I wonder at the comments about Ms. Jencks and racism, and how, in a school setting, literacy can be beneficially used as a site for depicting and negotiating race without teachers and others, including Whites, addressing students' cultural and racial experiences.

Beyond this response, however, and more reflectively, it is beneficial in thinking about Ms. Jencks and racism to consider her classroom in contrast to Ms. Smith's. In Ms. Smith's classroom, students could be successful writers without personally revealing or expressing themselves. In Ms. Jencks's classroom, students needed to be highly personal and reflective. This kind of reflection is demanding for anyone, let alone an adolescent, as the excerpts of conversation from that classroom suggest. How we interpret this demand is key to addressing the racism critique and key, too, to thinking about the nature of school literacy. Through the following questions, then, I am not so much inviting us either to admire or denounce either classroom, as to consider their complexities, their constructedness, and to consider what school literacy ultimately can be.

- Why should African American students (and other racial and cultural "minority" students) be expected to be self-aware in their literacy learning when students in the suburbs are expected to achieve in more conventional ways?
- Should the writing process as it gets orchestrated in classrooms to support students' writing also function explicitly to foster students' emotional and intellectual growth outside the bounds of writing itself?
- Is a personalized approach to teaching and learning, such as the approach in Ms. Jencks's classroom, a context-sensitive way of fostering students' critical thinking and intellectual engagement, or is it just an imperfect way to cross the socially constructed boundary that separates what can occur inside and outside classrooms?
- Perhaps most importantly, is there a tacit connection between the way that Whiteness comes to be normalized in school settings such as Ms. Smith's (let alone other societal institutions) and the way that a monolithic college-bound version of literacy comes to be normalized in the curriculum?

Taken together, these questions evoke an old but viable educational concern: What topics, what activities, what territory, are the proper province of the school? What should school be for? But to propose a single answer to this question is to deny the nuanced social complexities of schooling and society implied by the others.

In light of these questions and in light of my encounters with context in this study, I want to revisit the sociocultural theory that frames my work. It is essential for cross-racial or cross-cultural research that hinges on sociocultural theory to read or interpret this theory unabashedly robustly. Specifically, (1) when we say that writing is a socially constructed meaning-making activity, I believe it is incumbent to remember that this activity has sociopolitical consequences. There is no meaning-making without such consequences. Likewise, (2) when we say that students' writing processes are undergirded by an interrelated web of social and cultural experiences that get expressed through language, it is incumbent to remember that these social and cultural experiences are laden with values that sometimes harmonize, sometimes conflict. The language that expresses the experience is so laden as well. Therefore, it does not suffice simply to compare discussions across classrooms and believe that literacy events have been studied or understood. And (3) when we say that the writing-learning process is fostered by teaching that acknowledges students' social and cultural experiences, we need to remember that we are studying issues of equity and discrimination as much as literacy when we study cross-racially or cross-culturally.

A FINAL WORD: THE SOCIOPOLITICAL CONSEQUENCES OF WRITING AND LITERACY

I want to end this chapter by thinking of the difference between my role as researcher of writing and literacy and that of others who may face the difficult sociopolitical consequences of writing and literacy every day. I think again of the mother in the parking lot, shaken by her newly discovered view of the school her daughter went to. Like this mother, I was seeking to make sense of this community and its inequities. But as a researcher I enjoyed a luxury that she did not, the luxury of choice and time. I could choose to focus on Ms. Jencks's classroom and not on the one down the hall, and to study it for as long as I needed to, in order to get information that I felt was useful and that I could think about for a long time. I could step back from this classroom, and Ms. Smith's, and ask what some might call existential questions, for example, about ideal literacy— not if there was such a thing, because I would quickly have said no, there's not, not if literacy is, as theorists suggest, both a concept and a process socially and culturally shaped. But I could ask whose literacy was seen to be more ideal than the other's, and wonder what we tell ourselves as teachers and students such that falling short of an ideal can happen so easily to certain students, particularly working-class students of color. I could say that it is tempting from a conventional perspective to see Ms. Jencks's classroom as limited, yet that it is also critical to see Ms. Smith's as limited as well, if from this perspective we recognize that her students were underprepared to speak to and interact with diversity, to talk across cultural boundaries, and arguably, to participate richly in a global economic and political scene. If race, beyond skin color and other physical characteristics, is a marker of difference, what markers of difference, I could end up asking, are getting constructed in these classrooms? And is it possible for the educational community to recognize these classroom differences so that classrooms across schools, and throughout the grades, can speak to and foster literacy richly conceived for the range of children in them?

But these are not the mother's question, the what-am-I-to-do-now question. Hers both goes beyond and is prior to my study and requires anyone answering it to make use of all the practical wisdom about schools and schooling at their disposal. It is in the service of such practical wisdom that I want my research in the two classrooms ultimately to make sense. In doing so, it must also make sense to Zakia's mother, the anthropology student who cast me, at least in our phone conversation, as untrustworthy "other" when what I want as a researcher and as a human being is to be just about anything but that.

NOTES

1. My thanks for the acutely perceptive and challenging comments made about drafts of this chapter by the editors of this volume and by my colleague Anne DiPardo.

2. Key to transcription conventions throughout this chapter:

. . . perceptible pause

italics speaker's emphasized word (author's emphasis is noted when it occurs)

[brackets] author's comments or clarification

= latched conversational turns

REFERENCES

Applebee, A. N., Langer, J. A., Mullis, I.V.S., Latham, A. S., & Gentile, C. A. (1994). *NAEP 1992 writing report card* (Report No. 23-W01). Washington,

DC: Office of Educational Research and Improvement, U.S. Writing Department of Education.

Bakhtin, M. M. (1986). *Speech genres and other late essays*. Austin: University of Texas Press.

Labov, W. (1972). *Language in the inner city: Studies in Black English vernacular*. Philadelphia: University of Pennsylvania Press.

Ladson-Billings, G. (1994). *The dreamkeepers: Successful teachers of African American teachers*. San Francisco: Jossey-Bass.

Mitchell-Kernan, C. (1973). Signifying. In A. Dundes (Ed.), *Mother wit from the laughing barrel: Readings in the interpretation of Afro-American folklore* (pp. 310–328). Englewood Cliffs, NJ: Prentice-Hall.

Moll, L. (1992). Literacy research in community and classrooms: A sociocultural approach. In R. Ruddell, M. Ruddell & H. Singer (Eds.), *Theoretical models and processes of reading* (pp. 179–207). Newark, DE: International Reading Association.

Sizer, T. (1985). *Horace's compromise: The dilemma of the American high school*. Boston: Houghton Mifflin.

Smitherman, G. (1977). *Talkin and testifyin: The language of Black America*. Detroit, MI: Wayne State University Press.

Sperling, M. (1995). Uncovering the role of role in writing and learning to write: One day in an inner-city classroom. *Written Communication, 12*, 93–133.

Sperling, M., & Woodlief, L. (1997). Two classrooms, two writing communities: Urban and suburban tenth-graders learning to write. *Research in the Teaching of English, 31*, 205–239.

Valdes, G. (1992). Bilingual minorities and language issues in writing: Toward professionwide responses to a new challenge. *Written Communication, 9*, 48–136.

Vygotsky, L. S. (1962). *Thought and language*. Cambridge, MA: MIT Press.

Vygotsky, L. S. (1978). *Mind in society: The development of higher psychological processes*. Cambridge, MA: Harvard University Press.

CHAPTER 7

Reading Discrimination

Patricia E. Enciso

In classrooms across the United States, upper elementary-age children are expected to demonstrate fluent reading, show interest in and interpretive skill with regard to a wide range of narratives and genres, and reflect on and articulate their experiences and ideas related to these texts.[1] Although learning to read and interpret narrative forms is in itself a daunting achievement, children must also traverse the politics of classroom hierarchies and the discourses of difference and ability expressed in society and schools. In effect, children are expected to learn the implicit rules for "being a reader" while they also interpret and negotiate classroom friendships, meanings of race and gender, and the multiple, shifting rules constructed by children, schools, and society, which include, exclude, categorize, and assess (Davies, 1993; Dyson, 1993; Enciso, 1997, 1998a; Finders, 1997; Lensmire, 1993; Lewis, 1997).

As a literacy scholar, interested in the ways in which children draw on the dynamic interplay of languages and relations to establish their own and others' legitimacy as readers, I wanted to understand how I might document and interpret the sociopolitical landscapes through which upper elementary children learn to read. Furthermore, as a scholar and educator, well aware of the potential for intellectual growth and achievement that is often shut down and closed out of schooling (Ladson-Billings, 1994; Weis & Fine, 1993), I am also committed to research that simultaneously inquires into and interrupts blatant and subtle hierarchies of status and achievement (Tyson, 1998). To these ends, I designed research that allowed me to be both coteacher and researcher in a fourth and fifth grade classroom throughout the 1996–1997 school year. The research followed in the tradition of ethnographies of literacy that seek to understand the practices and purpose of literacy from the participants' (including my own) point of view (see for example, Cherland, 1994; Dyson, 1996).

The research design and methods were premised on sociocultural and poststructural theories of language, race, and social relations (Bakhtin, 1981; Barrera, 1992; Britzman, Santiago-Valles, Jiménez-Muñoz, & Lamash, 1993; Gee, 1990; Ellsworth, 1992, 1997). In many respects, these perspectives have been integral to my evolving understanding of what it means to teach and do research in an unjust society. Following a description and analysis of the research context and methods, I will focus on five insights from linguistic, antiracist, and poststructuralist theories of identity and social relations that have helped me make sense of my work as a teacher, reader, and researcher in the midst of social inequities and daily, local constructions of discrimination. These insights, listed below, will be addressed in turn:

1. The "real" is mediated.
2. Racist and sexist frames of reference require dichotomies, coherence, repetition, and rationality to sustain the assumption that these are natural (unquestionable) principles for organizing and interpreting relations among people.
3. Relations can be transformed by making "the making of meaning" the object of study.
4. The discourses that support racism and sexism within a particular community must be interpreted, in part, through the immediate relationships, histories, and activities of that group.
5. Assumptions of knowing a stable, fixed "other" and "self" close down strategic spaces for reconstructing inequitable relations.

RESEARCH CONTEXT, DATA COLLECTION, AND ANALYSIS

I was both a coteacher and researcher in a fourth and fifth grade classroom during the 1996–1997 school year. The classroom was part of an alternative school with a 25-year history of serving children from across the large urban center of a midwestern U.S. city. Children were enrolled through their parents' application and then selected to attend by a district-run lottery. In 1996–1997, the district was formally released from a federal desegregation plan so that, in effect, school administrators were no longer obligated to achieve a racial balance in their school's population.

I selected this classroom because it was a place where, despite increasing segregation of children by race and class in the city's schools, students in this school perceived and expressed diverse cultural affiliations. Six children (three girls and three boys) identified as African American, although two were also affiliated strongly with European American perspectives through their parents. One child, Evan, openly addressed his identity as biracial, though not bicultural. He affiliated most frequently with European American communities and peers. Fourteen children identified as European American (five girls and nine boys) and lived within close proximity to one another, thus facilitating overnight parties, shared after-school activities, and parental involvement with one another's children. This was true, too, of several of the African American children who knew one another's families and saw one another at church, on the bus, and at their neighborhood community center.

The positive, active feel of their classroom was shaped by the sturdy beliefs and experiences of a veteran teacher. Mrs. Tzagournis grew up in a working-class Greek family close to the inner city and had taught in the school district for 23 years. She was very clear in her expectations and respectful of children's rights and capacities to learn. Informal conversations I conducted with parents and the school principal indicated that she had established a very positive reputation among African American and European American families who believed that she would offer their children a strong, disciplined preparation for middle school. She was regarded, among other teachers, as somewhat less "informal" and somewhat more "traditional" in her teaching methods. The children viewed her as the "strict" teacher in the upper grades, but they soon learned that she was never sharp or arbitrary in her treatment of any child. Given the potentially provocative mediations and interpretations of reading and discrimination I imagined would be introduced through literature selections and discussions, I needed to know that the classroom teacher would establish and sustain underlying patterns of respect, clear expectations, and caring that would be consistently upheld. Mrs. Tzagournis provided this kind of setting for children as well as an active, enthusiastic approach to talking and learning together. Together, we were committed to extending our understanding of how we might engender greater interest in and accomplishments with reading, for all the children. This commitment required that we pay attention to the inequitable relations constructed in the class that could account, in part, for children's disinterest in reading.

As the school year began, children entered a new context, with new peers and new official and unofficial rules for belonging. Like all classes in the school, theirs was formed to create a heterogeneous group representing African American and European American racial affiliations, a balance of genders, socioeconomic conditions, and history of school success. Every child had formerly attended the school for at least 3 years. However, many children in the class stated in interviews that they did not know one another as friends from previous years and they were uncertain who their friends might be as the school year began.

On one level, variations across the children could be described through their proficiency and interest in reading. Using conventional language to describe them, the class would be typical of many upper elementary groups:

Twelve children were fifth graders and 10 were in their fourth grade year. (One girl left the school in January.) According to my field notes, the teacher's and children's descriptions of their reading and standardized assessments, nine children (four boys and four girls) read a wide variety of books with fluency and pleasure, three boys read well but focused on only one or two genres (e.g., R. L. Stine's *Goosebumps* series), five children had difficulty with word decoding and tended to make efforts to read picture books during sustained individual reading times, and four children tended to engage in "pretend reading" by skimming through the pictures of magazines and books but never seriously making an effort to decode or interpret the text. Of the nine children who struggled as readers, five received in-school tutoring; four of these children had been retained in first grade or kindergarten.

Another view of the children, informed by sociocultural theories of identity and hierarchical relations, enables me to see them as active participants in their social worlds. They participate in, but are also subject to, unstated social rules about what counts as normal. As they/we participate in making and sustaining these rules, the specificity of our cultural and social alignments are usually managed and bounded to conform to definitions of normality. All of this can happen during reading because it is a public, valued site for determining competency in schooling. The narrative presented below offers a sense of the complexities all of us faced to disrupt the assumption that reading was an isolated, individual activity available to a lucky few who fit a dominant narrative of "normal" and who seemed to possess certain secrets about being a reader. Consider the diverse histories and practices of reading among five of the fifth graders:

> From the time he was in first grade, Evan actually got in trouble for reading too much. He reported that other kids would tell the teacher that he was "reading again." His third grade teacher punctuated her story of his avid reading by demonstrating the way Evan could hold a book upside-down and to the side during clean-up time so he could read and push a broom at the same time. He continued to read constantly in our classroom. Evan was also socially isolated from his peers—the last to be picked for any social group. Yet I was sure he had a lot to teach us all about what reading meant to him, how he so readily "got into" books, and how he interpreted what he read. He also had a lot to teach us about the tensions and possibilities of growing up biracial in a society that is determined to construct Black/White definitions of identity.

Leanne, a young girl who could slug a softball but barely whisper an answer in class, struggled with the mechanics of reading. She was quite happy to have others read to her and particularly enjoyed scary stories, but the effort of decoding outweighed the potential pleasure of reading a book on her own. Besides that, she had few friends she could trust at the beginning of the year. Although she traversed diverse groups of girls, she sought the company of the "popular," middle-class girls who, like her, were European American, but unlike Leanne were comfortable in their ability to read and "do school." They also kept their reading selections and interpretations close and bounded from the rest of their classmates. Leanne wanted to be their friend; but it seemed impossible to build that friendship so that it included the "popular" girls' ways of selecting books, talking about characters, and generally sharing the work of reading.

Ebony was well-liked by male and female peers who, like her, were African American, but she was generally excluded by European American girls and boys, unlike other African American girls in the class. Her African American heritage and her mother's love of books led her to read all she could find about women and being Black in America. But her teachers and peers did not appear to acknowledge that Ebony loved to read or that her insights were startling, critical, and just beginning to be more consciously intertextual.

Ray struggled with reading, and was tutored through several years of Title I reading instruction. Despite his lessons he never really understood a consistent strategy for word analysis, and he didn't read books in the room. He skimmed through magazines during silent reading time and read with children who, like him, did not read well. Although he enjoyed talking with his African American peers during most parts of the day, his primary reading partner was Dan, a European American boy who rarely talked with Ray; he giggled and flipped through magazines, even though he could read fluently. At home, Ray read the Bible daily and learned to recite passages and interpret the moral order prescribed by the Bible. Interpretation in the room was a different matter. During read-aloud times when children would discuss their predictions and interpretations of key events, he often seemed to have completely lost the plot and characters until he was pressed to state and clarify what happened to whom when.

But getting Ray or his friend Matt to say what they valued or understood about a text meant quieting the other boys, particularly Jacques, who, like Ray, was a quick wit who verbally taunted and teased whenever the opportunity arose. However, during official read-aloud and discussion times Jacques, unlike Ray, initiated and dominated debates about texts, and answered questions of fact rapidly and successfully. He formed the unstable center of a group of European American boys who valued chess and Beatles music—and expressly rejected rap and R&B music. Despite their fluency in reading, this group of boys rarely completed a chapter book. Jacques, for example, came to school with Stephen King novels but admitted he lost interest about halfway through; he preferred chess books during silent reading times.

As a researcher, studying hierarchies and exclusions in reading I had to notice and document the multiple, shifting relationships among the children. The narrative description just presented, for example, suggests that reading practices for each child were informed by their interests outside of school, their familiarity and comfort with particular cultural and popular cultural resources, and their facility with the mechanics of decoding and interpreting a variety of written texts. The sociocultural dimensions of each child's reading were further legitimated or marginalized in the classroom depending on the stability of their relations with one another; our unspoken assumptions about racial, gender, and class status; and implicit classroom norms for being viewed as a reader. My work as a teacher and researcher required that I seriously attend to the intersections of these norms and relations as I began the day with the children and as I planned for and revised our ways of working together on reading. I wanted to understand how their affiliations were constructed, how their participation in reading contributed to these affiliations, and how their perceptions of themselves and others could be disrupted as we learned to examine and invent openly new ways to read together. Furthermore, I needed to understand how I contributed to any of these constructions.

These questions about affiliation, status, and disruption of social norms required ethnographic data collection methods and discourse theories for data collection and analysis. In addition, every step of the research, from proposal to analysis and writing, required extensive reading in the areas of cultural studies; identity politics; current research in reading education; and antiracist history, philosophy, and pedagogy.

Data were collected from the beginning of the school year in September 1996 through the end of the year in June 1997. During the beginning and ending months of the school year, I was involved in the classroom as a participant observer 3 to 4 days per week, focusing on the ways in which children and their teacher organized and interpreted reading practices and one another's reading interests and abilities. I also attended all arts-based classes (music, art, dance) and eventually worked with the arts teachers to find new ways to involve the children in interpretations of the books I read aloud to them. Each observation was audio recorded and accompanied by my field notes. From December through March I worked every day as a coteacher and researcher, using two video cameras, two to three audio recorders, and field notes to document the multiple relations, norms, and cultural resources that informed our shared reading events.

Analyses of data were ongoing and informed by performance theory (Baumann & Briggs, 1990) and poststructural theories of language that are interested in how we use language to define status and normalcy (Bakhtin, 1981; Butler, 1990; Ellsworth, 1997; Felman & Laub, 1992). Analytic categories included our use of intertextuality, dichotomous language, and language use to preserve or challenge what was implicitly but repeatedly referred to as universally accepted values and interpretations (Bloome & Egan-Robertson, 1993; Hodge & Kress, 1993). Analysis also followed the ways the children and I framed racism as a "real," natural construction versus a socially constructed and constantly managed, sustained set of relations (Enciso, 1998b).

As a teacher researcher, I also noted patterns of exclusion or discrimination and how I planned to disrupt them while deepening children's commitment to and understanding of multiple ways of reading. As several practitioner researchers have attested (Ballenger, 1998; Gallas, 1998; Herr, 1994; Paley, 1992), such teaching requires shifts in thinking and practice that can expose the systemic, institutionalized protections of status and power in which we, as educators, participate. As I considered the limits of my understanding and pedagogy I had to confront the realization that I, too, was always potentially complicit in supporting the very ideologies and exclusionary practices I hoped to interrupt and transform.

PRINCIPLES GUIDING RESEARCH AND TEACHING

The data analysis, then, included not only multiple readings of the texts and transcripts collected over time, but also examinations of the *ways* that I read those texts as I considered my own and the students' experiences of injustice—specifically, the construction and effects of racism in school and society. In the following sections, I describe five principles that guided the research and teaching. These principles arose out of multiple readings of an interpretive event during which I was a key, and I think, unreliable mediator of our assumptions about racism, intertextuality, and the meaning of reading.

The "Real" Is Mediated

Central to linguistic, poststructural, antiracist, and antisexist theories of everyday life is the idea that our social relations and the ways we accomplish life are always "in the making." What we see and experience shapes us and is being shaped by us all the time. Thus, whatever we do or perceive is not "natural" or "real" but rather a product of our assumptions about the way things should be. Our assumptions are "in the background" but always informing the way we make our lives together. One of those constructions is reading education, which is, in turn, shaped by larger, unstated, or unexamined societal ideas about who is a reader, what counts as reading, and what social arrangements seem "right" as reading is practiced.

During the first 3 months of the school year I paid attention to the ways in which children and Mrs. Tzagournis used language, reading materials, space, and groupings to accomplish reading. I was interested in how the children legitimated one another's ideas—or not—how practices such as self-selection of literature and independent reading times benefited some children and not others, and how they made all of these practices seem "real," normal, and unquestionable, as though "this is just the way reading is done." I noticed, for example, that Ray never answered or initiated questions during whole class discussions of a book being read aloud. Neither did one of the African American boys or three African American girls, including Ebony. Of all the African American children, Matthew was definitely the most eager to share an idea or question in front of the whole class. Similarly, Leanne never volunteered an answer or question while other girls were also relatively quiet compared to a small group of European American boys. Yes. Even though no one said it, race mattered. And sexism mattered. During the second week of school, Sara confided that she wasn't sure if it was "alright to not know something in this class, yet. Mathias and Steven are really smart." Accompanying Sara's observation are unstated relations of gender and race that were becoming visible and available to the children as they defined the taken-for-granted norms for how they should evaluate one another's legitimacy as learners in the classroom.

Children were also grouped for reading each week when Mrs. Tzagournis would ask five or six children to read out loud and respond to more closed comprehension questions (in "lower groups") or discuss a book's meaning and its connections with their lives (in the "higher group"). Furthermore, the grouping of higher readers included children who were already viewed as "good students" from the same European American, middle-class community. Although Ebony was a part of the high reading group, too, it was often the case that she was so silent that people forgot she was a participant. The children recognized that they were called into different groupings that, invariably, divided them by race and class. However, they did not know that their groups were receiving different degrees of high-level and low-level questions. Neither did they know what they might need to do to change groups.

In a matter of 4 weeks, a pattern of silence and sound was established that continued for 3 more months and that appeared to the girls and boys to be "just the way it is." Mrs. Tzagournis and I were concerned that all of the children gain fluency and joy in reading, but we were not certain how to disrupt what seemed to be an already settled pattern of strength and weakness, interest and disinterest. Although I knew that children would benefit from making reading processes more visible and open to shared consideration, I recognized that these processes alone would not effectively challenge the unspoken norms of inclusion and exclusion that children experienced. Even if we could make reading a more accessible process of inquiry, it would still be mediated by the children's expectations of legitimacy and hierarchies of status so that the same children might still feel they had no way—and no right—to be readers.

I was interested in the ways that discrimination operated through the class's public and private reading events, and how children's relationships with reading and with one another could be altered through deliberate attention—during reading events—to the meaning of discrimination in our lives and in society. What would happen to reading and to our relationships with one another if we made reading practices less settled? If we began to see that we make reading happen, that it isn't simply a natural practice that everyone understands and accepts?

My question was informed by the perspective of performance theorists Baumann and Briggs (1990), who argue that children and teachers and all the materials and policies associated with reading are engaged in a *contextualization*—making the group and its relations of status and legitimacy as they go along. As Baumann and Briggs (1990) define it, a contextualization

> involves an active process of negotiation in which participants reflexively examine the discourse as it is emerging, embedding assessments of its structure and significance in the speech itself. Performers [in this case, the children and teachers as readers and interpreters] extend such assessments to include predictions about how the communicative competence, personal histories, and social identities of their interlocutors will shape the reception of what is said. (p. 69)

This view of the ongoing reflexive examination of discourse and evaluation of participants' competence was central to my data collection and analysis. Such a view enabled me to document and reflect on how children, their teacher, and I made assumptions about reading competence, about the adequacy of particular reading practices, and about one another's right to participate in particular practices.

At the same time, I believed that although it is through language and action that reading practices are made "normal," language by its nature constantly opens the possibility of "recontextualizing" texts and relationships, as particular uses of language and positioning are contested during the moment-to-moment relations and practices that children and teachers enact. In the teaching I did from January through March, I intended to mediate children's negotiations around reading so that it would be possible, through language and art, to rework access to reading, claims of legitimacy, and performances of competency.

However, I needed to be aware that while I might want to alter the terms of inclusion for the children, I might also reinforce the very discourses that held us in fixed positions. As Davies and Harré (1990) argue in their analysis of social positioning,

> Any narrative that we collaboratively unfold with other people . . . draws on a knowledge of social structures and the roles that are recognizably allocated to people within those structures . . . Social structures are *coercive to the extent that to be recognizably and acceptably a person, we must operate within their terms.* (p. 52)

What knowledge did I take for granted? What did I not know that could render a child "unrecognizable?" Could I participate in coercive and corrosive social structures because they allow *me* to be recognizable? What if the contextualization I construct with the children is part of a social structure like racism? What if racism, as a discourse, is not examined and renders children "unacceptable" despite our efforts to make every child a part of the construction of reading practices?

The work I began in December with small groups and then developed in January with the whole class was directed, in part, by the principle that no one would be excluded from participation in the multiple ways of reading we might explore. As I read novels, picture books, and nonfiction aloud to the class I insisted that all the children would not only participate in the politics of interpreting literature together, but also openly discuss and examine *how* we constructed our relations with one another during reading. To maintain inclusion, I rejected the disciplinary strategies of ordering children to take a "time out" or "leave the group."

We also read and interpreted fiction and nonfiction literature not only through discussion, but also through the performing and visual arts so that every child had the opportunity to explore and express the sense of the texts we read together. In addition, the content of our reading focused on the histories of and challenges to discrimination in American society. Through this focus on discrimination we were able to consider how our own cultural affiliations were subject to constructions of racism and sexism in society and in our classroom.

For example, when we read a novel that introduced the Federal Removal Act of 1810, we participated in improvised dramas that portrayed a community and government's systematic construction of economic demands, stereotypes, fear, and violence, leading to the "natural" conclusion that the people indigenous to the United States should be "removed" from their land. These constructions paralleled the less tragic, but nonetheless ongoing exclusions experienced by class members during reading and other classroom events. Over several months we were able to view discrimination through an historical lens and the lens of our own ways of shaping daily classroom relationships. We attempted to do more than correct stereotypes; we tried to understand how and why stereotypes, silences, and discriminatory practices are made real and used against people in the first place.

By February, we were able to generate a list of the practices that promote discrimination and those that challenge and confront discrimination. Shown in Figure 7.1., many of these were directly applicable to our classroom life insofar as they made visible discriminatory practices that deeply hurt children's feelings, took them off guard, or silenced them. Often children who were faced with these experiences believed they were somehow wrong or deserving of verbal taunts and affronts. It was hard for them to see otherwise when discrimination was practiced and interpreted as though it were a natural part of schooling. This chart was a useful way to hold our thinking in place. It did not mean, however, that our ways of being and reading together could be simply addressed, mediated, and improved. Our address to discrimination was not a finished product.

However, the principle of no exclusion disrupted the familiar, apparently natural relations of those who could read, those who liked to read, and those who really didn't read much at all. By refusing exclusion as a structure of our relations, it was possible to begin to expose and change patterns of categorization and legitimization so that the multiplicity of voices and values in the class could be seen as part of the complexity of reading.

Racist and Sexist Frames of Reference Require Dichotomies, Coherence, Repetition, and Rationality to Sustain Their Construction as Natural

Despite a policy of no exclusion, people still get left out and the strategies for maintaining a "natural" racism and sexism still perform their acrobatics through the movement and thoughts of our lives. Thus, in field notes and in data analyses, I asked: How do exclusions and definitions of legiti-

Figure 7.1. Understanding and Fighting Discrimination

How Does Discrimination Start to Happen?	*What Can We Do to Resist and Fight Discrimination?*
Fear—People use lies, exaggeration, and propaganda to make people afraid of a person or a group of people. *Fear leads to hate. Hate leads to war.*	*Speak up!* Ask people in leadership roles to speak up.
Fear is taught. *Prejudice is taught.*	Talk to other people—form a group that supports one another.
People want some things that other people have; or they want to be sure other people don't get the same things. Kids get jealous or make fun of other kids' clothes. Adults sometimes only think of themselves and don't want everyone to have as much food, clothing, money, or education. It's *hard to share!*	*Listen.* *Have hope.* *Laws*—remember the Civil Rights Act; remember that some laws are not just even though they are laws. We can fight unjust laws.
Intimidation = I'm bigger than you are. I can hurt you.	*Seek support* from family, church, and community leaders.
Harassment = constantly making someone feel bad about themselves or like they should do something against their will.	Peaceful protest. Have *faith.*
Dehumanization = name calling, making a face, whispering about someone in front of them, not listening, walking away—all of these things make someone feel like they do not exist.	*Show respect* for yourself and others. *Nonviolent response*—a violent response can have serious consequences for you and may make other people ignore or dismiss you and the problem.

macy get enacted and sustained among children learning about reading together? What might disrupt patterns of exclusion and discrimination within this group? Who benefits when exclusive relational practices are maintained? Who benefits when exclusive relational practices are disrupted? What happens to definitions and practices of reading when exclusions are maintained or questioned?

Feminist and antiracist theorists, including Judith Butler, Toni Morrison, Gloria Anzaldúa, Patricia Williams, Audrey Thompson, and Liz Ellsworth, have helped me name the coercive and corrosive strategies that exclude, limit, and define our sense of who we can be in the world. All of these writers point to discursive practices that construct a superior category of person through its contrast with "the other." This dichotomous construction insists on a categorically privileged group that has deserved its rights, while the designated "other" group must prove its claims to approximations of the same rights and privileges. As Thompson (1997) states in her analysis of racism as a frame of reference,

> Racism . . . insists on the otherness of outsider groups. Indeed, it specifically *generates* the category of race as an organizing principle of social meaning and then works to naturalize hierarchical relations so that oppressed minorities appear inherently inferior, suspect, or undeserving. (p. 11)

The groups or individuals defined in these hierarchical, dichotomous relations are expected to maintain these relations through their complicity with numerous discursive practices. Ellsworth (1997), for example, points to the problem of "continuous dialogue," which requires the maintenance of coherence and convergence of viewpoints. Through the expectation of consent to a shared perspective, continuous dialogue excludes any question of its premises. Similarly, Butler (1990) identifies repetition in our everyday language, and popular culture as a practice that names and reinforces what is included while it simultaneously points to what is excluded. In Butler's analysis of gender constructions, she argues that repetition is an indication that something else, something either not recognized or "unacceptable," exists. The repeated effort to define what is included is, at the same time, an effort to deny the existence of what is less stable or fixed. Ellsworth (1997), Williams (1991), and Anzaldúa (1987) also question those strategies that attempt to rationally, objectively provide evidence for particular interpretations of events and viewpoints. According to these scholars, the evidence and rationales mobilized to assure "clear thinking" often issue from inherently racist and sexist standpoints. Furthermore, their function is to silence and to win.

The groups or individuals defined in these hierarchical, dichotomous relations are expected to maintain these relations through their complicity with numerous discursive practices. Ellsworth (1997), for example, points to the problem of "continuous dialogue," which requires the maintenance

Thus, if we wish to challenge racism and sexism as corrosive, constructed frames of reference for our participation in the world, it is futile to do so in terms of an already established method of rational explanation since these methods are often founded on principles of interaction that constructed racism and sexism in the first place. In addition, rationality easily slips into apparently obvious, ready-made solutions for ridding ourselves of discrimination. For example, teachers and children often attempt to correct one another's racist and sexist talk or actions by personalizing these "errors" and showing that someone's experiences or perspectives are simply insufficiently empathetic (Thompson, 1997; Williams, 1991). Eventually the site for the construction of racism is located solely with students or other individuals rather than in the systematic construction of dichotomies, coherences, repetitions, and rationales.

During the time period of January through March, I engaged students in discussions and interpretations of texts that would unsettle the assumption that everyone should agree or share similar standpoints from which to interpret the world. The children did not find this to be an easy or comfortable change, particularly for seven boys who affiliated with European American, middle-class values and who achieved a high degree of visibility and legitimacy as they "proved their points" in debates about the literature we read. When I read aloud and encouraged discussion of a book they took this as an opportunity to show one another their ability to predict an outcome or identify a detail while everyone else made futile attempts to challenge their answers.

In contrast with their view and practice of discussion, my goal was to engage everyone in looking at reading and our work together as the site for multiple, often contradictory positions and interpretations. We had to allow ourselves to be surprised and uncertain. This was successful in many respects, though not without a lot of wondering among the children about why reading in the classroom had changed. Eventually, referring to a series of books in which the characters study science through various unpredictable adventures, the children described our reading as "The Magic School Bus Ride" through a book. We never "got to the point." We exposed viewpoints and ways of reading that enabled a book to become a site for many forms of play and interpretation.

But I want to stop here, with the sort of sanguine sense of change I just described. I want to turn to a moment in the year when dichotomies, coherence, rationality, continuity, and repetition effectively operated to deny legitimacy to children who were on the verge of becoming more confident, fluent readers.

The event occurred in early February and focused on a class discussion of *The Gold Cadillac* by Mildred Taylor (1987). I selected this short story to read aloud to the whole class as part of an ongoing study of the production of and resistance to discrimination in our society. Up to this point, I think it's fair to say, we were working almost daily to name and explore the production of difference and discrimination by governments, people in their everyday lives, and by media. We tried to understand how people are targeted for discrimination, how a group of people become the beneficiaries of discrimination, and how discrimination is related to interests in property rights.

The Gold Cadillac shows one family, and particularly one man's struggle with all of these dimensions of discrimination. The story follows the decisions and actions of David Logan, an African American man, living and working in the 1950s. Mr. Logan buys a gold Cadillac to claim his right as a citizen and worker. He asserts that he has earned it. He openly challenges the Jim Crow construction of limited agency in the African American community by not only buying the car but also by announcing that he will drive it from Toledo, Ohio, to Mississippi, accompanied by his wife, children, and extended family. I selected the book to connect the children with and deepen their understanding of the history and injustices of race relations in the United States. (Note that I believed *I could understand* this experience to such an extent that I could mediate *their* understanding. In fact, I have had no firsthand experience with Jim Crow practices, no experience with police profiling, no experience with the Black community's mediation of stories of this nature, and no experience with the fear of crossing state lines or borders).

In the story, Mr. Logan and his family are stopped by the police as they cross the state line into Tennessee. Mr. Logan is ordered out of the Cadillac, into a police car, and driven to the police station where he is held for several hours, charged with speeding, and then released. (The mother and children are left in the Cadillac and driven by a second policeman to the station). Although physical harm is not evident, all of the characters express psychic pain as they reflect on the event and support one another toward a sense of strength. In many respects, the ending is unresolved as David Logan imagines a future in which he must answer his daughters' questions about racism and live and work within and against societal expectations of his civil and human rights.

The moment in the story that evoked the greatest debate among the boys in the class was Mr. Logan's reaction to the police when the police searched and intimidated him. Ray and Matthew, both children who affiliated primarily with African American culture, announced that they wanted David to fight back. Ray spoke first and was mildly challenged by his peers and me:

> PAT: Who's going to have . . . what would you fight with Matthew?
> RAY: My butter knife. [Laughter]. (This is a reference to the carving knife from the picnic basket held by one of the girls in the backseat of the car.)
> PAT: What would the police have, Matthew?
> RAY: They have the guns.
> [Many, overlapping voices describing the range of weapons police might have.]

PAT: Let me talk to Matthew. What else would the police have?
MATTHEW: Handcuffs, that metal bar, mace. [He has heard these
    from classmates.]
PAT: Who's going to win that fight?
MATTHEW: I got kids. (He is referring to the two children in the car,
    in the story. Note his use of "I," meaning "I am the father,
    now.") There's two cops right? I gotta wife with me.
RAY: I got my whole CREW.

Dichotomies, repetitions, rational evidence, and coherences shaped our
continuing dialogue—and our relations with one another—as we debated
David Logan's actions and motivations during his encounter with the state
police. Ray and Matthew argued that David Logan should have fought
back when confronted and harassed by the police.

I considered and tried to be sensitive to the conflicted positioning this
story might produce for Ray and Matthew and other African American
children—David Logan is a dignified, proactive character, yet he is placed
in a compromising, humiliating position in front of his family. How could
I mediate the possible desire for some children to be affiliated with this
man and his family while attending to their positioning in the class and
society as possibly deserving of discrimination? How could racism, as a
taken-for-granted frame of reference, be undone in this discussion? I was
not completely surprised by Ray and Matthew's stance that Mr. Logan
should and could fight the police. I had assumed that they would position
themselves near or alongside him and that they would want him to take
action. However, I surprised myself by my own level of investment in my
desire for the African American boys, in particular, to think through the
consequences of a violent response.

My presence and performance as an adult in the classroom lent social
force to the questions and values I raised. By questioning the boys' interpretations of the story, I offered legitimacy to interpretations that could be
confirmed by the text and that fit rationalist and perhaps conformist perceptions of racism. In contrast, Ray and Matthew insisted on interpretations that were confirmed by their own experiences and that fit values of
social justice.

In order to construct and assert an interpretation of the Logan family's
actions that fit their views and ideas, Ray and Matthew had to shift the
story across their contemporary experiences and settings to the historical
moment during which the story takes place. This is a difficult move to
make if you are not an experienced participant in the interpretative debates
that often occur in classroom book discussions. Furthermore, to shift the
terms of the discussion from that of a matter of literally interpreting the

text to that of historically and metaphorically interpreting the text requires a high degree of social power within a group. In this book discussion, Matthew and Ray were not seen by other members of the class (or me, at that point) as having the authority to claim a legitimate interpretation or the power to remake social relations.

> PAT: Matthew, who is going to win the fight?
> RAY: The people. The dad is.
> MATTHEW: I am.
> JACQUES: The White man.
> MATTHEW: I am.
> JACQUES: Okay, Matthew. (Said sarcastically, as if to say, "That's enough. You can't possibly believe that.")

These excerpts from our extended conversation are illustrative of the repetitions and dichotomies that were constructed and challenged several times over. Each effort to point to a stable meaning of power in the story (the police are inevitably more powerful; Mr. Logan is ultimately most vulnerable), denied an effort by Ray and Matthew to examine the less stable possibility that a fight could be justified. Despite the insistence of the other boys that fighting back was impossible, Ray and Matthew offered a number of compelling arguments for Mr. Logan's need and right to fight back. They referred to different meanings of "fight" through references to Rosa Parks, Malcolm X, Rev. Martin Luther King, and their struggle, in the face of violent protest by White activists, to do what was right, not what was safe.

In this contextualization of reading and interpretation among these children, legitimacy as a reader was afforded to those who could "think clearly." In other words, the right interpretation was a rational one, based on the story's facts. Yet this rationale was grounded in the premise that racism is, in many respects, unavoidable and unassailable.

What would it have meant to Ray and Matthew to insist on an interpretation that was centered in their vision of dignity, activism, and discrimination? As Matthew's frustration grew, he introduced the argument, through a pointed rhetoric, that God's justice would protect a man in danger. Meanwhile, Ray attempted to reposition the police when he interjected that they may not be as aggressive or dangerous as they appear— they merely hide behind their guns. But again, Ray and Matthew's arguments were dismissed when the facts of the story were posed by Aaron, who insisted that Ray examine and account for a picture in the book of armed policemen.

MATTHEW: But look. But look Pat. I'm not trying to be no religious person . . . But MAN . . . (He was frustrated with multiple voices talking over and around him.)

PAT: Excuse me. Matthew is talking.

MATTHEW: But even if they got a gun don't mean . . . or a crow-bar . . .

RAY: Some polices hide behind guns.

MATTHEW: 'Cause that man got something on his side. He don't have to have his family. He got GOD.

RAY: Some polices hide behind guns.

AARON: (Looking at the book and showing Ray.) Matthew and Ray. Look at all his bullets and the gun.

RAY: I don't care. I would have snatched it out of his hand! (Lee and Tanya and others rise up to look at the picture.)

MATTHEW: Nah! But Aaron you don't understand. God is much powerful than a bullet. He's got God on his side. He don't have to have his family on his side.

Frustration with being misunderstood and devalued resulted in Ray's appeal to me to "just read the book." On reflection, Ray's request seems to me to be an effort to both point to and escape the premises of the debate and the assumptions among his peers that only certain interpretations could be recognizable as reading. As Thompson (1997) points out in her analysis of the foundational philosophy and practice of antiracist education, too often the terms of inclusion and debate about racism rest upon the premise of a "naturally" racist society that must, simply, be corrected or amended. Thus, "racism [continues] to set the terms for what will count against it" (p. 19). Both the terms of our debate about resistance to racism and our contextualization of one another as effective or ineffective purveyors of evidence, and therefore effective or ineffective readers, positioned Ray and Matthew's cultural knowledge and reading as inadequate. "Just reading the book" would make it possible, in Ray's view, to diminish the entrapping effects of a debate premised on the rationality of racism and the necessity of only one kind of evidence.

As our discussion seemed to reach an impasse, Matthew insisted that I should continue to read the story because, as he said, "It's true, too." He realized that this book and discussion closely mirrored the identities and assessments he and his peers constructed for one another. The debate exposed the children's differential rights to legitimacy and the obvious differences in their sense of security and agency in a racist society. He argued, finally, that the positions he and his friend took up relative to the story were mirrored in the class's social relations. In a final attempt to persuade his peers of the legitimacy of his interpretation, his alienation from his classmates and potentially from reading were confirmed:

> MATTHEW: Well, Pat, they seem like they don't care if *they* was the cops and someone pulled *them* over. How would they feel? [He turns to his classmates.] Like say, if we was White and you all was Black how would you all feel?
>
> BRIAN: I would feel bad but I wouldn't just go up and start punching him.
>
> MATTHEW: I didn't say that. I'd fight back.
>
> BRIAN: I wouldn't.
>
> MATTHEW: If he hit me or something then I'd . . .
>
> JACQUES: But he didn't.
>
> LEE: But he didn't.
>
> MATTHEW: I didn't SAY that.
>
> BRIAN: HE MAY HAVE disrespected him and he told him a lie but he never attacked him.
>
> MATTHEW: I didn't say that the cop went just like [He hits his hand] that with a stick. Did I say that? No.
>
> BRIAN: Yeah. But that's what you're sounding like. You're sounding like . . .
>
> RAY: Well, Matthew is saying if the cops hit him then he would hit them back, unless the cops don't do nothing to him he don't do nothin' to them.
>
> TANYA: I respect your voices, but . . .
>
> MATTHEW: It seems like *you* all *want* the cops to pull us over, man.

The paradox for Matthew was that he had achieved what Bakhtin (1981) calls an internally persuasive telling of the text, through which he could "retell the text in [his] own words, with [his] own accents, gestures, modifications" (p. 424). Yet every move he made to support a more multivocal interpretation was read against him. He called upon multiple texts to lend authority to his interpretation, he appealed to his peers to listen and he made powerful emotional and cultural connections with a key character and event in the story. Yet despite the fact that these strategies were not only legitimate but sophisticated characteristics of insightful reading and interpretation, he was trapped by the repetitions, dichotomies, continuities, contextualization, and premises of our reading.

Make the Making of Meaning the Object of Study

Thompson (1997) argues that antiracist education must challenge the kinds of entrapments we constructed. Following the work of the philosopher

Alain Locke, Thompson proposes art as an alternative to the reproduction and naturalization of racism in education. In her view, artistic, performative pedagogies have the potential to create

> [their] own terms for understanding and appreciation, allowing us to sidestep the received, conventional terms of meaning, and to take up new possibilities presented to us in the work of art. (p. 19)

As a way of refocusing the debate and moving out of the bounds of our contextualization of reading and one another, I asked the children to make symbolic representations of their interpretations of the story. This request draws on my years of experience with this method as a way of opening meanings within literary texts. More recently I have recognized this method as a way of showing children how they make meaning, by situating themselves within the events of the story. They are asked, through this method, to represent or point to "where they are" or how they are positioned within this story's descriptions and relations. Furthermore, this method relies on metaphor, not literal interpretation for making meaning. Through metaphor, more meanings are suggested and explored rather than stated and confirmed, as they are in a more literal approach to interpretation.

As our discussion reached an impasse, I gave small groups and pairs of children three pieces of paper—one gold, one black, and one white—and asked them to tear or cut the paper and arrange them together to show how the characters were related to one another and to the gold Cadillac at a key point in the story. A crucial part of this process was to make a symbol for themselves and place it within these relationships, so we could literally see the social position(s) from which they made their interpretation (see Enciso 1992, 1998a).

The symbolic representation work they began and later shared with one another effectively shifted them into another set of assumptions about what counts as a legitimate reading. Where continuous dialogue, filled with repetitions, dichotomies, and rationalities, exposed the efforts of many children to stabilize positionings, artistic, metaphoric work focused attention on the possibility of multiple positions, the layers of meaning, and experience that informed and shaped their perspectives, and the generative possibilities of their images and ideas.

To construct a metaphor for the story's events and relationships, the children had to rely both on their interpretation of Taylor's narrative propositions and on the cultural resources and experiences they viewed as most capable of "holding" the meanings of those resources and experiences. The metaphors they made became markers for meaning but not directives to singular meanings.

I am not suggesting, here, that racial politics are erased or completely escaped through artistic mediation of interpretations. However, the following excerpt suggests that Ray and Matthew used metaphor to help us step back from the assumption of a singular text and a rationalist, predictable interpretation. Through their symbolic interpretation we could begin to construct fresh, surprising insights around a story that had previously yielded a litany of evidence and counterevidence.

When Ray and Matthew received their set of colored paper, they worked together to represent and describe their understanding of the story's most significant symbol, gold.

> RAY: Pat see. Look. Look. This is for me and Matthew. Look this is the Black people and the White people. [He overlays half of the black sheet of paper onto half of the white sheet.] And the gold Cadillac. [He places the gold sheet in between the sheets of black and white.] But it's the Black people's [car] but the police think they stole it. They took them in and it's like covering half and half cause the police think they stole it so they took them . . . but it's really the Black people's car. It's kind of like half and half.
>
> MATTHEW: Let's have half of this can be the Cadillac and half of this can be God. And see and see . . .
>
> PAT: Okay. Here's some more paper if you want to add to this.
>
> RAY: Me and Matthew's is going to be good.
>
> PAT: It is going to be good. You've got a very clear idea.

In their metaphoric representation of the story's themes and events, gold began to stand for possession, contested possession, and the presence of God in the midst of all the strife. In many ways, the analysis they built quickly and effectively through the paper symbols took them to the heart of the story and the heart of their own conviction about social and moral justice. Ray understood that the gold Cadillac was claimed by both the White police and the Logan family for different reasons. Although the symbol they made emphasized a very concrete material relationship in the story, it was also the critical site for interpreting racism in this story. Indeed, as the class learned in the ensuing months, seizure or invalidation of property rights has been and continues to be a prime strategy for enforcing and institutionalizing discrimination based on race, gender, or sexual orientation (Williams, 1991).

Furthermore, Ray and Matthew's interpretation had a sense of ownership, energy, and commitment that I had not seen previously in class discussions. In a reversal of Ray's request to "just read the book," they claimed the value of and desire for their own interpretation. Ray even volunteered to stay in for recess to complete their creation.

After recess, we gathered as a whole class to share the art we had made. As children, in pairs or threes, went around a circle sharing their representations of the story, questions and possibilities were raised about the meaning of color, space, size, and movement. We grew interested in how we made sense of racism and how racism was made in the story. When Matthew and Ray were asked to share their work, shown in Figure 7.2, they elaborated further on their interpretation of God's presence in the tense, potentially violent event that faced the Logan family. Matthew spoke first without interruption from any of his peers.

> MATTHEW: This (gold) represents the gold Cadillac and the Black people and the White people (points to either side of their paper) . . . and what happened in the discrimination in the book . . . and this (overarching piece of gold, attached to both black and white paper) represents God and he's on both sides.
>
> PAT: That's interesting that you place God on both sides. Why did you do that, Matthew and Ray?
>
> MATTHEW: Because nobody got hurt.

FIGURE 7.2. Ray and Matthew's Symbolic Representation

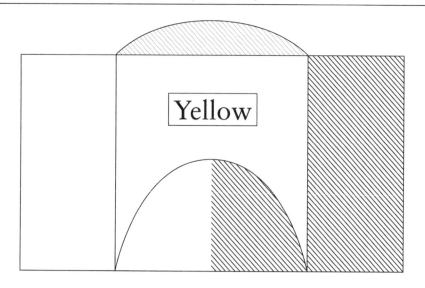

RAY: Even though God don't like what White people doing to the Black people but he still loves them even though he don't like what they're doing.

PAT: So there's a loving God watching this.

CHERI: It's like a blessing.

PAT: That's a lovely, thoughtful interpretation of a very difficult situation.

PAT: Where are you?

RAY: [He taps the gold of God]

PAT: Where would you like to be?

MATTHEW: [He smiles] In the Cadillac.

[Laughter]

The three-dimensional image they made was simple in form, conveying an understanding of the racial conflicts, psychic pain, loss, and hope that racism and discrimination have meant for people throughout American history. The tension and strife are clear, but it is not a "natural" relationship that humans should accept or promote. As the discursive ground of our reading discussion shifted from one of defending evidence to generating possible perspectives, we were able to consider Ray and Matthew's cultural resources as an avenue into a story that was, to that point, understood almost exclusively in terms of an acceptance of racism as a regrettable but natural set of relations. In the forthcoming weeks, as we read about, interpreted, and developed a class book about discrimination and the fight for civil rights, we repeatedly encountered the significance of church, God, and the struggle between the desire to retaliate physically and maintain pacifist resistance in the face of dehumanization and brutality. Ray and Matthew knew a way of interpreting these texts that was unfamiliar to many of the other children. Our class, together, was just beginning to understand how to recontextualize our social relations and thus the multiple narratives that could be claimed as legitimate while we read and learned together.

This was a critical moment in our history as a group of people of culturally diverse resources and affiliations who were engaged in reading across time, space, and identities. If Ray and Matthew continued to face their peers by defending themselves from a position that was rendered unrecognizable, they could not imagine that their presence mattered to reading practices. Conversely, as categories of legitimate reading were destabilized, it could become possible for all of us to contribute to a proliferation of meaning—meaning that does not have to be premised on racist or sexist frames of reference. We could find ourselves in a position to learn that what we do with texts, among peers, is interesting, puzzling, and engaging.

Interpreting Immediate Relationships and Histories

Knowing is part of the research process. The goal is to document repeated events, relations, and meanings until they become visible to the researcher as a constructed practice, not something taken for granted and in the background of classroom life. I worked with the children and their teacher for a year, and during that time came to see all of us as unique collections of participants in a contextualization, making reading, racism, and other discriminations visible and invisible in particular ways. We were a group that shared a particular history of participating or intervening in playground battles, bus ride fights, best friends, best friend betrayals, and numerous realignments of friendships and status. These were often linked with broad constructions of class, race, and gender, but they were also related to this specific group's geographical locations in the city, family histories within the school and city, and the racial and gender politics of our city and school district.

As I conducted research and teaching, I often relied on the belief that I had seen enough and documented enough to be able to move to a "confirming" phase of data gathering and analysis. I could see Evan being excluded throughout the day, every day by different children. I could see Jacques at the center of several unstable friendship groups, orchestrating the day's skirmishes with teachers and peers. I could see Ebony quietly picking up books and sinking into their world. I could see Leanne listening to a peer read aloud and hear her say afterward, "I don't like to read." The specificity of each child's way of participating and their ways of reading and being together became visible through systematic documentation and review of data.

By the time I began teaching with *The Gold Cadillac*, I believed I understood enough about Jacques and Ray and the ways that they participated in reading to be able to recognize (even predict) the pathways they might take in their interpretations of the story. I believed I knew enough about multicultural literature, research, reading, and kids in general to be able to mediate—stand between or within—their worlds and offer guidance toward mutual understanding. Despite my understanding that each communicative act is drenched in old meanings and histories (which are often unstated, unseen, and undetermined), and language is directed in each new setting by the participants' histories together and by the particularities of their immediate relations, I treated the reading event as a known set of relations and communications. I also imagined the possibility that if we could know enough about one another's views and experience, we might achieve some kind of mutual understanding and equity.

I did not count on the unstated and ever-present possibility that the pathways they might take would not converge; that instead, their talk and gestures would provoke surprising discontinuities and challenges to reading, relationships, and knowing.

Assuming a Stable "Other" and "Self" Closes Down Exploration

As this insight suggests, you can become familiar and believe you are "knowledgeable" about these relations and histories in such a way, as happened to me, that you imagine everyone as being fixed and stable; you forget the ever-present premises and frames of reference of racism and sexism that persist; you think you've addressed them and now you can move on; you think "I know enough now" to escape these terms of exclusion. In those moments of deception, those moments of believing you know—you have closed down the possibility of disrupting discursive strategies. You have stopped looking for the strategic spaces that expose and possibly interrupt the construction of hierarchies of status, difference, and meaning.

Across my reading of theories related to racism and sexism, I have found that many theorists have some very clear interests in and ideas about messing up taken-for-granted relations of power, identity, and knowing. They are all committed to pedagogies that account for the absurdities, gaps, and excesses that spring up when difference is regulated by assumptions of a fixed, stable self and other.

I am interested in Butler's (1990) view, for example, that because we assume and predict a given gender, we also produce the possibility of a multiplicity of gender configurations. By our prediction we are, in effect, pointing to all of the configurations that must be kept outside and unknowable. And, she argues, our efforts to contain multiplicity requires a lot of effort that appears as repetitions. As many filmmakers and often children know, a proliferation of repetitions can become parodic and thus an exposing, destabilizing space for otherwise fixed assumptions.

In the face of silences, rationalities, and categorical exclusions, Patricia Williams (1991) and Gloria Anzaldúa (1987) use poetry, parables, and also parody to make their way through the moments of incoherence and exclusion in their daily lives. These pedagogies and strategies are deliberately constructed to create a space for the possibility of not knowing. When not knowing—as a paradox—is invited into the experience of learning, it makes it possible to explore what is supposed to be fixed, true, standard, or predictable (Ellsworth, 1997). My intention in offering the children colored construction paper was, in part, to open up a space that could not be determined, unlike the discussion we had that was premised on knowing something true and shared about racism, identity, and justice.

Given the paradox of knowing and not knowing in teaching and research, I have to see myself as always an unreliable mediator of what children believe and imagine. I have to remind myself often that what I am seeing, indeed what I am integrally involved with, is not transparent—not readily available for mediation. Nor are my ideas and imaginings transparent and available as I teach. This is work happening in each moment as I try to be aware of gaps and breaks in corrosive, exclusive strategies. It does not mean the absence of any strategies or efforts to make discrimination visible. Rather, the effort is to keep meaning in motion.

What alerts us to the numbing coolness and the smooth hand of fixed, exclusive discourses? For me it is children's statements, parading as evidence, that get split apart by bits and pieces of construction paper and drama. For children, maybe it will be another book, another take on reading or another glimpse in the direction of one another that reminds them to consider an identity in process that is "other than the already given self" (Bakhtin, 1981). In the particular site where research and teaching converge to intervene in racist, discriminatory discourses, we can look for resources such as community artists, or a walk across the street that will unfix our taken-for-granted belief that we know ourselves, the children we teach, or the histories through which we define our social relations.

CONCLUDING THOUGHTS ABOUT RESEARCH AND TEACHING THAT IS COMMITTED TO ANTIRACIST EDUCATION

I am one of many people over the decades who has tried to tell this same story, to indicate to others that it is unbearable to see children sinking or drifting away because "who they are" is so frequently and persistently discounted. I have to wonder why the story has to be told again, and whether or not it is me who should be telling it.

I think I have learned to be a better educator as I have gained a surer sense of my intention to interrupt and deny the veil of racism in schooling. Still, being there, and trying to make a difference by documenting the struggle involved in really grasping one another's possible meanings—not one another's social category—is a humbling endeavor. I know that what I am writing is never going to account for enough—enough of societal frames of reference, enough of the dynamic swirl of popular cultural images, or enough of the cultural threads that give our lives weight and meaning. And the words that capture a child's expression or energy seem too small and awkward. Words often diminish children's vitality and courage in the face of misunderstanding, denied friendships, and blunt refusals to listen. I am not sure that research articles, in their standard form, are actually going to help us express or explain the gestures, noises, and surges in classrooms that bear the rhythm of racism and discrimination. New forms of writing, art, and ways of questioning the world around us will, perhaps, be more insistent that we construct a great deal more space for more possible lives.

NOTE

1. This research was developed through the support of a Spencer Postdoctoral Fellowship 1996–1997, funded by the Spencer Foundation and the National Academy of Education.

REFERENCES

Anzaldúa, G. (1987). *Borderlands/la frontera: The new mestiza*. San Francisco: Aunt Lute Books.

Bakhtin, M. (1981). *The dialogic imagination*. M. Holquist (Ed.); C. Emerson & M. Holquist (Trans.). Austin, TX: University of Texas Press.

Ballenger, C. (1998). *Teaching other people's children*. New York: Teachers College Press.

Barrera, R. B. (1992). The cultural gap in literature-based literacy instruction. *Education and Urban Society, 24*, 227–243.

Baumann, R., & Briggs, C. (1990). Poetics and performance as critical perspectives on language and social life. *Annual Review of Anthropology, 19*, 59–88.

Bell, D. (1992). *Faces at the bottom of the well: The permanence of racism*. New York: Basic Books.

Bloome, D., & Egan-Robertson, A. (1993). The social construction of intertextuality in classroom reading and writing lessons. *Reading Research Quarterly, 28*, 304–333.

Britzman, D., Santiago-Valles, K., Jiménez-Muñoz, G., & Lamash, L. (1993). Slips that show and tell: Fashioning multiculture as a problem of representation. In C. McCarthy & W. Crichlow (Eds.), *Race identity and representation in education* (pp. 188–200). New York: Routledge.

Butler, J. (1990). *Gender trouble: Feminism and the subversion of identity*. New York: Routledge.

Cherland, M. R. (1994). *Private practices: Girls reading fiction and constructing identity*. Bristol, PA: Taylor & Francis.

Davies, B. (1993). *Shards of glass: Children reading and writing beyond gendered identities*. Cresskill, NJ: Hampton Press.

Davies, B., & Harré, R. (1990). Positioning: The discursive production of selves. *Journal for the Theory of Social Behaviour, 20*, 43–61.

Dyson, A. H. (1993). *Social worlds of children learning to write in an urban primary school*. New York: Teachers College Press.

Dyson, A. H. (1996). Cultural constellations and childhood identities: On Greek

Gods, cartoon heroes, and the social lives of schoolchildren. *Harvard Educational Review, 66*, 471–494.

Ellsworth, E. (1992). Why doesn't this feel empowering? Working through the repressive myths of critical pedagogy. In C. Luke & J. Gore (Eds.), *Feminisms and critical pedagogies,* (pp. 90–119). New York: Routledge.

Ellsworth, E. (1997). *Teaching positions: Difference, pedagogy, and the power of address.* New York: Teachers College Press.

Enciso, P. (1992). Creating the story world: A case study of a young reader's engagement strategies and stances. In J. Many & C. Cox (Eds.), *Reader stance and literary understanding: Exploring the theories, research and practice* (pp. 75–102). Norwood, NJ: Ablex.

Enciso, P. (1997). Negotiating the meaning of difference: Talking back to multicultural literature. In T. Rogers & A. Soter (Eds.), *Reading across cultures* (pp. 13–41). New York: Teachers College Press.

Enciso, P. (1998a). Good/bad girls read together: Young girls' coauthorship of subject positions during a shared reading event. *English Education, 30*, 44–62.

Enciso, P. (1998b). *Reworking reading positions among African American and European American fourth- and fifth-grade boys and girls.* Paper presented at the annual meeting of the American Educational Research Association, San Diego, CA.

Felman, S., & Laub, D. (1992). *Testimony: Crises of witnessing in literature, psychoanalysis, and history.* New York: Routledge.

Finders, M. (1997). *Just girls: Hidden literacies and life in junior high.* New York: Teachers College Press.

Gee, J. (1990). *Social linguistics and literacies: Ideology in discourse.* New York: Falmer Press.

Gallas, K. (1998). *"Sometimes I can be anything": Power, gender and identity in a primary classroom.* New York: Teachers College Press.

Herr, K. (1994). Empowerment and practitioner research: An example. In G. Anderson, K. Herr, & A. S. Nihlen (Eds.), *Studying your own school: An educator's guide to qualitative practitioner research.* Thousand Oaks, CA: Corwin Press.

Hodge, R., & Kress, G. (1993). *Language and ideology, 2nd Edition.* New York: Routledge.

Ladson-Billings, G. (1994). *The dreamkeepers: Successful teachers of African American children.* San Francisco: Jossey-Bass.

Luke, A. (1991). Literacies as social practice. *English Education, 23*, 131–147.

Lensmire, T. (1993). *When children learn to write: Critical revisions of the writing workshop.* New York: Teachers College Press.

Lewis, C. (1997). The social drama of literature discussions in a fifth/sixth-grade classroom. *Research in the Teaching of English, 31*, 163–204.

Morrison, T. (1992). *Playing in the dark: Whiteness and the literary imagination.* Cambridge, MA: Harvard University Press.

Paley, V. G. (1992). *You can't say you can't play.* Cambridge, MA: Harvard University Press.

Taylor, M. (1987). *The gold Cadillac*. New York: Dial.

Thompson, A. (1997). For: Anti-racist education. *Curriculum Inquiry, 27*, 7–44.

Tyson, C. (1998). A response to "Coloring epistemologies: Are our qualitative research epistemologies racially biased?" *Educational Researcher, 27*, 21–22.

Weis, L., & Fine, M. (1993). *Beyond silenced voices: Class, race, and gender in United States schools*. New York: State University of New York Press.

Williams, P. (1991). *The alchemy of race and rights: Diary of a law professor*. Cambridge, MA: Harvard University Press.

CHAPTER 8

Diversity Discourses: Reading Race and Ethnicity in and around Children's Writing

Colette Daiute and Hollie Jones

Social problems like racism often remain tacit in everyday interactions, even though understanding racial and ethnic conflict has been a national preoccupation in the United States for many years.[1] In fact, relatively little attention has been paid to school-aged children's public and private discourse about race and ethnicity. Our experience as readers of children's writing has involved us in work to develop strategies for "reading" discourse about issues of racial and ethnic relations.

Insightful and equitable reading of children's writing requires knowledge about the history and complexity of what we refer to as "diversity discourses." Diversity discourses are the stated or implied assumptions, expectations, and goals about social relations in oral and written language. Recognizing a statement like "they insulted your race" as a diversity discourse may seem straightforward, but such explicit statements are relatively rare in the discourse of elementary school classrooms, while implicit diversity discourse like "that's a strong statement" is more common. Failure to recognize diversity discourses in research and practice is, unfortunately, sometimes due to a desire to maintain race-based inequities, yet even educators and researchers working from a social justice perspective may read myopically because we lack theory and methodology to help us recognize unfamiliar social understandings and realize what we don't know about familiar ones.

Our attempts to improve readings of children's writing about social conflict—specifically racial and ethnic discrimination—occurs within the context of a research project designed to analyze how children and teachers in multicultural urban schools understand racial and ethnic conflicts. Toward this end, our research involved collecting writings and audio recordings of discussions by African American, Latino, and White children, and teachers in seven third and fifth grade classrooms using a literacy, ethics, and prevention program based in high-quality children's literature (Walker, 1997). This program, which involved discussing strategies for dealing with racial and ethnic conflicts described in literature as they extended to children's and teachers' own lives, seemed an appropriate context in which to learn about intergroup relations. We examined oral and written texts created in this context from several theoretical perspectives to gain insights about the complexity of children's understandings of race and ethnicity.

DISCURSIVE CONSTRUCTION OF RACE AND ETHNICITY

Some scholars have argued that children's understandings depend on whether and how they are socialized to think about race and their own racial identities more than they depend on cognitive-developmental capacities and limits (e.g., Daiute, Buteau, & Rawlins, 2001). Socialization to low- or high-race salience in homes, schools, and other contexts plays a formative role in how young people deal with crises described in racial identity theory (Cross & Fhagen-Smith, 2001), and such socialization can lead to understandings sophisticated beyond what cognitive-developmental theory predicts for school-aged children (Daiute et al., 2001). This socialization perspective is consistent with discourse theories, which provide the basis for reading the wisdom of children who have experienced racial and ethnic discrimination in their young lives.

The following text by John, a fifth grader who identified himself as "Black," was written as part of his work in the classroom literacy, ethics, and prevention program mentioned above:

> One day I was walk in the croner store and manni [manager/clerk] said get out for no resana at all so I walked out of the store and manni was walking right behid me and he tryed to hit me so he hit me and I truned a round and I punched him in the face and he stared to cry. He was feeling bad and I was not so happy me self becaues I now that I could have talked it out and not punched him. He walked away crying.

When the purpose of reading such a text is to assess it for markers of standard, edited English, readers can identify misspellings, a lack of clarity about purpose, a lack of narrative resolution, and a lack of explicitness about the protagonist's and antagonist's understandings of racial aspects of the conflict. But when we want to consider social developmental bases of instruction, we must read from a different interpretive stance, drawing on knowledge about the author's history, the context where the text was produced, contemporary issues of race and ethnicity, and awareness of our own perspectives.

We must also read for what the young author knows and for what he does not know, especially when one of the goals of reading is to create a theory of development that is sensitive and smart about creating instructional theory for students in multicultural societies. Since John wrote this story in the context of a curriculum analyzing discrimination conflicts and strategies for dealing with them, one reading of this story could be that it is a compassionate reflection on surveillance, which is all too familiar to Black males. Such a reading, however, must be considered with other readings.

Focusing on race and diversity in theme, author, or reader runs the risk of stereotyping, as one of the teachers in our research project pointed out. Our approach to the dilemma of reading diversity discourses without reducing them to stereotypes is to objectify our own research perspectives. For this reason, we have analyzed classroom discourse through multiple readings. These readings create different meanings in the focal texts— different meanings that may be echoes of one another, may be complementary or contradictory. By interpreting texts with sensitivity to different ways of expressing racial and ethnic relations, research and teaching can, in at least a small way, seek social justice in the classroom. As researchers, we have crafted a process of gaining interpretations from teachers and children in the contexts we have studied. In the end, however, we take responsibility for the integration of readings, and do our best to explain the criteria and circumstances of those integrations.

A CONTEXT FOR CONSTRUCTING RACE AND ETHNICITY

As part of an experiential curriculum implemented in two schools in a large northeastern city, seven third and fifth grade classes read and discussed two literary works about racial or ethnic discrimination in the fall and spring. The students then wrote related expository and narrative texts about social conflict, individually and with peers. High-quality literature of social conflict by authors from diverse cultural groups provided the context for discussion of racial and ethnic discrimination, literary analysis, and writing activities in these classrooms (Walker, 1997).

Our research involved gathering and analyzing program-related writings and transcripts of class discussions in the seven classrooms. The schools where the principal and teachers volunteered to implement the experimental curriculum included a Chapter One school with over 50% of the families it serves qualifying for financial assistance, and a non-Chapter One school serving children from a slightly broader range of economic backgrounds. Students came from a variety of racial and ethnic backgrounds. For the research, we gained permission to tape record program-related class discussions and program-related writings as they occurred in the context of the curriculum activities.

Our analyses of racial and ethnic relations focused on works by students who had identified themselves as belonging to one of the three major racial and ethnic groups in the city school system, who had also completed curriculum-related writing activities. From among the children who met these criteria, we randomly selected 44 individuals whose work was compiled into a database of discourse by 21 third grade and 23 fifth grade boys (20 altogether) and girls (altogether 24) working with different teachers across the African American, Latin, and White groups. This systematic selection of data allowed us to make comparisons relevant to diversity discourses.

Each social issues unit in the experimental curriculum revolved around a literary work depicting peer conflicts in a U.S. cultural setting where children and their families deal with conflicts and learn about themselves and others as they deal with discrimination conflicts. The sociocultural contexts of the stories were chosen to represent racial and ethnic groups like those of children in the study, as well as to provide diversity across the readings. Literary selections included, for example, in the third grade, *Angel Child, Dragon Child* by Michele Maria Surat (a story about verbal and physical discrimination involving a White boy and a recently immigrated Vietnamese girl), and in the fifth grade, *Mayfield Crossing* by Vaunda Michaux Nelson (a story about a group of African American children who must transfer to a White school when the only middle school in their community closes).

As outlined in a teacher's guide for each literary selection, discussion questions focused on identifying the central conflicts in the stories from different characters' perspectives about causes, resolutions, and consequences of conflicts. Writing activities were designed for students to interpret the curriculum with their own experience and included: (1) responding to literary interpretation questions, (2) collaboratively writing original endings to the literary selection, and (3) individually writing narratives about conflict experiences.

Analyses involved three phases of "reading" children's writing and classroom discourse transcripts. Grounded in different theoretical perspectives about race and ethnicity, we defined one phase of reading as "identifying race and ethnicity strategies," another phase as "reading genre," and a final phase as "reading culture." "Identifying race and ethnicity strategies" involved categorizing implicit and explicit discourse strategies. Such categorization of race and ethnicity discourse is important because much of it is implicit and has not, surprisingly, been analyzed before. "Reading genre" involved examining how those strategies occurred across teacher-led class discussions, responses to literary interpretation questions, peer literary reconstructions, and personal conflict narratives. Our third reading is where researchers often begin—and end—by analyzing texts in terms of the race and ethnicity of their authors. We called this final reading in our study "reading culture," which we applied to the personal conflict narratives. This reading was based on assumptions that people from similar race and ethnicity groups have similar ways of knowing that are expressed in their discourse.

READING RACE AND ETHNICITY DISCOURSE STRATEGIES

Previous theory and research indicating how patterns of talk and silence shape meanings suggests the need to read explicit and implied messages and to do different theory-based readings as a way of testing interpretations. Explicit discourses include words, phrases, and other objective text features expressing the focal content (Smith, Feld, & Franz, 1992), in this case race and ethnicity. Implicit discourses include text organizations, implications, and interpretive meanings marked in evaluative devices (Labov & Waletzky, 1967/1997). Based on prior research (Daiute, 1998), we expected that much of the recognition of race and ethnicity would be implicit. After one researcher generated and described the various strategies, the other independently applied these categories, and together we wrote definitions with examples of each category. With this process, we identified nine strategies of race and ethnicity discourse: Identifying, contextualizing, broadening, practicing, empathizing, universalizing, distancing, avoiding, and personalizing. We then analyzed teachers' and students' uses of these strategies as they occurred across the transcripts and written texts in the study corpus.

Identifying

The most explicit race and ethnicity discourse strategy is identifying, which involves using the terms *race* and ethnicity or other forms of these words, such as in *racism* or *ethnic groups*. Identifying also means mentioning specific groups, such as "Blacks" or "Puerto Ricans," and racial or ethnic attributes, such as skin color or language. In addition, identifying is the explicit naming of processes or issues surrounding race and ethnicity, such as "prejudice," "discrimination," the use of epithets, and acts that are explicitly related, such as "group hatred."

The following comment by a fifth grade teacher in the study mentions racism explicitly, when she says, "Who creates a racist? Is a baby born a racist?" An example of identifying from a third grade teacher's story about an experience of discrimination in her life is explicit about differences within an ethnic group: "Well, the professor, for one, had kind of told us that we were going to come across people that didn't like people from New York, especially Puerto Ricans from New York." Given this type of modeling by a teacher, it is not surprising that examples of identifying also appeared in children's writing. In response to interpretive questions about the literary selected, read, and discussed in class, one child wrote, "I learned alot from discussing this book about alienation and racism," and another wrote, "You shouldn't judge people of their skin color."

Contextualizing

Contextualizing is a race and ethnicity discourse strategy of mentioning institutional, environmental, historical, relational, or other causes of racism, prejudice, and unkind acts without explicitly labeling these *injustices*. In the following example of contextualizing, a third grade teacher in our study mentions several circumstances that may have led to a sense of entitlement among the girls who had discriminated against her many years ago:

> the other girls lived there, so they had family and friends. They just lived in the boarding house because it was closer to the university, but they actually lived in the town and the owner of the building knew their parents and were close friends, and the owner of the building said, we got there later than they did, they had been there already. We came in October, so we had to leave.

In this comment, the teacher offers several context-related reasons for her being asked to leave the boarding house, when she says "the owner of the building knew their parents and were close friends" and "the owner of the building said we got there later and they had been there already." These reasons are grounded in the entitlement of the local Puerto Rican girls— knowing the owner, being from the place, and thus being in the house first. Although she did not explicitly call the owner of the building a racist, the teacher offered historical and cultural information that she suggests led to excluding the New York Puerto Ricans in favor of the locals.

Children's contextualizing strategies typically involved using geographic location to represent group membership, as in the following example: "Raymond teases Hoa because she comes from Vietnam and she wears like almost pajamas." But social processes were also mentioned in narrative dialogue, such as, "Just because you went to school here first doesn't mean you own it!"

Broadening

Broadening is a discourse strategy that mentions race and ethnicity via synonyms for difference, such as "newcomer" and "outside looks," or descriptions of circumstances of difference, such as "immigrant," "speaking a different language," "wearing unfamiliar clothing," or consequences of difference as occurs in the attribution of conflicts to those who are different. The following is an interactive example of broadening related to a character in *Angel Child, Dragon Child*, a literary selection the class is studying. As the teacher prompts the children to explain why the main character Hoa is sad, children refer to her as "pajamas," which is how the antagonist in the story, Raymond, refers to Hoa's ethnic clothing:

> CHILD: And a red-haired boy, they call her, she misses her Mom, and a red-haired boy calls her "pajamas."
> TEACHER: Okay, this red-haired boy teases her?
> CHILD: Yea, and called her "pajamas."
> TEACHER: Pajamas, because of ah, *ao dai*, that's what she's wearing, right?

Later, as the children expand their attention to intergroup conflict, the teacher implies that their language is too strong.

> CHILD: Then Hoa, Hoa and the boy hate each other.
> TEACHER: Okay, well hate is a powerful word.
> CHILDREN: They don't like each other.
> TEACHER: Okay, dislike each other, good. What is some of the things that the author uses to tell you that?

The teacher's comment could reflect her judgment that the events in the book might not warrant a description as strong as "hate" or that she does not think such language is appropriate in classroom talk. Later, in this discussion, the teacher seems to identify implicit racism in a child's statement: "Raymond thought it was not right for them to . . . spoil the country with their clothing." These examples illustrate teacher and student interactions addressing race and ethnicity with synonyms for physical characteristics and actions. Broadening is thus another relatively implicit classroom discourse strategy for opening up the potentially sensitive analysis of discrimination as it relates to other curricula, in this case literary analysis of character motivation.

Practicing

Practicing is a strategy particularly common to children's discourse, which is not surprising since children often approach intellectual work with concrete examples rather than abstract analysis. Practicing involves using language associated with a particular group rather than naming the group, as in "She thinks she's all that"; and "Don't fight unless you have to protect yourself." "She's all that" is often used by African American youth to refer to someone who is conceited.

Empathizing

Empathizing is a strategy that focuses on the psychosocial consequences of difference or discrimination. Since the curriculum was based on addressing social conflict via perspective-taking, it makes sense that teachers' use of the empathizing strategy was frequent and dramatic. In the following interaction, an experienced fifth grade teacher who identified herself as Italian American brought the characters' feelings in the face of discrimination to life.

> TEACHER: I want you to really think about your being, come on, you know when you do that you always say to me that when you're reading you try to think about how the character feels. You connect to the story. You say, "I think about you," you know you say, "I relate to the character." Do that, don't just yell out, "Saaaaaad, baaaaaad." Okay, Zinna?
>
> CHILD: Terrible.
>
> TEACHER: She feels terrible, and what's terrible?
>
> CHILD: It means like both of them, like bad and sad.
>
> TEACHER: Sad and bad put together equals terrible? That's a—
>
> CHILD: Kinda.
>
> TEACHER: Kinda? Okay, Siandra?
>
> CHILD: Depressed.
>
> TEACHER: Yeah, that's a great [word missing] word. You think she feels a little depressed? She starts think about.

Empathizing has a subtle but important relation to racial and ethnic discrimination, since it states feelings that could result from exclusionary or discriminatory interactions. In our study, empathizing was a preferred strategy of children, as well as of teachers, and boys became increasingly empathetic in the discursive representation across the school year.

Universalizing

Universalizing involves generalizing beyond issues of difference to broader human values. Universalizing often invokes values like "love thy neighbor" without reference to specific histories and interactions that have made it difficult for neighbors to acknowledge each other's presence, let alone love each other.

As noted by other scholars (Enciso, 1997; Gates, 1992; Morrison, 1992), embedding racial and ethnic issues as though they were the same as any interpersonal relation is a strategy particularly common to Whites or others in power. Expressing a universal perspective on conflict, a third grade teacher counseled her students, "If you just take the time to talk it out, you can always work out your differences," without reference to issues of race or ethnicity, which may make discussion and resolution difficult or impossible. Another fifth grade teacher emphasized universal human similarity over racial and ethnic differences that may be captured in appearance, when she said, "We're all the same, no matter what we look like."

Although children typically talk in specifics, they also expressed universal moral discourses that do not acknowledge race and ethnicity issues: "We're all the same"; "Treat everyone the same no matter what"; "Treat all people with respect and as you would want to be treated"; "Everybody should get along with everybody else." Such comments are inclusive and ethical, reflecting a mainstream U.S. morality, but they could also be interpreted as masking the real and prevalent issues of racism that occur in this country. Recent developmental research indicates that school-aged children distinguish issues in intergroup conflict from broad human values (Turiel, 2002).

Distancing

Distancing is a strategy that belies attempts at self-justification or self-protection, referred to as "buffering" by Cross and Strauss (1998). Distancing emphasizes difference just as universalizing emphasizes similarity. For example, in the following comment, a teacher observes that it takes time to become friends and that relationships take work. In this way, the teacher resists the idea that all conflict is the same and that all conflict can be resolved via talking. Just as universalizing may be a common strategy of those in groups who have not experienced much discrimination, distancing may be borne of painful discrimination experiences (Cross & Strauss, 1998). What is being resisted is, in short, the tendency to mask racial and ethnic discrimination in generalizations.

> TEACHER: And how is Raymond reacting to her now?
> CHILD: Ah, nice.
> TEACHER: Okay, he's being a little bit more accepting?
> CHILD: Yeah.
> TEACHER: You think they're going to become best friends? Okay, now becoming best friends is that something that happens right away?
> CHILDREN: No.
> TEACHER: No, it takes some time, yes?
> (Intervening comments)
> TEACHER: Now they're not friends.
> CHILDREN: Some say friends, some say close.
> TEACHER: At least they are communicating with each other, yes?
> CHILD: I communicate with everybody except with my brother.
> TEACHER: Okay, then you need to work on that relationship with your brother, yes? Uh-huh (laughs) because that's not everybody and family is most important. Okay, now they need to work on their relationship.

Children also use the distancing strategy, as in, "Don't do what they want. Don't hate because they want you to be ugly like them"; and "Words can't hurt if you say they're not true." Children use this relatively subtle strategy across genres.

Avoiding

Avoiding is a strategy in teacher-led discussions that involves denying that race and ethnicity are factors or never directly discussing race, ethnicity, or discrimination in a context where it was an explicit theme, such as in a curriculum or literature related to the curriculum. One example of avoiding comes from children's responses to literary interpretation questions, such as the comments, "I have not learned anything"; "Everybody should just get along very good." An example of avoidance that contradicts the goals of the curriculum is a fifth grade teacher's comment, "In multicultural contexts, kids don't worry about race. They just deal with kids based on whether they get along."

Personalizing

Personalizing is a strategy based primarily in personal experience, such as, "it happened to me." This occurs mostly by children who state it quite literally, as in this comment by a grade student involved in a fifth grade class discussing discrimination in the book *Mayfield Crossing*: "I know it's true because it happened to me."

These strategies occurred differently across genres and participants.

READING GENRE

After identifying the nine race and ethnicity discourse strategies in our sample of classroom discourse, we examined how these nine strategies occurred across the different forms of classroom discourse we had available: transcripts of teacher-led class discussions, children's written responses to literary interpretation questions, and children's written narratives.

We define *genre* as social interaction embodied in discourse (Cope & Kalantzis, 1993). Rather than serving as a mere carrier of meaning or a specific text format, this sociocultural notion of genre defines texts as specific moments in social relations occurring across time, situations, and participants. Genres are infused with the cultures and sociopolitical relations where they occur. This notion of genre, thus, means that interpreting a transcript of individual pieces of writing like teacher-led class discussions means paying attention to power relations, such as the purposes and values promoted by the teacher. Whether stated or not, values like "all conflicts can be resolved if you try hard enough" have a powerful influence in framing children's expressions and sometimes even their memories of personal experiences.

Readings that conceptualize genre in this way acknowledge that what participants say or write in one situation is not necessarily what they say or write in another situation. Such variation occurs because of the interaction between messages about race and ethnicity stated or implied in assignments, participants' interpretations of these assignments, and messages from other aspects of their lives. If different genres constitute different social relations, then an analysis of children's and teachers' understandings of race and ethnicity must include a range of genres. Children's mimicry of curriculum values in teacher-led class discussions compared to their questioning of those values during peer interactions (Daiute, Stern, & Lelutiu-Weinberger, in press), for example, suggests that there may well be differences in how children understand race and ethnicity across different written genres.

Our analysis showed that the race and ethnicity strategies defined above differed dramatically across genres. In particular, children addressed issues of race and ethnicity more explicitly in their responses to literary interpretation questions than in literary reconstructions or in personal conflict narratives. Moreover, literary reconstructions addressed issues of race and ethnicity with a number of relatively explicit strategies, while the conflict narratives focused on other issues. Teachers tended to extend race and ethnicity representations over the course of class discussions as they tried to integrate students' comments into their own representational strategies. In this process, most teachers expressed race and ethnicity in terms of empathizing, but they differed in whether and how they used other strategies.

Teacher-Led Class Discussions

Empathy was the most common strategy when leading class discussions, used by six of the seven teachers. Engaging children to imagine, model, and reflect upon how characters in literature and participants in personal conflicts thought and felt about issues of race and ethnicity was consistent with the perspective coordination theme in the curriculum. Empathizing is also a value in U.S. culture and one that is typically used as a basis of mainstream education, where morality has for a long time been grounded in "do unto others as you would have done unto you." Multicultural education has, in part, extended this somewhat myopic perspective to something like "find out and keep in mind what others think or need, which may differ from your view of the world."

Four teachers expanded beyond interpersonal relations to intergroup relations, defining groups in terms of "difference" and national status; and four addressed racial and ethnic intergroup relations directly. A few mentioned universal values and context. Attesting to diversity by individual participants, all the teachers avoided racial and ethnic conceptualizations at some point, even though most teachers also used some other identification strategy. Thus, while a teacher might have cited racism in relation to a specific character or situation, she also might have refused to make race and ethnicity an all-encompassing factor in conflicts.

Identifying and broadening were the next most frequent strategies among the teachers, indicating that four of the seven teachers in this group explicitly discussed issues of race and ethnicity, as was appropriate given the literature and the curriculum, and four broadened to other ways of describing cultural differences like "newcomer," "different," "looks," etcetera.

Interestingly, two teachers used identifying and universalizing discourse, but none of the teachers who identified issues of race and ethnicity explicitly organized the class discussion in ways that we coded as avoiding. Discussing the causes and injustices of racism explicitly, for example, co-occurred with discussions about universal values of treating everyone the same no matter what. Some teachers found a way, for example, to deal with racial and ethnic discrimination by considering how specific characters felt about issues of difference, which were named in terms of national or geographic status rather than race, ethnicity, or skin color.

Avoiding was the only strategy used uniquely by a teacher. This teacher worked with the literature and curriculum in a way that focused exclusively (in the transcripts we examined) on issues of language, writing process, and reading strategy. Instead of discussing the content of characters' racist comments, this teacher engaged children in generating adjectives and identifying plot structure.

This range of orientations to race and ethnicity by a culturally diverse group of teachers is consistent with teacher research, indicating that working with students on intergroup relations reveals the sociopolitical nature of teaching across subjects (Freedman, Simons, Kalnin, Casareno, & The M-Class Teams, 1999).

Children's Responses to Literary Interpretation Questions

To examine how children represented race and ethnicity in an expository mode, we collected responses to 176 literary interpretation questions by the 44 children whose work we examined for this study. Among children's responses to the literary interpretation questions about literature, the most frequent strategy was practicing, expressed in 19 of the 44 examples. The next most frequent strategy was universalizing, in 13 of the 44 examples, followed by 9 examples of identifying, the explicit mention of race and ethnicity. Instances of broadening and distancing were the next most frequent approaches, at 8 mentions each. Although more than one race and ethnicity discourse strategy could occur in a response, children tended to address a question in one way or sometimes with two strategies.

When the questions probed their thinking about injustice and racial and ethnic identity explicitly, children tended to mention issues of race and ethnicity most explicitly—as identifying, contextualizing, and broadening. This was particularly true in the question, "Why did Raymond tease Hoa?" in the third grade literary selection *Angel Child, Dragon Child*—and response: "Because she comes from vietnam [sic] and she wears like allmost like pajamas and she talk vietnamese." The prompt following the fifth grade selection *Mayfield Crossing* also tended to elicit relatively explicit discussion of race and ethnicity. Another example of a question that tended to elicit the more explicit discussion of race and ethnicity was the following: "After the fight with Clayton," Meg thinks, "People always say words can't hurt you, but that isn't true. They can hurt worse than a punch in the eye" (p. 67). What does Meg mean? Do you agree with her? Why or why not?

Reading Culture in Written Narratives

Our third reading was organized in the way that much research interested in race and ethnicity is organized—around the race and ethnicity of the participants. When the race and ethnicity of the participant is the primary (or only) organizing factor for analyses, the assumption is that differences across texts will be caused by differences across the racial and ethnic groups. For the readings presented above, we have already seen how race and ethnicity discourse can vary in relation to discourse context, but we now present a more traditional analysis to learn about whether and how children's racial and ethnic backgrounds may point to differences in the ways they describe social conflict. Analyzing whether and how children identifying as African American, Latino, or White describe social conflicts in terms of race and ethnicity is based on the assumption that children from different groups would have experienced racial or ethnic discrimination differently. Given our previous analyses, however, we entered this examination with the awareness that racial and ethnic discrimination experienced by children from African American, Latino, and White backgrounds would interact with the context, such as many of the teachers' tendency toward universalizing and empathizing discourses and children's penchant for practicing race and ethnicity.

As part of their work in the curriculum, children wrote autobiographical narratives and, since this narrative task involved extended, individual writing, it was appropriate for readings based on the individual child's stated racial and ethnic background. The prompt for this writing activity mentioned conflict but not racial and ethnic issues: "Write a story about a time when you or someone you know had a conflict or disagreement with someone your age. What happened? How did the people involved feel? How did it all turn out?"

Our initial finding was that the narratives made little or no explicit reference to race and ethnicity, so we examined them to identify characteristic ways of knowing that organized the story.

The theory behind this phase of analysis was that socialization into race and ethnicity groups occurs through verbal and non-verbal discourse (Vygotsky, 1978). This method of reading commonalties in discourse by racial or ethnic group assumes that children internalize racial and ethnic belief systems and discourse patterns. The values, practices, and expectations underlying the narrator's shaping of characters' motivations and actions can be represented, at least in part, as social systems.

This analysis revealed dramatically different representations of social-relational structures and social conflicts across stories by African American, Latin, and White children. The narratives about personal experiences described a range of conflicts, from fights about toys to debates about fairness in jump rope games, to emotional appeals about exclusivity in friendships, and intense reflections on physical and psychological bias. In turn, we found differences in how African American, Latino, and White children organized social systems in their personal conflict narratives. In particular, these groups of children created individual/society relationships that differed in terms of how individuals depended on social systems and in terms of individuals' personal responsibility to others as well as to oneself.

The possibility that racial and ethnic background would shape children's narratives in subtle but profound ways had been observed previously; therefore, we expected to see some similarities. Nevertheless, we hoped that differences would not be so pronounced—given the heterogeneous nature of the schools in the study, the explicit instruction toward perspective-taking and conflict-resolution strategies, and the opportunity for multiple writing experiences.

SOCIAL CONFLICTS EMBEDDED IN SYSTEMS
OF RIGHTS AND RESPONSIBILITIES

Rather than expressing conflicts as fights between individuals, African American children tended to present conflicts among characters in terms of social contingencies, like rights and responsibilities. Conflict participants, including the author, tend to operate in social systems beyond their interpersonal interactions. Embedding conflict in social systems sometimes meant describing the rules that were broken or created in interpersonal conflicts, sometimes meant characters appealed to authorities like parents, teachers, or older kids, and sometimes meant the author reflected on the moral or justice significance of interactions in the story. These stories organized in terms of social systems also often, interestingly, depicted multiple points of view within the story and sometimes self-critique.

The following story, written by a boy in third grade who identified himself as African American illustrates how this process operates.

The Bike Fight

One day me and my friend had an argument. We had an argument about my bike. He alwaysed hoged it allot and I never got to ride it.

Since I never got to ride it we made a time schechuite. He had it outside for 1 hour and I had it for 1 hour.

In this story, the author assumes a solution where he and his antagonist will both have access to the resource (his bike), and he comes up with an institutional solution—a schedule—to mediate conflicting desires for the bikes. The author acknowledges the differing perspectives, stating that his friend "hoged" the bike and the injustice that he, the author, "never got to ride it," but he distributes justice to both needs.

In other stories, authors represent the conflict in terms of their own responsibility which is often self-reflective or self-critical, such as, "But I can't believe that I did not say I'ame sorry. But I felt bad I konw she fet bad to. So I jest had to stop. I could not go on."

The following example shows how author responsibility involved expressing the point of view of an antagonistic character. A story by a girl in the third grade who identified herself as Black included the following dialogue: "My friend said 'You always get what you want' and [that] whatever I say has got to be done. That's not even true though, so she [my friend] said, 'This time I'm not listening to you.'" After apologizing, the author described what the girls did and concluded her story by saying, "It sure was fun doing it her way for a change."

Conflicts as Interactive Bonding

Conflict stories by Latino authors tended to focus on relationship issues, with conflicts represented as conversations among participants around issues like bonding, betrayal, and devotion. The process characteristically offers a back-and-forth description with verbal elements prominent and tending to end with the participants being friends again. The interactive process seems to constitute a resolution process rather than requiring an appeal to mediations outside what are typically presented as dyads. Interpersonal resolutions seem consistent with the conflicts since the issues are often interpersonal rather than intergroup.

For example, in the following story, the author and her best friend Jimmy engage in reciprocal pushing, getting mad, name calling, stopping, saying sorry, and picking each other up.

Fight with my Friend

One day Jimmy. Jimmy was Best Friend but now he my Best Friend Because he push me into the mud and I Push him water. and then we got Mad and called each other names he call me bad girl and I call him Pig. So we got into a Big Fight he Bushed me and I Push. and

Bused him so then we stop each other and said Sorry. and then I pick him he pick me up So then we Became Best Friend agin.

In addition to representing reciprocal actions, young Latino authors also tended to solve conflicts through reciprocal interaction rather than through a separate and mediated resolution process, as tended to occur in the conflict narratives by African American children.

The Phone Call

One day I went to my Friend's house and her other Friend made a phone call to a girl that we were all mad at. The girl said you are such a slut and a damn dog then she hung up. Then the girl that we called, called me in the park and told me why did you call me that and I told her I didnt call her that I was so mad because the girl that I went to her house told the girl that was acusing me in the part that it was me when it was her friend. After that I went home. The next say the girl said sorry and we became friends.

Social Conflicts at a Distance

Conflict stories by authors who identified themselves as White tended to situate the conflict outside the author, although the authors were represented as participants in a variety of ways. This perspective is conveyed in several ways: (1) authors were often portrayed as victims of someone else's aggression, misunderstanding about an accident; (2) authors play the role of fixer or judge; (3) authors take an analytic or curriculum-based approach to resolving the conflict; and (4) authors tell stories from the distance of time or emotion.

The following story by a White girl in another class offers an elaborate description of the problem, its development over time, and the resolution. Although elaborate in some ways, the author situates herself as the first-person participant in the conflict at a social distance from her interlocutor.

Secrets

A while ago my friend Nicole and I had a fight that was larger than life, it was all about secrets. You see Nicole liked to take people over and tell them secrets in fron and about every one else. For a while this was okay, but soon it got out of hand, Nicole was telling more secrete thant he entire population of Japan could in a year. If nobody was going to stop her I would! I felt as though I was carrying the world on my shoulders, but I told her calmly how I felt and she appeared to listen. I found out a couple of weeks later that she was acting, she was at it again, secrets, secrets, secrets, everywhere you looked, secrets, and Nicols behind each of there front doors. I coulnd't take it anymore! Then ony day Hannah told me about a really bad secret about me. I blew up right in her face, I made her promise never to tell a secret again, and she didn't for awhile.

The author describes Nicole as the perpetrator of the conflict and situates the problem in Nicole to the point where "secrets" seems to symbolize Nicole. The author describes her own reaction indirectly, saying "it got out of hand." In turn, she depicts her involvement as taking the situation under control, pointing out that, "If nobody was going to stop her I would!" This intervention is described as one of teaching Nicole rather than working with her to exchange views about the problem or work out a social resolution. The author's reflection ("I thought I was carrying the world on my shoulders") in fact characterizes the similarity we found across the texts by the White children on this task.

These cultural readings have identified dominant social discourses by assuming similarity within groups and diversity across groups. The particular patterns we have identified are, however, unique and focused specifically on social relational issues.

CONSEQUENCES OF READING RACE AS TEXT

We have tried to subordinate any single analysis on how race and ethnicity are discussed in elementary school classrooms by imposing several different theoretical frames on the texts we have examined. In this way, we identified different ways of explaining conflict and offer these insights to urge other researchers and teachers to provide a range of contexts and supports for discussions about racial and ethnic conflict.

Our work for this chapter has, moreover, affected our knowledge about research in addition to yielding some insights about the complexity of children's understandings of discrimination conflicts. Focusing on literacy through the lens of racial and ethnic discourses has offered several ways to probe for social issues in classroom contexts where racial and ethnic conflicts were the subject of inquiry in and around literacy activities. Our approach to figuring race and ethnicity into literacy research has transformed our own understandings.

As a young African American woman from a working-class background, I (Hollie Jones) was raised in a household that was very "race conscious." In my youth, I was socialized to embrace the idea that the past and present actions of those at the top of the racial and ethnic hierarchy were responsible, in part, for the lack of resources and opportunities afforded many ethnic minority communities. I have not had difficulty discussing the issue of race or naming racism or ethnocentrism when I see it. Early in my graduate career I realized that the recognition of social and cultural norms and the location of individuals, and groups, in relation to these norms must undergird my scholarly work on the psychology of race and ethnicity. My research into racial and ethnic issues and identity has led me to question my own role as an African American researcher.

While analyzing the children's narratives by ethnic group, I realized that it was impossible to separate the political and the subjective from the research task. I thought very deeply about how my own personal experiences, history, biases, and interests influence the interpretation of data and what data I felt were "most" valuable. I found myself looking for explicit examples of children's understandings and naming of race and ethnicity. Because I was raised in a household that was politicized, and sometimes polarized around these issues, I expected to find explicit identification of these issues and mention of racial and ethnic discrimination by the African American and Latino children in the study. I did not have the same expectations for the White participants.

As the study progressed, I moved my expectations beyond my own experience and focused on implicit differences among the groups. I realized that children's discussion of racial and ethnic issues is not always explicit; understandings of race and ethnicity can appear in more subtle or implicit forms and not all ethnic or racial minority children are politicized around these issues. Some ethnic minority children may avoid discussing their experiences with race and ethnicity as a way of resisting the dominant discourse that says they will be disadvantaged by virtue of their group membership, or they may not see themselves or their ethnic or racial group as being disadvantaged. I had a personal stake in hoping that the African American and Latino students would explicitly discuss race and ethnicity and related experiences. This expectation was based on my belief that children and adults' recognition of disadvantage and racial and ethnic discrimination can hasten the action we are willing to take to end unfair practices. A great deal of knowledge can be gained from children's understandings and experiences with race and ethnicity from those groups who experience racial and ethnic disadvantage and privilege.

Throughout the study I also struggled with wanting to recognize and focus on in-group differences. As in psychology and other disciplines, there has typically been a problem with essentializng group differences. As such, I found myself wanting to focus on the diversity of experience and narrative within each racial and ethnic group and questioning whose knowledge and representations would be held forth and privileged. In order to recognize the diversity of experiences within racial and ethnic groups, one necessarily needs to incorporate a more complex analysis into such a complicated topic. For despite their similarities, racial and ethnic group dynamics are mediated by socioeconomic and gender factors and are continually being reshaped and readjusted.

For me (Colette Daiute), this process has been one of foregrounding and backgrounding personal issues of ethnicity and class in relation to participation in diverse multicultural communities. As for many European Americans, my ethnic awareness grew, at least in part, through insights from the Black power movement. Understanding of and by White ethnics in my own Irish and Italian traditions is an ongoing learning process that has been enriched by teaching and research. In particular, a personal process of racial and ethnic identity has continued to evolve through evaluating my qualifications as a teacher—first as a teacher of writing and English and then as a professor of psychology with students from mostly African American and Latino backgrounds. A question by the director of my first teaching job is a constant reminder about the importance of perspective-taking: "How can you as a White woman reach and teach these students of color?" My response was that we, especially I, would have to work hard to understand and to communicate, although just how people with different social histories do that is the subject of intense inquiry even today and in this volume. This process has revolved around the dilemma of recognizing the need to express and maintain cultural differences, which I continue to learn from my students and research participants, and hoping for universality.

The discussions with teachers in our project resonated with this range of feelings. One middle-aged White teacher said that the kids were "not as obsessed with racial and ethnic difference" as we made them with the curriculum and that being a person of color is privileged over being from an ethnic group. An African American teacher, on the other hand, was worried that reading, talking, and writing about racial and ethnic discrimination could happen too early in the life of a child, especially a Black child, who would have to live that reality forever. Somewhere between these extreme cautions about the role of race and ethnicity in children's lives as refracted through our differently seasoned perspectives was the view of another teacher who said we're always the same and always different. Questioning our views through research with different readings can help us with the difficult task of recognizing similarity and difference and learning about when each is important. By examining the group narrative patterns, which I resisted as a form of stereotyping, I experienced how deeply historical White entitlement is and how mature are the reflections of a child who internalizes her parents' and grandparents' experiences to recent personal experiences of discrimination. At the same time, each group pattern incorporated in its own way the designs of the curriculum toward moving from the unexamined social orientation. The experience that being a good reader means being bold yet humble is the lesson from this study—bold enough to take a stand about what one expects to hear and bold enough to read for what we don't want to hear, and humble enough to accept that these multiple readings offer complexity.

Finally, and most importantly, we hope that the consequences for the other participants in the study have been served by getting several hearings about their ideas and feelings. If we have been able to explain a process of reading for diversity and if this makes sense to our readers, we think that the interpretive enterprise that has offered so much play to experienced authors may benefit child authors and their teachers with having voices that express complex identities and resist simplification to stereotypes. For the teachers who invited us into their classrooms, these readings are also inspired by their patience with the process of teaching the relatively new subject matter of social issues and nurturing growth in their students, themselves, and the researchers looking over their shoulders by accepting their role as authorities without expecting it to be an easy job.

CONCLUSION

The readings presented in this chapter illustrate how children represent race and ethnicity in a variety of ways, depending on their backgrounds and on specific discourse contexts. Readings that assumed children's racial and ethnic backgrounds would shape their description of social conflicts did in fact yield dramatically different ways of organizing social analysis. Although these 7- to 10-year-old children tended to describe conflicts around interpersonal rather than intergroup issues, children echoed group perspectives on race and ethnicity in the ways that they described social conflicts. Organizations of social relations in conflict narratives across the groups differed strikingly in terms of the interdependence among participants in the narratives rather than in what they said about race and ethnicity. In contrast, readings across genres indicated that the same children who embedded racial and ethnic knowledge in the organization of personal conflict stories wrote explicitly about race and ethnicity when asked to do so.

We propose that children create racial and ethnic categories interactively. Children need opportunities to explore and to transform historically scripted orientations into their own hopeful orientations for future inter-group relations. Reading, writing, and talk in the classroom can play a formative role in such transformations, and these need to be supported by activities over a long time. Equally important is the implication that re-searchers and teachers must be aware of how our readings of race as text can construct identities for others.

By reading race as a text, one is given a glimpse of how it is repre-sented by complex discursive constructions and practices. Furthermore, it shows how "language use signifies the difference between cultures and pos-sessions of power, thereby spelling the difference between subordinate and superordinate, and between bondsman and lord" (Gates, 1992, p. 51).

NOTE

1. The research reported on in this chapter was supported in part by the Wil-liam T. Grant Foundation.

REFERENCES

Billig, M. (1997). The dialogic unconscious: Psychoanalysis, discursive psychology, and the nature of repression. *British Journal of Social Psychology, 36,* 139–159.

Bogdan, R., & Biklen, S. (1992). *Qualitative research for education: An introduc-tion.* Boston: Allyn & Bacon.

Cope, B., & Kalantzis, M. (Eds.). (1993). *The powers of literacy: A genre approach to teaching writing.* Pittsburgh, PA: University of Pittsburgh Press.

Cross, W. E., & Strauss, L. (1998). The everyday functions of African American identity. In J. Swim & C. Stangor (Eds.), *Prejudice: The targets perspective* (pp. 268–278). New York: Academic Press.

Cross, W. E., Jr., & Fhagen-Smith, P. (2001). Patterns of African American identity development: A life space perspective. In C. L. Wijeyesinghe & B. W. Jackson (Eds.), *New perspectives on racial identity development: A theoretical and practical anthology* (pp. 243–270). New York: New York University Press.

Daiute, C. (1998). Points of view in children's writing. *Language Arts, 75,* 138–149.

Daiute, C. (2000). Youths' construction of social consciousness. In M. Fine & L. Weis (Eds.), *Construction sites: Excavating class, race, gender, and sexual-ity among urban youth* (pp. 211–234). New York: Teachers College Press.

Daiute, C., Buteau, E., & Rawlins, C. (2001). Social-relational wisdom: Develop-mental diversity in children's written narratives about social conflict. *Narra-tive Inquiry, 11,* 1–30.

Daiute, C., Stern, R., & Lelutiu-Weinberger, C. (in press). Negotiating violence prevention. *Journal of Social Issues*.

Enciso, P. E. (1997). Negotiating the meaning of difference: Talking back to multicultural literature. In T. Rogers & A. O. Soter (Eds.), *Reading across cultures: Teaching literature in a diverse society* (pp. 13–41). New York: Teachers College Press.

Freedman, S., Simons, E., Kalnin, J., Casareno, A., & The M-Class Teams (1999). *Inside city schools: Investigating literacy in multicultural classrooms*. New York: Teachers College Press.

Gates, H. L. (1992). *Loose canons: Notes on the culture wars*. New York: Oxford University Press.

Labov, W., & Waletzky, J. (1997). Narrative analysis: Oral versions of personal experience. *Journal of Narrative and Life History, 7*. (Original work published 1967)

Morrison, T. (1992). *Playing in the dark: Whiteness and the literary imagination*. New York: Random House.

Rogers, T., & Soter, A. O. (Eds.). (1997). *Reading across cultures: Teaching literature in a diverse society*. New York: Teachers College Press.

Smith, C. P., Feld, S. C., & Franz, C. E. (1992). Methodological considerations: Steps in employing research content analysis systems. In C. P. Smith, J. W. Atkinson, D. C. McClelland, V. Joseph (Eds.), *Motivation and personality: Handbook of thematic content analysis*. New York: Cambridge University Press.

Turiel, E. (2002). *The culture of morality: Social development, context, and conflict*. New York: Cambridge University Press.

Vygotsky, L. (1978). *Mind in society* (M. Cole & S. Scribner, Trans.). Cambridge, MA: Harvard University Press.

Walker, P. (1997). *Introduction to voices of love and freedom*. IA: Prescription Learning.

Afterword

Sonia Nieto

Between 1882 and 1968, an estimated 4,742 Blacks (mostly men, but also a small number of women) were lynched in the United States (Allen, Als, Lewis, & Litwack, 2000). Chattel slavery, legally abolished in 1863, mutated into other forms of inhumanity—including Jim Crow segregation—toward people of African descent. And although purposeful segregation by race is now legally prohibited, it is nevertheless still obvious in all areas of life from housing to health care to education (Crenshaw et al., 1995; Orfield, 2001). Numerous other situations in United States history are emblematic of a racist past, a past that continues into the present. The genocide of Native Americans is a graphic example of exploitation, as is the fact that from the 18th to the 20th centuries, the federal government appropriated millions of acres of land, first from Native Americans and later from Mexicans, effectively stripping the people who lived on those lands of their political and human rights (Spring, 2000). And at the close of the 19th century, imperialism became a fact of life in our country as lands populated by non-Europeans—including the Philippines, Puerto Rico, Hawaii, and Alaska—were either "purchased" from other colonizers, "liberated," or won as spoils of war (Wei & Kamel, 1998). Whatever the method, lands that had not previously been part of the United States were seized and colonized, and some remain so today.

Given this woeful history, proclamations characterizing the United States as a land of unbridled opportunity and equality for all ring hollow. A recent case in point took place in November 2002, when Senator Trent Lott, at a party celebrating the 100th birthday of Senator Strom Thurmond, grew misty-eyed about the fact that Thurmond had lost his bid for the 1948 presidency. But because Thurmond, a staunch segregationist, had become an embarrassing reminder of a past steeped in White supremacy and blatant institutionalized racism, President George Bush quickly repudiated Lott's comments. Bush was forceful in his rebuttal, saying, "Recent comments by Senator Lott do not reflect the spirit of our country . . . Every day that our nation was segregated was unfaithful to our founding ideals" (Sammon, 2002). Bush went on to say that "any suggestion that the segregated past is acceptable or positive is offensive and it is wrong" (Cameron, 2002). Although these words were reported in the media as a vigorous refutation of racism, they can be read instead as an attempt to whitewash a shameful history of racism, a history all too evident even today. Bush's words helped to uphold the historic amnesia so crucial to perpetuating the myth of colorblindness.

In fact, it is some of the founding ideals to which Bush referred that have helped to sustain inequality and racism. For instance, no less venerable a document than the U.S. Constitution, often lauded as the epitome of equality and freedom, set the framework for preserving and protecting the institution of slavery by counting each enslaved African as three-fifths of a person. Yet in his statements, nowhere did Bush mention how some groups of people have historically benefited from institutionalized racism, or how the unpaid labor of Blacks and the low-paid labor of immigrants built our nation. Nowhere was there an acknowledgment that racism is not an aberration, but rather built into the fabric of our society, or that it is a problem that has yet to be solved. In reality, rather than a slur on a heroic past, Lott's statements reflected a reprehensible history of inequality and racism.

Given this reality, it is reasonable to ask just how research about literacy can lead to racial understanding. It seems naïve, even disingenuous, to believe that research on literacy can make a difference in any appreciable way. The task seems too overwhelming, and to enlist university researchers and classroom teachers in righting the wrongs of racial inequality seems such a small step. Perhaps it is for just this reason that *Making Race Visible* is such a welcome addition to a field that is often loathe to take on political issues in any direct way. Yet turning a critical eye on those areas of life where power resides is exactly what needs to be done, and research on literacy is as good a place to begin as any. We could conceivably begin the journey for racial understanding in the areas of housing or health care or justice; these are all places where people in our society are racialized and, based on that racialization, disenfranchised and disempowered. As educators, we need to begin where we are, and literacy is at the center of what many of us do, no matter what we teach.

While many people in academia want to talk about race (the achievement gap, the growing segregation in schools, affirmative action in higher education), few want to talk about racism. This is not surprising. Why bring up the issues that led to the achievement gap, segregation, or to the need for affirmative action in the first place? Somehow, these problems are approached as if they just "happened," as if they came to us fullblown, for no apparent reason. As a result, most discussions concerning race in education are focused on the need to fix the symptoms of the problem. This is one reason that *Making Race Visible* is a welcome contribution to the field. The editors and authors of this volume insist on speaking the unspeakable: They argue that racism is part and parcel of our society, and that it is deeply embedded in all our institutions' policies and practices. And they maintain that this situation did not happen overnight but instead was created from the very roots of our history.

As Gloria Ladson-Billings correctly points out in the Foreword, in our nation literacy has been a core symbol of power and prestige, as well as a major gateway out of poverty for many. At the same time, literacy has frequently been withheld from the least powerful. This situation is obvious in the so-called achievement gap, a gap that was closing during the 1970s when some attention (and money) were being focused on equal educational opportunity. The gap is now greater than ever, and it is most obvious in the area of literacy: Today, the average 12th grade low-income student of color reads at the same level as the average 8th grade middle-class White student (Kahlenberg, 2000). Unless we hold to the belief that genetics or culture are to blame for this discrepancy, we must turn to an exploration of racism to help guide us in solving this problem.

This book adds a significant dimension to the conversation about literacy, social justice, and racism in our nation. As you have seen throughout the chapters, the authors and editors all strive to make racism and privilege visible, whether it is in their teacher education courses, in work with young people, or in questioning their own assumptions. Researchers tend to hide behind proclamation of neutrality and colorblindness. These proclamations shield us from criticism and responsibility for the work we do. In these chapters, in contrast, the authors demonstrate in numerous ways that research is not neutral, and they show how it can be used either to uphold the status quo or disrupt it. In so doing, they challenge the claims of objectivity that have for too long characterized our profession. The majority of the authors are White, and this is, I believe, as it should be for a volume of this kind. After all, the responsibility for exposing and confronting racism has for too long been on the shoulders of African Americans and other people of color. It is time to share the burden, and it is up to teachers and researchers of all backgrounds to do so. If this is to happen, White educators need to make the problem of racism *their* problem to solve. This means nothing less than directly engaging in difficult conversations and actions that seek to address racism. This volume is a promising step in that direction.

As a society, we will have taken a big step forward when researchers demonstrate a willingness to engage in unsettling conversations and actions, conversations and actions that may in the end jeopardize their own privilege. It is not easy to own up to privilege, yet this is precisely what the authors in this text ask of themselves, and of other educators. They demonstrate the many ways in which Whites—in some cases, themselves, in other cases, teachers and prospective teachers—come to understand how literacy practices benefit some students over others. They write about how, through their teaching and research, they may be complicit in creating negative outcomes in literacy learning. The authors also write about how they face the discomfort of this understanding. In the words of the editors, "We make ourselves vulnerable in the stories we tell." The stories told in this volume are unsettling and even arduous to read, yet they serve as a model for other researchers and educators for the type of work that must be done. This kind of reflection and analysis is difficult but necessary, and it is refreshing to see it so often in a text that focuses on literacy learning.

This book also challenges the Black/White binary that for hundreds of years has defined race relations in our society. Although we have never been a nation of just Black and White, this image—for historic and other reasons—is a difficult one to dislodge. Yet the experiences of indigenous people, Asians, Latinos, and those of biracial and multiracial backgrounds also have deep roots in our history. By including the voices and stories of some of these groups, the authors ask educators to understand racial understanding beyond the Black/White paradigm.

At the same time that this volume asks teachers and researchers of all backgrounds to engage in the struggle for racial justice, it also has the potential to privilege Whiteness. In fact, one of the greatest dilemmas related to racism in education is the ease with which Whiteness can once again become the central focus, even among those concerned with racism and inequality. This problem is obvious, for instance, in the growing number of books and scholarly articles aimed at White teachers. Although this focus is necessary (White teachers make up the vast majority of our teaching force and most have had little experience with diversity of any kind), it becomes too easy to fix our gaze on White teachers rather than on children of color. Thus, books about Whites' epiphany concerning racism abound, but few books center on the academic successes of Black, Latino, and other children of color in our classrooms. This shift from Blacks and "Browns" to Whites should come as no surprise; it is simply a replication of what has happened all along. But as a field we need to guard against focusing simply on soul-searching about and recriminations for racism. Instead, we need to direct our attention to what needs to happen for children in our classrooms.

Fortunately, for us, the authors of this book have not focused solely on their own consciousness. Instead, they have provided direction for those of us who do literacy research, whether it is with teachers or with young people. The major lessons to be learned from their research are to *develop insight* about the problem in the first place. In each of these chapters, the authors discuss the sometimes painful process of developing awareness about the role of race and racism in literacy research. They also illustrate how we need to *work up the courage* to change what we do in our research studies and in our classrooms. Probably most important, these researchers have written about the importance of *assuming a stance of humility*, not always an easy thing to do in a profession characterized by big egos and personal agendas. Finally, they encourage us to join them by *engaging in social change*. Talk is cheap, as we know, but action is much more difficult. Rather than just talking about literacy, or just theorizing about racism, Stuart Greene, Dawn Abt-Perkins, and the superb writings they have gathered in this volume make it clear that this is the time for action.

There is no turning back. Racism is a problem that must be confronted in research, in classroom practice, in the assumptions and beliefs that researchers and teachers have about the intelligence and capabilities of children of color, and even in the very way we understand literacy. But the road ahead is not an easy one. *Making Race Visible* confronts difficult issues that cannot be resolved in one book, or even in a thousand. Racism and privilege are not going to disappear overnight. But the people whose voices are reflected in this volume have taken a bold step in pointing out how to use literacy as a tool for social justice. This is a fine beginning.

REFERENCES

Allen, J., Als, H., Lewis, J., & Litwack, L. (2000). *Without sanctuary: Lynching photography in America*. Santa Fe, NM: Twin Palms Publishers.

Cameron, C. (December 13, 2002). Bush calls Lott's remarks offensive. *FoxNews.com*.

Crenshaw, K., Gotanda, N., Peller, G., & Thomas, K. (1995). *Critical race theory: The key writings that formed the movement*. New York: New Press.

Kahlenberg, R. D. (2000). *Economic school integration*. New York: The Century Foundation Idea Brief.

Orfield, G. (2001). *Schools more separate: Consequences of a decade of resegregation*. Cambridge, MA: The Civil Rights Project at Harvard University.

Sammon, B. (December 12, 2002). Bush scolds Lott for remarks. *Washington Times*.

Spring, J. (2000). *Deculturalization and the struggle for equality: A brief history of the education of dominated cultures in the United States* (3rd ed.). New York: McGraw-Hill.

Wei, D., & Kamel, R. (Eds.). (1998). *Resistance in paradise: Rethinking 100 years of U.S. involvement in the Caribbean and the Pacific*. Philadelphia: American Friends Service Committee.

About the Contributors

Dawn Abt-Perkins is associate professor and chair of the Education Department at Lake Forest College, and is also serving as chair of the Conference on English Education for the National Council of Teachers of English. Her main areas of interest in research and scholarship are the preparation of teachers to work with students of color, supervision practices in teacher education, and the design of English Education programs. She has published works in *The Teacher Education Journal, Journal of Curriculum and Supervision, English Journal, English Education, Language Arts, International Journal of Education,* and *Women and Language,* as well as authored several book chapters.

Deborah Appleman is the Class of 1944 professor of educational studies and liberal learning at Carleton College in Northfield, Minnesota, where she teaches courses on literacy, schooling, and adolescence. She also directs Carleton's Summer Writing Program for high school students. A secondary English teacher for 9 years, Professor Appleman works regularly in high school classrooms and has presented workshops to secondary teachers throughout the United States, and in Japan and Australia. She has published many journal articles and book chapters on adolescent response to literature, multicultural literature, and contemporary literary theory in high school. Her recent book, *Critical Encounters in High School English,* focuses on teaching literary theory to secondary students. Professor Appleman has served as president of the Minnesota Council of Teachers of English and is currently on the executive committee of NCTE's Conference on English Education.

Courtney B. Cazden is the Charles William Eliot Professor of Education (emerita) at Harvard University. Her teaching and research has focused on language learning and literacy for all students. Her most recent book is the second edition of *Classroom Discourse: The Language of Teaching and Learning* (2001).

Colette Daiute is professor of psychology and urban education at the Graduate Center of the City University of New York (CUNY). Dr. Daiute joined the Graduate Center faculty in 1994, after having taught at the Harvard

Graduate School of Education since 1983. Colette Daiute's research focuses on social development among youth living in urban contexts, in particular as they use the cultural tools of literacy, technology, and the arts. Dr. Daiute's recent publications include a series of articles about children's understandings of racial and ethnic discrimination: "Social Relational Wisdom: Developmental Diversity in Children's Written Narratives about Social Conflict" (with E. Buteau & C. Rawlins), published in *Narrative Inquiry* (2001), and "Writing for Their Lives: Children's Narrative Supports for Physical and Psychological Well-Being" (with E. Buteau), published in the American Psychological Association publication, *The Writing Cure: How Expressive Writing Promotes Health and Emotional Well-Being*. Dr. Daiute is also currently working on the book *Narrative Analysis: Studying the Development of Individuals in Society* (with C. Lightfoot), which is forthcoming from Sage Publications; and a series of books on *Global Perspectives on Youth Conflict and Resilience*.

Patricia E. Enciso is an associate professor at Ohio State University where she teaches courses in literacy, culture, and sociocultural theory. She completed her master's work in England with Dorothy Heathcote, a pioneer in drama in education, and continued this strong interest in arts and literacy connections through her doctoral work on fourth and fifth grade children's engagement in reading. Dr. Enciso has published widely on issues of reading and mediating multicultural children's literature in elementary classrooms. She is currently writing a book on sociocultural and equity aspects of reading education at the middle level.

Stuart Greene is associate professor and Frank O'Malley Chair of the University Writing Program at Notre Dame University. His expertise is in the area of rhetorical theory, writing in the disciplines, and literacy. He is the lead author of a textbook on written argument, *Inquiry and Argument*, and coeditor of *Teaching Academic Literacy*. His research has also appeared in such journals as *Research in the Teaching of English* and in a number of edited collections on composition theory, research, and theory. He is past president of the National Council of Teachers of English (NCTE) Assembly on Research and is currently a member of the NCTE Commission on Composition.

Hollie Jones is currently a level 2 doctoral student in the social personality program at the Graduate Center of CUNY. Hollie has diverse research experience and has worked on several federally funded research projects. Many of these projects have focused, in some manner, on the role culture and ethnicity play in psychological phenomena, including identity and literacy. She is currently working as an associate for a New York-based evaluation research firm. Her dissertation research will examine the ways in which racial and ethnic identity buffer and mediate the effects of general and race-related stress.

Gloria Ladson-Billings is a professor and H. I. Romnes Fellow in the Department of Curriculum and Instruction at the University of Wisconsin-Madison. She was a former senior fellow in urban education at the Annenberg Institute for School Reform at Brown University. Her research interests concern the relationship between culture and schooling, particularly successful teaching and learning for African American students. Her publications include *The Dreamkeepers: Successful Teachers of African American Children, The Dictionary of Multicultural Education* (with Carl A. Grant), *Crossing Over to Canaan: The Journey of New Teachers in Diverse Classrooms* (May 2001), and numerous journal articles and book chapters.

Joanne Larson is associate professor and chair of the Teaching and Curriculum Program. Her research focuses on microanalysis of classroom language and literacy practices and examines the ways in which literacy as a social practice mediates literacy learning. Her teaching includes courses on curriculum, discourse analysis, qualitative research methods, and literacy learning. A recent State Department of Education Eisenhower professional development grant allows Larson to work with teachers at a local urban school to develop more meaningful language arts curricula. She has been published in numerous professional journals, including *Research in the Teaching of English, Language Arts, Written Communication, Discourse and Society, Linguistics and Education*, and *Harvard Education Review.* She has recently edited *Literacy as Snake Oil: Beyond the Quick Fix*, published by Peter Lang.

Sonia Nieto is professor of education at the University of Massachusetts–Amherst. Her research focuses on multicultural education and the education of Latinos, immigrants, and all students of culturally and linguistically diverse backgrounds. Her books include *Affirming Diversity: The Sociopolitical Context of Multicultural Education* (3rd ed., 2000), *The Light in Their Eyes: Creating Multicultural Learning Communities* (1999), *Puerto Rican Students in U.S. Schools* (an edited volume, 2000), and *What Keeps Teachers Going?* (2003). She serves on several national advisory boards that focus on educational equity and social justice, and she has received many academic and community awards for her advocacy and activism. She is married to Angel Nieto, an author of children's books and a former teacher. They have two daughters and six grandchildren.

Melanie Sperling is associate professor of education at the University of California–Riverside, where she currently serves as chair of the School of Education faculty. She is coeditor of *Research in the Teaching of English*, an international research journal published by the National Council of Teachers of English (NCTE). She is the author of numerous articles and book chapters on writing and literacy, including a chapter entitled "Research on Writing," which appears in the current *Handbook of Research on Teaching*, published in 2001 by the American Educational Research Association (AERA). Sperling is a winner of the NCTE Promising Researcher Award, the Steve Cahir award for research on writing given by AERA's special interest group in writing research, and the University of California–Berkeley outstanding dissertation award in education. She has served on numerous boards and committees on literacy education and regularly consults for national organizations in the area of reading and writing.

Marilyn S. Sternglass is professor emerita of English at the City College of the City University of New York. Her book *Time to Know Them: A Longitudinal Study of Writing and Learning at the College Level* (published by Erlbaum in 1997) was a cowinner of the Mina Shaughnessy Prize of the Modern Language Association in 1998 and winner of the Outstanding Book Award of the Conference on College Composition and Communication in 1999. She currently resides in Pittsburgh.

Arlette Ingram Willis received her Ph.D. from the Ohio State University. She is currently a professor at the University of Illinois at Urbana-Champaign, in the Department of Curriculum and Instruction, the division of Language and Literacy. Her research interests include the history of reading research in the United States, sociohistorical foundations of literacy, preservice teacher education in English and Language Arts, and teaching/learning multicultural literature for grades 6–12. Among her publications are *Teaching and Using Multicultural Literature in Grades 9–12: Moving Beyond the Canon, Multiple and Intersecting Identities in Qualitative Research* (with Betty Merchant), and numerous articles that have appeared in *Reading Research Quarterly, Language Arts*, and *Harvard Educational Review*.

Index

Abt-Perkins, Dawn, 1–31, 27 n. 1, 205
Acceleration approach, 5
Achievement gap, Black-White, 4–6, 9, 39, 43
Adger, C. T., 48 n. 4
Adolescence: A Farewell to Childhood (Kaplan), 72
African-American students. *See* Black students
African American Vernacular English (AAVE), 44–47, 95–97, 102–103, 136–137
Alderson, P., 81
Allen, J., 201
Als, H., 201
American Knees (Wong), 64–65
Anand, Bernadette, 19, 39–40
Anderson, James, 5
Angel Child, Dragon Child (Surat), 181, 184–185, 190
Angelou, Maya, 1, 64
Antiracism, 25, 160–161, 166, 174–175
Anton-Oldenburg, M., 41
Anzaldúa, Gloria, 13, 60, 69, 160–161, 173
Apple, M., 75, 81
Applebee, A. N., 134
Appleman, Deborah, 19, 21–22, 71–85, 73, 74, 76, 77
Atkinson, G. M., 104 n. 2
Attitudes
  defined, 38
  teacher expectations of minority students, 6, 23, 38–44
  toward language variation, 44–47, 95–97, 102–103, 136–137

AVID (Advancement via Individual Determination; San Diego), 43–44
Avoiding discourse strategy, 187, 190
Ayers, William, 81

Bakhtin, M. M., 23, 135, 149–150, 155, 167, 174
Ball, A., 2, 103
Ball, Deborah, 37
Ballenger, Cynthia, 19, 40–41, 155
Barrera, R. B., 149–150
Basic-skills pedagogy, 94
Baugh, J., 48 n. 4
Baumann, R., 155, 157
Behar, R., 14
Bell, D., 8
Beseler, C., 41
Best practices, 15
Bizzell, Patricia, 107
Black English, research on attitudes toward, 44–47, 95–97, 102–103, 136–137
Black students
  and Black-White achievement gap, 4–6, 9, 39, 43
  desegregated education for, 2, 4, 17
  embedded conflict and, 25–26, 192–193
  exclusionary practices toward, 5
  high school graduation rates, 9–10
  language variations among, 44–47, 95–97, 102–103, 136–137
  marginalization of, 93, 102
  as percentage of school population, 4
  teacher expectations for minority students, 6, 23, 38–44
  use of Black English, 44–47, 95–97, 102–103, 136–137

Black-White Test Score Gap, The
  (Jencks & Phillips), 39, 43
Blind vision (Cochran-Smith), 15–16
Bloome, D., 155
*Board of Education of Oklahoma City
  v. Dowell*, 4
Briggs, C., 155, 157
Britzman, D., 149–150
Broadening discourse strategy,
  184–185, 189, 190
Brown v. The Board of Education, 4,
  17
Bryant, Betty H., 45
Bush, George H. W., 4
Bush, George W., 4, 9, 201–202
Buteau, E., 179
Butler, Judith, 155, 160–161, 173

Cameron, C, 202
Canto, M., 57
Carter, Sonya, 42
Casareno, A., 6, 190
Cazden, Courtney B., 2, 18–21,
  35–50, 45
Chambers, D., 81
Chan, C., 63
Change, value of research process in,
  11–12
Charlotte, NC, dismantling of integra-
  tion, 17
Cherland, M. R., 149
Child Development Group of Missis-
  sippi (CDGM), 44–45
Christian, D., 48 n. 4
Citizenship schools, ix
City College, City University of New
  York, 23–24, 107–128
Civil Rights Act (1964), 2
Civil rights movement, ix, 2, 4, 17
Clark, Septima, ix
Class, literacy as function of, 138–141
Cochran-Smith, M., 3, 9, 15, 18,
  22–23
College Board, National Task Force on
  Minority High Achievement,
  38–39

*College Composition and Communica-
  tion* (Bizzell), 107
Conflict. *See* Social conflict
Context
  in literacy research, 15–16, 26–27,
    89–104, 138
  in reading process, 157–159, 165
  of representation, 74–79
Contextualizing discourse strategy,
  183–184
Continuous dialogue (Ellsworth), 161
Cope, B., 188
Corbin, J., 13, 14
Cornelius, J. D., ix
"Corporateization," x
Crenshaw, K., 201
Crichlow, W., 11
Critical race theory, vii–ix
  defining racism in, 8
  emergence of, 52–53
  feminist approach to, 20
  historical view of, 16–18
  narrative in, 21
Cross, W. E., Jr., 179, 186–187
Culturally informed literacy practices,
  2
Cultural racism (Tatum), 59–60
Cultural relevance, 137
Culture
  literacy as function of, 138–141
  reading in written narratives,
    191–192
  in writing about life experience,
    141–144

Daiute, Colette, 10, 24, 25–26,
  178–200, 179, 182, 188
Darling-Hammond, Linda, 19–20,
  38–39
Davies, B., 91, 101, 149, 158
Deficit model approach, 93, 100, 102,
  103–104
De La Luz Reyes, M., 5
Delgado, R., viii, 8, 13, 18, 53
Delgado Bernal, D., 13–14

Delpit, Lisa, 5, 10, 48 n. 4, 60, 73, 77, 97, 101
Desegregation
  dismantling of, 17
  education concerning, 2
  legislation, 4, 17
Detracking, 19
Discussion
  masking diversity of students, 100–101
  of race, resistance to, 1–4, 53–58, 60–63, 66–69, 202–203
Distancing discourse strategy, 186–187, 190
Diversity discourses, 178–199
  on construction of race and ethnicity, 179–182
  nature of, 178
  strategies for, 182–188
Douglass, Frederick, 16–17
Dreamkeepers, The (Ladson-Billings), vii
Du Bois, W. E. B., 13, 92
duCille, A., 2
Duranti, A., 90, 91–92
Dysconscious racism (King), 61
Dyson, A. H., 2, 90, 149

Eaton, S., 5
Ebonics, 44–47, 95–97, 102–103, 136–137
Edelsky, C., 90, 99
Egan-Robertson, A., 155
Ellsworth, Elizabeth, 149–150, 155, 160–161, 173
Elsasser, N., 97
Embedded conflict, 25–26, 192–193
Empathizing discourse strategy, 185–186, 189
Enciso, Patricia E., 16, 19, 24–27, 149–177, 155, 168, 186
English as a Second Language (ESL) students, 107–108, 115–122
Enriquez-Beitler, Magda, 36
Epistemology, 12–14, 20

Equity, goal of, 19–20
Ethics, of research process, 11
Ethnicity
  context for constructing, 180–182
  discourse strategies for, 182–188
  discursive construction of, 179–180
European American worldview, 13
Expectations
  of students for schooling, 141
  of teachers for students, 6, 23, 38–44

Fecho, Bob, 46–47
Feld, S. C., 182
Felman, S., 155
Feminist theorists, 20, 160–161
Ferguson, R. F., 6, 39, 43
Fhagen-Smith, P., 179
Finders, M., 149
Fine, Michelle, 2, 3, 7, 12, 14, 19, 39–40, 71–73, 149
Fires in the Mirror (Smith), 35
Flagg, B., 8, 26
Focus group strategy (Delgado Bernal), 14
Fordham, Signithia, 46
Foucault, Michel, 13, 23, 91
Fourteenth Amendment, 2
Franz, C. E., 182
Freebody, P., 90
Freedman, S., 6, 190
Freeman v. Pitts, 4
Freire, Paulo, 52

Gallas, K., 41, 155
Gates, H. L., 186, 199
Gay, G., 5
Gee, J. P., 90, 91, 149–150
Geertz, C., 12
Genre
  defined, 188
  reading, 188–192
Gentile, C. A., 134
Gilbert, P., 90
Giovanni, Nikki, 73–74

Giroux, Henry, 52
Goffman, E., 23, 90, 91–92
Goldberg, D., 91, 94
Gold Cadillac, The (Taylor), 162–172
Goodburn, A., 11
Goodwin, C., 91–92
Goodwin, M., 91–92
Gordon, Edmund W., 38
Gordon, N., 2, 4, 6
Gotanda, N., 201
Grant, Tim, 44
Greene, Stuart, 1–31, 205
Griffin, S., 41
Grundy, Pamela, 17
Guiton, G., 6, 24
Gutierrez, K., 2, 90, 98

Halbfinger, David, 17
Handbook of Multicultural Education
     (Darling-Hammond), 38
Hanks, W., 95
Hansen-Krening, Nancy, 54
Harré, R., 91, 101, 158
Harvard Project on School Desegrega-
     tion, 5
Head Start, 38–39, 44–45
Heath, Shirley Brice, 2, 37, 41, 72, 90,
     94, 97
Helm, Janice, 55
Heritage, J., 104 n. 2
Herr, K., 155
Higginbotham, E., 56, 66
High school graduation rates, 9–10
Hispanic students. *See* Latino students
Hodge, R., 155
Horatio Alger exercise, 56–58, 60
Horning, A., 116
Hubbard, Lea, 43–44
Hynds, S., 73, 74, 76, 77

Identifying discourse strategy, 182–
     183, 189
I Know Why the Caged Bird Sings
     (Angelou), 1
Indexicality

assumed shared indexical field, 102
example of racialized indexing,
     94–97
nature of, 91–92
in power relations, 91–92
Insider/outsider perspective, 20–21,
     35–47
complementarity in racial issues, 47
contradictory assumptions and, 138
on teacher attitudes toward student
     use of Black English, 44–47,
     95–97, 102–103, 136–137
on teacher expectations for minority
     students, 6, 23, 38–44
Insider research, defined, 37
Institutional racism, 65, 67
Interlanguage (Selinker), 116
IRE (Initiate Response Evaluate)
     approach, 23, 98
Irvine, P. D., 92, 95, 97, 104 n. 1

Jefferson, Thomas, 16
Jeffries, Dexter D., 127
Jencks, C., 4, 39, 43
Jencks, Kristin, 131–135, 138,
     141–147
Jenkins, Esau, ix
Jiménez-Muñoz, G., 149–150
Johnson, Lyndon Baines, 44–45
Jones, Hollie, 10, 24, 25–26, 178–200
Jonsberg, Sarah D., 1
Jordan, Carlton, 19, 39–40
Journals. *See also* Self-reflection
of preservice teachers, 58–60,
     61, 64–66

Kaestle, Carl, 5
Kahlenberg, R. B., 203
Kalantzis, M., 188
Kalnin, J., 6, 190
Kamel, R., 201
Kaplan, Louise, 72
Keating, A., 11
Kincheloe, J., 3
King, Joyce, 61

King, Rodney, 136, 139
Kingston, Maxine Hong, 133
Knobel, M., 90, 91
Kohl, Herbert, 61–62
Kornhaber, M., 9
Kozol, Jonathan, 59
Kress, G., 155
Kwanzaa and Me (Paley), 41, 42–43

Labeling, 19
Labov, W., 136, 182
Ladson-Billings, G., vii–xi, viii, 5, 7–9, 13, 16–18, 53, 60, 67, 103, 137, 149, 203
Lamash, L., 149–150
Lampert, Magdalene, 37
Landsman, J., 7
Langer, J. A., 134
Language practices in classroom, 90–97
    attitudes toward language variation, 44–47, 95–97, 102–103, 136–137
    writing and ESL students, 107–108, 115–122
Lankshear, C., 90, 91
Larson, Joanne, 23, 89–106, 90, 92, 95, 98, 99, 104 n. 1
Latham, A. S., 134
Latino students
    case studies of college-level writing students, 109–126
    and conflict as interactive bonding, 25–26, 193–194
    desegregated education for, 2
    ESL, 107–108, 115–122
    exclusionary practices toward, 5–6
    high school graduation rates, 9–10
    identity issues and, 110, 114–115, 122–126
    marginalization of, 102
    as percentage of school population, 4
    self-esteem of, 110, 119–121
    stereotyping and, 109–115

teacher expectations for minority students, 38–44
    worldview in studies, 107–128
Laub, D., 155
Lee, C., 2, 5, 90, 103
Lelutiu-Weinberger, C., 188
Lender, Helen, 140
Lensmire, T., 149
Lewis, C., 149
Lewis, J., 201
Lewis, Sharon A., 1
Lintz, A., 43–44
Literacy
    expectations for schooling, 141
    as function of race, culture, and class, 138–141
    invisibility of race issue in, 12
    problems of urban public schools and, 132–133
    racism critique of, 144–146
    as site of racial struggle, ix
    sociopolitical consequences of writing and, 146–147
    in tenth-grade class, 131–147
Literacy events in classroom, 90, 97
Literacy instructional practice, 2
Literacy pedagogy, 23
    excluding student literacy knowledge, 97–100
    as form of surveillance, 91
    language arts textbooks in, 92–97
    language practices in classroom, 90–97
Literacy research
    on attitudes toward language variation, 44–47, 95–97, 102–103, 136–137
    contributions of, 10–12
    on diversity discourses, 178–199
    features for racial understanding, 15–16
    invisibility of race issue in, 12
    on language arts textbooks, 92–97
    language practices in classroom, 90–97

Literacy research (*Continued*)
  potential betrayal in, 73–74
  power relations in, 72–73, 75–76
  on preservice teachers, 51–69
  race in context of, 26–27, 89–104,
    138
  racial epistemology of, 12–14
  on reading discrimination, 149–175
Litwack, L., 201
Locke, Alain, 167–168
Long-term approach
  to literacy research, 16, 108–109
  value of, 126–128
Lopez, Gerardo, 8, 9
Lopez, I., 7
Lorde, Audre, 52, 67
Lott, Trent, 201–202
Luke, A., 90–91, 91, 101
Lutrell, W., 83

Macedo, Donald, 52
Maier, M., 90
Majors, Y., 103
Malcolm X, 139
Mann, Horace, 16
Mayfield Crossing (Nelson), 181, 190
McCarthy, C., 11
McIntosh, Peggy, 60–61
M-Class Teams, 6, 190
McLaughlin, M., 72
Meaning
  in reading process, 167–171
  through writing process, 135–136
Mehan, Hugh, 43–44, 98
Meredith, James, 17
Michaels, S., 2
Mitchell-Kernan, C., 136
Moll, L., 137
Morris, A. D., ix
Morrison, Toni, viii, 67, 160–161, 186
Moss, B., 11
Mullis, I. V. S., 134
Multicultural literature
  preservice teachers and, 64–66
  representation problem, 71–84

Narrative. *See also* Reading; Stories;
    Writing
  in critical race theory, 21
  journals of preservice teachers,
    58–60, 61, 64–66
  objectification through, 79–81
  reading race as text, 195–198
  reconsideration of, 80–81
  teaching multicultural literature,
    64–66
National Assessment of Educational
    Progress (NAEP), 5–6, 134
National Council of Teachers of
    English (NCTE), 1–3, 109
National Research Council, 36
Native Americans, 201
Natriello, G., 9
Nelson, Vaunda Michaux, 181
New literacies, 69
New London Group, 23, 90
Nieto, Sonia, 10, 201–205
No Child Left Behind Act, 9
"Not-learning," 61

Oakes, J., 6, 24
Objectification, 79–81
Ochs, E., 92, 100
Ogbu, John U., 45–46
Olson, Lynn, 36
Orfield, G., 2, 4, 5, 6, 9, 201
Other, concept of, 2, 75, 92, 161, 173
Outsider research, defined, 37

Paley, Vivian G., 19, 40, 41–43, 77,
    155
Pallas, A., 9
Pappenheimer, R., 41
Paulson, Lou, 44
Peller, G., 201
Performance theory, 155
Perry, T., 48 n. 4, 97
Personalizing discourse strategy, 108
Peshkin, A., 39, 78, 79, 83–84
Phillips, M., 4, 39, 43
Pollock, M., 48 n. 3

Poverty, 5–6
Powell, L., 3
Power relations, 13
    attitudes toward language variation,
        44–47, 95–97, 102–103,
        136–137
    deconstructing social inequalities
        and, 56–58
    discursive practices in masking diver-
        sity, 100–101
    excluding student literacy knowl-
        edge, 97–100
    indexicality in, 91–92
    language practices and, 90–97
    in literacy research, 72–73, 75–76
    teacher talk and, 92
Practicing discourse strategy, 185, 190
Practitioner research, as insider
        research, 37
Prendergast, C., ix, 17

Questions
    children's responses to literary inter-
        pretation, 190–191
    "what," 97–98

Rabinow, P., 72–73
Race. See also Diversity discourses
    context for constructing, 180–182
    in context of literacy research,
        26–27, 89–104, 138
    defining, 7–10, 37
    difficulty in discussing, 1–4, 53–58,
        60–63, 66–69, 202–203
    dilemmas of negotiating, in the class-
        room, 101–104
    discourse strategies for, 182–188
    discursive construction of, 179–180
    importance of, 4–6
    invisibility of, 12, 22–24
    literacy as function of, 138–141
    masking discontent in discussing,
        61–63
    masking diversity of students,
        100–101

racial identity of researcher, 89
reading as text, 195–198
    in the theater, 35–36
    in writing about life experience,
        141–144
Race-conscious market, 7
Racial identity development theory
        (Tatum), 55
Racism, 7–10
    acknowledging, 53–58
    challenging, 161–162
    in critique of literacy practices,
        144–146
    cultural (Tatum), 59–60
    current examples of, 201–202
    deconstructing, 56–58, 65–66
    defining, 8, 37
    difficulty in discussing, 1–4, 53–58,
        60–63, 66–69, 202–203
    "dysconscious" (King), 61
    institutional, 65, 67
    narrative in contextualizing, 53,
        58–60
    natural, 159–160
    permanence of, 8–9
    racist frames of reference, 159–167,
        173–174
Rawlins, C., 179
Reading
    context in, 157–159, 165
    discourse strategies for race and
        ethnicity, 182–188
    genre in, 188–192
    multicultural literature and, 64–66
    about race, resistance to, 63
    race as text and, 195–198
Reading discrimination, 149–175
    antiracism and, 25, 160–161, 166,
        174–175
    hierarchies in, 152, 154
    interpreting immediate relationships
        and histories, 172–173
    making of meaning to combat,
        167–171
    mediation of "real," 155–159

Reading discrimination (*continued*)
  performance theory and, 155
  practices that promote, 159
  racist frames of reference in, 159–
    167, 173–174
  research context, 150–155
  sexist frames of reference in,
    159–167
  social positioning and, 158
  student profile, 153–154
  understanding and fighting, 160
Reciprocal distancing (Larson &
  Irvine), 92
Remediation approach, 5
Representation, 71–84
  context of, 74–79
  examples of, 75–78
  objectification, 79–81
  potential betrayal in, 73–74
  problem of, 71–73
  reconsideration of, 78–79
  symbolic, 168–171
Roberts, Benjamin, 16
Roberts v. Boston, 16
Rodriguez, N. M., 3
Rodriguez, Richard, 112
Roithmayer, D., 52–53

Sammon, B., 201–202
Santigao-Valles, K., 149–150
Santow, M., 4
Schaafsma, D., 2
School-based community of writers,
  139–140
School choice, 16–17
Schooling, expectations for,
  141
Self-reflection
  on discourse, 157–159
  in literacy research, 16, 19
  by preservice teachers, 58–60, 61,
    64–66
  stories and, 18–22
Selinker, L., 116
Serna, I., 6, 24

Sexism
  challenging, 161–162
  feminist theorists and, 160–161
  sexist frames of reference, 159–167,
    173–174
Sherman, Dana, 19, 39–40
Shor, Ira, 52
Silence in classrooms
  of preservice teachers, 60–61, 67–68
  reading discrimination and, 173
  as weapon, 21, 60
Silko, Leslie Marmon, 64
Simons, E., 6, 190
Sizer, T., 141
Skelton, T., 72, 81
Slavery, ix, 201, 202
Smith, Anna Deveare, 35, 37
Smith, C. P., 182
Smitherman, G., 95, 136
Social class, literacy as function of,
  138–141
Social conflict, 25–26, 192–195
  at a distance, 25–26, 194–195
  embedded, 25–26, 192–193
  as interactive bonding, 25–26,
    193–194
Social positioning, 158
Sociocultural theory of learning, 103,
  152–153, 154, 181, 188
Special education, non-White students
  in, 93
Sperling, Melanie, 24–25, 131–148,
  135, 136, 139
Spina, S., 51–52
Spring, J., 201
Steinberg, S. R., 3
Stereotyping, writing as means of
  coping with, 110–115
Stern, R., 188
Sternglass, Marilyn S., 23–24, 107–
  128, 110, 115–116
Stine, R. L., 152
Stories. *See also* Narrative
  in contextualizing racism, 53, 58–60
  value of, 18–22

Strauss, A., 13, 14
Strauss, L., 186–187
Street, B., 90, 93, 97
Surat, Michele Maria, 181
Swain, J., 41
Symbolic representation, 168–171

Tai, R., 51–52
Talk to Me (Smith), 35
Tate, William F., vii, 8, 13, 53
Tatum, Beverly D., 7, 37, 38, 55,
    59–60, 63, 113–114
Taylor, Mildred, 162–171
Taylor, O., 48 n. 4
Teacher Quality, 51
Teachers. *See also* Power relations;
    Practitioner research
  assumptions of, 6
  attitude toward student use of Black
      English, 44–47, 95–97, 102–
      103, 136–137
  characteristics of typical, 51–52
  discussions led by, 189–190
  expectations for students, 6, 23,
      38–44
  practices of, 10
  preservice literacy education, 51–69
  stories of, 18–19
  theorizing own racial position,
      10–11
Teaching Other People's Children
    (Ballenger), 41
Textbooks, literacy research based on,
    92–97
Theoretical sensitivity (Corbin and
    Strauss), 13–14
Thomas, K., 201
Thompson, Audrey, 160–162, 166,
    167–168
Thought and Language (Vygotsky), 38
Thurmond, Strom, 201–202
Tillman, Melissa A., 45
Tilly, Charles, 39
Tracking, 6, 24
Treacy, C., 63

Tribal secrets, 13
Turiel, E., 186
Twilight Los Angeles (Smith), 35
Tyack, Davie, 5
Tyson, C., 149

Universalizing discourse strategy, 186,
    189–190
University of Mississippi, 17
University research, as outsider
    research, 37

Valdes, G., 134
Valentine, G., 72, 81
Villanueva, I., 43–44
Vygotsky, L. S., 38, 135, 138, 139,
    191–192

Waletzky, J., 182
Walker, P., 178–180
Walters, K., 11
War on Poverty, 44–45
Warrior, R., 13
Ways with Words (Heath), 41
Wei, D., 201
Weis, L., 2, 3, 7, 14, 71–72, 149
Wells, A., 6, 24
Weseen, S., 2, 7, 14
West, Cornel, 58, 81
"What" questions, 97–98
White privilege, ix, 197–198, 203–204
  deconstructing, 56–58, 65–66
  impact on teachers, 51–52
  insidious nature of, 22
  and preservice teachers, 56–58,
      60–62, 66–69
White Reign (Kincheloe et al.), 3–4
White students
  and Black-White achievement gap,
      4–6, 9, 39, 43
  and conflict at a distance, 25–26,
      194–195
  silence in classroom, 21, 60, 67–68
White Teacher (Paley), 19, 41–42
Whole-class-read-alouds, 97

Whole-language-based teaching, 93, 98
Whole-school reform, 36
Williams, Patricia, 160–162, 169, 173
Willis, Arlette Ingram, 19–21, 51–70
Wilson, William Junius, 39
Winant, H., 7
Wong, M., 2, 7, 14
Wong, Shawn, 64
Woodlief, L., 135, 136
Writing. *See also* Diversity discourses
    incorporating personal worldview
        into, 107–128
    as means of coping with stereotyp-
        ing, 110–115
    need for practice in, 127–128

of preservice teachers on race,
    54–55
about race, resistance to, 63
race and culture as sources of conten-
    tion in, 141–144
as socially constructed meaning-
    making activity, 135–136
sociopolitical consequences of liter-
    acy and, 146–147
teacher-based approach to, 99–100

Yon, D., 72
Yonezawa, S., 6, 24

Zelman v. Simmons-Harris, 16–17

DATE DUE

AG 27 '07			

DEMCO 38-296